Chalk Dust
on
My Shoulder

Line Drawings by
Donald Robison

Chalk Dust
on
My Shoulder

Charles G. Rousculp

Charles E. Merrill Publishing Company
Columbus, Ohio
A Bell & Howell Company

Standard Book Number: 675-09543-3

Library of Congress Catalog Card Number: 69-16501

2 3 4 5 6 7 8 9 10 - 74 73 72 71 70 69

Printed in the United States of America

PUBLISHER'S NOTE

Once in a great while, a book of immediate and universal appeal is written. The material communicates with conviction, deals in reality, touches the lives of people everywhere. Charles G. Rousculp's *Chalk Dust on My Shoulder* is just such a book.

Presenting educational philosophy and methods through lively essay and anecdote style, *Chalk Dust* is more than a memoir from the pen of a career teacher. It is an intensely human, plain-spoken document of the ordeals, the errors, and the triumphs that mark the teacher's day and that underscore his dramatic contribution to American society.

Chalk Dust is a milestone in Merrill's traditional and continuing efforts to upgrade and support education on all fronts in the midst of these chaotic, changing times.

Charles E. Merrill Publishing Company

To my beloved wife, daughter, and mother--
and to the youth of 106,
who have further enriched my life--
I dedicate this humble volume.

Foreword

In a different sort of world, Thomas Henry Huxley once found it possible to visualize and to dramatize the wonders of biological evolution by turning to a quite common, ordinarily unexciting substance—a piece of chalk. The essay which grew out of Huxley's speculation so stirred my schoolboy imagination that I will, I suppose, always associate the contrasting yet relative concepts of permanence and change with that same squeaking stylus. Over the years I have come to see an analogous identification between Huxley's chalk—a silent, unalterable witness to the changing forms of living creatures—and Truth, which stands immutable in the face of the often frantic, often incomprehensible evolution of human thought.

Though all this concern with chalk and Truth may seem excessively profound, I assure my reader that I am only doing an inadequate job of rationalizing my particular function in the world. For my business is with chalk dust, the tiny scrapings of Truth. The chalk dust on my shoulder is the badge of my fraternal order. The little mists of ideas which descend upon me every day as I write upon and erase the board in my room have given my existence a meaning and a direction.

Many hundreds of young faces have come and then gone away from my classroom, many of them to classrooms of their own, full of other faces and memories. Still, I like to feel that they have not really gone. All of them—the Fulbright scholar, the beauty

queen, the young doctor, the teacher on Midway Island, the avia-
tion machinist, the building contractor, the nurse, the car sales-
man, and another two thousand (including one whose chair will
never again be assigned)—are there in the dust of my room. And
regardless of how the custodian sweeps and waxes and washes,
the dust penetrates the wood, the glass, the plaster, and the tile
and will not wholly depart. When I leave my room at night, it is a
haunted place, full of the phantom sounds of questions and answers, ghostly rustlings of papers, airy chimes of laughter, and
the marvelous dreams of youth. These are my legacy—these and
the yellowing pages of abandoned gradebooks.

Apart from my profession there is nothing that is extraordinary
about my life. Nevertheless, when I see the chalk dust sprinkled
over my clothing, I like to imagine that I have been given a raiment
of distinction and been purified somehow by the only cloud that
can obliterate the mushrooming atom. The chalk dust invades
the pores of my hand, rains over my desk, and feeds my dry
cleaner; but my heart insists that it cloaks me with joy and honor.
When the chalk breaks and scatters annoyingly in bits upon the
floor and when I lean to retrieve them, I am in fact picking up the
pieces of my life. I am a teacher.

Worthington, Ohio
February, 1969   Charles G. Rousculp

Acknowledgments

It is altogether fitting that I express here my endless gratitude to Charles A. Jones, my good friend and advisor, for his faith in my work, his boundless effort in my behalf, and his continuing interest in extending and improving American public education. And to the officers and employees of the Charles E. Merrill Publishing Company, I wish to convey my sincere *thank-you* for their many kindnesses—indeed, for making me feel like one of that wonderful "family." Especially, I want to voice my deep appreciation for the superb editorial assistance of Madelon Aylwin, once my own student and now, some years later, my charming and efficient tutor in the exciting work of producing a book.

I am also indebted to a number of distinguished educators and authors for their encouragement and helpful suggestions: the late Dr. Kimball Wiles, Dean of the College of Education, University of Florida; Dr. Frederick Mayer, Fellow, Royal Society of Arts, London, England; Dr. Harold Spears, Visiting Professor and Educational Consultant, Indiana University; Dr. Alice Miel, Professor of Education, Columbia University; Dr. Wilfred Eberhart, Professor of Education, Ohio State University; Dr. Winston Weathers, Associate Professor of English, University of Tulsa; and Mr. Ernest Cady, Literary Editor, *The Columbus Evening Dispatch.*

The "Prologue" for this work originally appeared in the January 1, 1966 issue of *Read*, a school magazine published by American Education Publications, under the title "The Bitter Brine of the Soul." "Their Own Commencement" appeared in part and under this title in the *Ohio Schools* of April, 1959. Portions of "The Soul of a School" were published by *The Worthington News* in several issues. For permission to reprint or to paraphrase copyrighted materials, I thank the following publishers, authors, and agents:

American Scientist: "Address before the Student Body" (California Institute of Technology, 1938), by Albert Einstein.

Columbus Evening Dispatch: a news article of March 9, 1966.

Contents

Prologue: March 14, 1945—
   The Shoulder Is Prepared 3
From Volcanic Ash to Chalk Dust 11
The Chalk Begins to Talk 21
Room for Improvement 29
The Soul of a School 37
Out of Time, Out of Place 49
The Windsor Knot 61
The Trial of a Teacher 71
His Eye Was on the Pigeon 89
Their Own Commencement 99
The Father-Image 109
The Big Cage Called a "Study Hall" 119
The Chalkboard Set 127
The Devil's Advocate 137
The "Key" to a Better Understanding 151
The Rebel Stranger 161
Cecil B. and I 173
TGIF: Thank God It's Fun 185
Chalk Dust Gets in Your Eyes 197
Classroom on Wheels 211
The Purloined Papers 223
The Kids from B.R.I.G.H.T. 237
Chalk Dust by Moonlight 249
The Teacher-Errant 263
The Many-Splendored Chalk 275

W-E-A Spells AWE   287

The How-to-Study Man   297

The Hairy Question   305

Every Man Has His Price   315

The Professional Defined   325

Epilogue: The Chalk-Blessed Shoulder Shared   333

Chalk Dust
on
My Shoulder

We made ready to push off at 1000 HOURS that morning. It was to be the last big drive, we were told. When the day's work had been finished, the "brass" fully expected us to have reached the shining Pacific, there at the northeast of Iwo Jima. There were a few left among us who, having been subjected to twenty-four consecutive days of perpetual dying and gnawing fear, had begun to doubt that Iwo was, in fact, an island.

We had been told back on the ships that we were headed for a target that would not take more than a dozen days to secure, but now it seemed that we were on some peninsula of Hell, some strand of ash and lava that had no end but merely led into a dark continent of burning, perforated, mutilated, bleeding Death. For a

Prologue: March 14, 1945-- The Shoulder Is Prepared

long time there had been a rumor among the men that we would be relieved by fresh troops. We had wanted to believe it—the idea that we might be snatched safely back from the terrible line, back to the beach and Life. The beach, once a nightmare to every man, had now become a beautiful dream, a vision of safety and security.

By this time, we had lost the ability to dream of Home. Home was the greatest myth of all; it was a kind of heaven where angels wrote letters to you from unattainable clouds. No, you'd never get Home; you'd settle for the beach and the sweet sensation of no longer being etched over another man's gunsight. Even Heaven was closer than Home.

The Lord is my Captain;
I shall not weep.
He maketh me to lie down in shallow foxholes;
He leadeth me through the corpse-strewn Valley;
He restoreth my ammunition.
He leadeth me past the paths of cave snipers
For my own sake.
Yea, though I walk through the Valley of the Shadow of
*   Death,*
I should fear no Evil,
For Thou art with me.
Thy presence and promise, they comfort me;
Thou preparest my C-rations before me in the presence of
*   mine enemies.*
Thou coverest my head with steel roundness.
My canteen runneth over.
Surely my need of Thy mercy shall follow me
In the shrinking calendar of my life,
For I shall dwell in this Valley forever.

I lay against a rock of hardened lava in the miniature canyon the men called the Valley of Death and listened to our barrage of machine-gun and mortar fire. They were certainly doing it up right, I thought; they were softening up the area that we had been expected to take the day before, when the terrain had abruptly sprouted Japanese by the scores—troops that were supposedly dead or sealed away in the multitudinous caves that our demolition had closed.

I didn't like to think of the events on the preceding day: Lindy's losing his mind in a shell crater, Zeb's bleeding to death upon a table of rock, and that moment when I had carved my name and the dates of my birth and anticipated demise in the stone as a last, futile effort to be remembered. The bullets tearing through the rags of a Japanese; Strain, my look-alike, who had changed firing places with me only to be shot in the head seconds later—these and a hundred other grisly snapshots were permanently impressed in the camera of my eye.

Then the word came over the walkie-talkie. Sundayman, the little Apache who had left a reservation for duty with the Marines, still carried the phone. He merely looked at me, and I checked my watch. It was 1000. There were just nine of us, less than a squad, who made up the remnants of Easy Company's third platoon, and when we stood up we didn't look very much like the billboard, recruiting-office Marines. Rather, we resembled a little herd of goats or at best a group of filthy, stinking, soul-seared caricatures of what God had presumably created in His own image.

As I passed the word, I felt that terrible fear again. I tried not to show it, and I studiously watched the faces of the other eight in an effort to discern whether they might have detected signs that my last reserves of strength were crumbling away. A great finger of my mind pointed accusingly at my cowardice. Wherever I looked, I could not avoid that digit of indictment and a voice that screamed in my ear: *Run and hide. Your guts are gone. You're done.* There was little sound among the others; each man was preoccupied with his own problems. No, they didn't know how I really felt but were concerned solely with their own fears and discomforts.

We left our sanctuary in the rocks, and our objective was the same as that of the day before—the Japanese bunker on the heights to the left of the draw. With the cessation of our barrage and screening fire, an ominous stillness fell over our sector. Maintaining our flank contacts, we moved rapidly ahead. I wanted it to be over fast, regardless of what it brought.

When we had pressed to less than a hundred yards away from the suspected pillbox, the men began to slow down. I knew why. Directly ahead of us lay a little prominence of rock. In crossing it, we would inevitably be targets. I stopped and looked around at Corporal Witt. He was kneeling and cutting a plug of tobacco, and I wondered where he had got it. None of us had been shopping lately. Had he taken it from a dead Jap? Did Japs chew tobacco? Maybe I should ask Witt for some. This might be my last chance to try. . . .

Then I saw the boy to my right, fidgeting with his rifle. His firing pin, he insisted, wasn't working. My voice was a lash. How did he know it wasn't working? It had worked yesterday, hadn't it? And the day before? It hadn't misfired today, had it? I pulled back the bolt and showed him that it was all right. And when he turned his eyes away from me, I knew that in my heart I blessed him for making me forget for a moment my own trembling. I sensed that he, like me, wanted to throw his weapon away and run until he had no breath, into some faraway land where there were no mirrors or eyes to reflect the weakness of the spirit. Among men the most unbearable moment of truth comes, perhaps, when they grow up only to see how far they miss heroic stature.

5

We hadn't stopped long before the walkie-talkie Apache came with the new colonel's voice—an official, clean-collar sound that wanted to know our progress. I told him about the hill, and when he said something that sounded like *so what?* I began to swear over the walkie-talkie in short, eloquent bursts. The officer must have been either very tolerant or hard-of-hearing. I could have been court-martialed, a dozen times, no doubt, for what I probably said.

It was obvious that someone had to go up the little hill, and it was equally apparent that I was the Number-One Candidate. There was probably nothing there, anyway, I told myself. I even tried to convince myself that mythical Japanese submarines had slipped by our ships in the mythical ocean and evacuated all the remaining Japanese troops. In short, I began to talk the actor, the fraud in me, into making a real "production" of the hill.

I glanced about at the others—helmet-topped faces that peered at me curiously, expectantly. But time was running out. Bending forward, I clambered awkwardly up the incline. A few seconds of peeking cautiously over the top revealed nothing but a lonely, thick-trunked banyan tree—I think that is what it was—which our naval gunfire had sheared off at the top.

> *I think that I shall never see*
> *A decent, full-boughed, green-leaved . . .*

I could hardly resist looking back down at my comrades, but something about that half-shattered tree held my attention. It had appeared to move slightly. It seemed to me that my imagination must be getting as shaky as my knees. I took one more step upward, exposing myself nearly to the waist. Simultaneously a Japanese stepped from behind the tree. He wasn't twenty feet away and his movement was one of determination. My BAR—normally sergeants carry carbines, but I had long since swapped mine—was firing now; the weapon appeared to work of its own accord. Then I felt a great sledgehammer strike my shoulder.

A Hollywood sequence would have had the leading man fall gracefully in some knightly manner. But Truth deals with counterfeits in her own way: not being a hero, I was dumped on the seat of my dungarees and made to look like a ridiculous child on a playground slide. The blow that I had felt spun me completely around, and I slid halfway down the hill in an undignified, embarrassing fashion. When I had come to rest, I looked down at the puddle of faces with open mouths. I accused Pek of throwing a rock at me. He crouched and stared silently with wide eyes and a wry moustache. It was an unreal scene out of a slapstick comedy. Then I reached for my throbbing shoulder and brought my hand away, red with my blood. Witt helped me down, the others taking cover and looking for hideous violence to spill over the top of the hill. On our flanks there was scattered firing now.

Any medical corpsman would have seen that, for the moment, I was in a state of shock. The condition lasted for five minutes or more. Nevertheless, I remember some details very vividly—having the right side of my combat jacket cut or torn off, seeing blood mingle with my dog tags, feeling Witt sprinkle sulfa powder over the two clean holes produced by the Jap's Nambu. I recall all too clearly the unpleasant moment in which Walters whispered somewhat too audibly that he thought I might have two bullets inside me. What followed remains vague to me, but they informed me afterwards that I got back on my feet and began hurling hand grenades over the hill with my usable arm and making unpleasant insinuations about Japanese society in general and their ancestry in particular. I prefer to doubt these reports of my behavior, but I must at the same time admit to equally stupid actions on other occasions. If I am to be honest, I must say that I probably owe my life to the several men who restrained me in those seconds.

There was a call from the CP then: "Easy Three, make contact." We had lost contact with the flanking units. Sundayman reported that I had been hit. The reply was an order for me to go back to the Battalion CP. I felt a surge of delirious relief; a miracle had happened—a marvelous, wonderful thing that would take me back to the beach.

My selfish, secret joy was short-lived. I looked at the little group scattered among the rocks around me. What would happen to them? I belonged here with them and the everlasting horror. I was guilty of being afraid and should be condemned, therefore, to the living death of Iwo. I turned to Witt and found in his eyes a look of envy, the envy I had felt when others had been evacuated with comparatively minor wounds. Out of my respect for him, I wanted his stamp of approval. He must have read my unspoken question.

"Go back," he said with the wisdom of four beachheads in his eyes.

"But I'm okay," I answered. "I know what's going on now, and I can still—"

"Listen," he returned, "just let me get one little scratch here, here on my finger, and I won't wait for an order. I'll evacuate myself." While Witt was still holding his finger dramatically in the air, Sundayman beckoned me to the walkie-talkie.

"Can you walk?" came the executive officer's voice.

"Sure, I can," I answered; "I'm staying here."

"You are like hell!" he snapped. "I'm sending up replacements. Come back to the first-aid station. Tell Witt to take charge and stay right there."

"But—" I had run out of objections. I had never really wanted to object in the first place.

"Don't argue with me, Sergeant; if you're all right, you'll be back with your bunch tonight. Now get back here."

I handed the phone to Sundayman, who grinned. "Now you better go back for sure," he advised. I gave my BAR to Witt. He already had one of his own, and he stood looking like a combination of clown and weightlifter. Then, after nodding a *so long* to him and waving one to the others, I turned and moved slowly down the draw.

I think I knew down deep that I wouldn't be back with them that night. The word was out that any and all wounded were being evacuated. At the Battalion CP they took one brief look at my shoulder and helped me into a jeep with a crayoned red cross on the side. The ride to the beach was a rapid one. I saw nothing but meaningless blurs along the route. My mind was too busy with remembering faces I had left behind.

At our beach destination there was a little tent for first aid and emergency surgery. Men stood or lay about outside the shelter with various degrees of hurt, both physical and psychological. A young man, the first I had seen with a clean shave for nearly a month, emptied a syringeful of penicillin into my arm and then fastened a white card to my dog tags. Soon, half a dozen or more of us were put onto an amphibious tractor which began moving rapidly away from the tent, away from Meat-Grinder Ridge and the Amphitheater and out into the water off Blue Beach.

I looked around as best I could at my new companions—a man staring wildly at nothing, a boy with a mangled leg, another with a bandaged hand that he seemed to converse with, and a poor devil with . . . I turned away. My neck and arm were growing stiff and throbbed rhythmically. I had been sitting, but now I rose with effort and moved to the side of the amphtrack to look back at the island. The full realization that I was actually leaving Iwo Jima hit me for the first time as I stood there.

The chaos of the beach, shell-beaten Suribachi, planes landing and taking off at Motoyama Number One, wreckage of landing craft, a tiny bulldozer still scooping graves—these were the panorama before me. And somewhere past the ridges on the right, in a weird, inferno-like landscape there were eight boys, any or all of whom I might not see again. And how many of my friends—Casey, Lane, Longo, and all the others—would rot here?

The tears came freely, noiselessly then. Unashamedly, they came like the tide, impeded only slightly by the reeds of my curled and tangled beard until they had covered my mouth with the bitter brine of my soul. I felt my whole body racked by great silent sobs. I wept for many things in those moments: for the friends I had left or lost forever on the island; for the irretrievable passing of boyhood dreams; for the kid in a black sweater who had stood in a row of catechism students and recited *Thou shalt not kill;* and for all the waste, transgression, and violence that had filled my twenty-one years. I did not see the great white hospital ship we were approaching. For in this instant I was concerned, not with the healing of my body, but with a catharsis of the spirit. And as I wept, the sickness inside me began to be purged.

It is well that my feelings of pain, guilt, and folly were never wholly purged. The immunity of the spirit, like that of the flesh, requires antibodies. Anyway, the soul cannot begin again. Homer was a romantic—after a Troy, a Ulysses can never really go back to his Ithaca. Tennyson knew it, and Tom Wolfe said it, and I soon discovered the truth for myself. I couldn't go home again, though I wanted to ever so badly. For Home is a state of mind.

When I first left the islands, the Corps, and the playthings of war, I was still a badly disoriented, thoroughly haunted young man without the vaguest glimmer of what I wanted to do with my life. Yet I felt a curious sense of obligation. The laws of probability, it seemed to me, had given way and had unexpectedly bestowed upon me the gift of survival. For a time, I did not know how to accept or to use that gift, and I spent my time rather aimlessly. If I had

From Volcanic Ash to Chalk Dust

any purpose at all, it was to immerse myself in pleasure and to drown the horrors with which I still walked. My Charybdis was labeled Old Overholt and my Scylla was a many-faced ghost confronting me at every turn. Fortunately, I wasn't long in learning that mere self-indulgence brings only fleeting pleasure and that he who has taken life does not easily evade Him who gives it.

I did not learn these lessons overnight, but during the three months in which I worked at trying to find my way Home. Almost osmotically, the knowledge of what I had to do filtered into my consciousness. I recalled the opportunities that I had cast aside before the war. At the time of my graduation from high school, I had won a four-year scholarship at an Eastern school and had received numerous other tuition offers. At seventeen, my life had been full of promise and activity. Apart from the great griefs of my youth—the separation of my parents had been one of these—I had had a rich, full, and rather satisfying adolescence. June, 1941 had not been a happy time for me, however. Like most high-school graduates of any year, I had felt great uncertainty and insecurity. Moreover, 1941 had seen many of my friends entering the armed forces, and Pearl Harbor had been only six months away.

Although the times had not been auspicious, my greatest problem had been my own muddled thinking. Even though I had enjoyed high school, I had reached a kind of saturation point in formal education, or so I thought. Though I might have surmounted the formidable financial obstacles in the way of college, the prospect of additional years in a classroom had seemed rather bleak. Besides, I was in a fun mood. As a result, I had taken a full-time job as a file clerk and apprentice cost-engineer. Had I gone to college the following September, I probably would not have done well. I had been too all-knowing, too narrow in my smugness, and too ridiculously arrogant in my manner. It would require the college of the bayonet and flamethrower to lend me greater wisdom. Now in March of 1946, I could see the past more clearly, but I was still a young man of 22, caught somewhere between resolution and indecision.

Curiously, February and March have always seemed to be two months of the year that are the most important in producing the crises and turning points of my life. Though I had already seen some dozen instances of this recurring magic, I had not yet put that mosaic of coincidence together. But the "Tides" of March, 1946, brought a vision that would alter my life in still another way.

Some women are merely beautiful. Some are attractive, too. It is a rare woman who combines these attributes with an unspoiled warmth and an absolute selflessness. On that March night when I first saw her, Alice was all these things and more. And she remains so today. Aglow with a vivacity, a prettiness, a wittiness, and a uniqueness beyond belief, she belongs, like her name, to that age in which the female had not yet "emancipated" herself into the listless, discontented, pseudo-sophisticated creature of the "feminine mystique."

When we were married, twelve weeks later, I did not know that Alice would be a "woman in white" for another twenty years, working as a private-duty nurse and later as a staff nurse at a badly understaffed hospital where patient care was subordinated to paper work and bond retirement. My wife would willingly work so that I could find and follow my calling. We could not see the hard work, sacrifice, and heartache that lay ahead. Yet, together, through it all, we would find laughter, *camaraderie*, parenthood, and the meaning of marriage.

By the time of our wedding, I had tentatively decided to enter Ohio State University in the fall quarter of that year. My gunshot wound had provided a small disability pension and now made it possible for me to attend college under Public Law 16, which had distinct advantages over the regular GI Bill. By strumming "Auld Lang Syne" on some political strings, the family obtained a part-time job for me in the Ohio Senate. Every step seemed almost pre-arranged in a pattern. Still, when I entered the arts college at OSU that year, I had absolutely no real plan for my life; in actuality, I went there to find a purpose.

Those people who attended college before or after the "Veteran Crush" of 1946-1950 can not imagine what those years were like in schools all over the country. It was as if Coxey's Army, Shay's Rebellion, and the Bonus Marchers had suddenly descended upon universities everywhere. Young men who would ordinarily have never had the opportunity for higher education now found that chance, and thousands of them took advantage of it. Clad in bizarre combinations of service and civilian clothing, they brought a surprisingly high order of seriousness and persistence to the schools where they enrolled. Some observers have argued that the whole face of American education was lifted during those post-war years. On the other hand, the pseudo-sophisticates and professional students of Fraternity Row lost much of their aplomb. Their usual antics seemed somehow ludicrous and downright childish. The perennial Big Man on Campus had been emasculated by the appearance of young men who had seen somewhat more of life and who were not easily impressed by the playthings of wealth and leisure.

To help serve this inundation of 1946-model freshmen, a number of sometime OSU professors came out of retirement; and others, excited by what was happening in classrooms, put off their plans for Florida and emeritus labels. Indeed, there were some first-rate teachers at OSU—no "Publish or Perish" dictum had discouraged their practice. E. L. Beck, the friend of Irish poet James Stephens, could patiently read the crude verses I handed him and still encourage my efforts. Warner F. Woodring's lectures in history were probably my favorite hours as a freshman. Sidney Fisher, an expert on the Byzantine, helped me to gain a sense of organization and time. Nevertheless, my principal concern remained an enigma—what was I to do with my future?

I suppose that every man is motivated toward leaving something of himself to the world, something that will live on after he has ended his stay here. In high school I had wanted to become a professional writer, to build some tower of prose or verse; but, recognizing my limitations and doubting my ability to break into that rather uncertain field, I had relegated the idea to my store of favorite reveries. While working as a cost-engineer, I had once more considered becoming a builder—of what, I didn't know. When I was asked to declare an objective by the Veterans' Administration guidance man at OSU, I had blurted, "Architecture!" Thus I found myself taking math, physics, and drawing courses which, while they were informative and not especially difficult, did not stimulate me nearly so much as my English and history classes.

I was sitting in the main library one March day, contemplating that miserable T-square that I had to carry all over the campus. It regularly alienated other people whenever I turned suddenly and unintentionally maimed them with the cross I bore. *No, it wasn't exactly a cross—just a great big capital* **T** *with a hump on top.* I turned it over rather ruefully and accidentally dropped it. I made a frantic grab for it but missed, and it clattered against a table leg across the aisle. Glancing up, I caught the librarian's gaze of displeasure, and I tried to look apologetic. I retrieved the offending instrument and slid back into my thoughts. **T** *for what? For* **T***ime, for* **T***ruth, for* **T***eachers?* The T-square even looked like one of my teachers, a bony cadaverous gentleman with a brilliant mind. He was a published author and an excellent instructor, and his whole appearance suggested peace of mind. But what did he build besides books? People? Yes, he *did* build people, in a way— even his books influenced, perhaps reconstructed lives. *People! What more important product could a man work with?*

I suspect that my thoughts that day were not quite so coherent as I have suggested, but this was as nearly as I can recall my moment of revelation and decision. They say that the Emperor Constantine saw a cross in the sky. Maybe he did and maybe he didn't. The point is that, whatever he thought he saw, the vision changed his life. I saw only wood and plastic in the form of a **T** and a teacher, yet I knew in that moment the means whereby I could read and write and grow and build.

I was going to teach in a high school. I believed then, as I believe now, that the most important events in a young person's life can happen during those four years. I had enjoyed my own experiences in high school. My first real love for literature began there. I remembered, too, the teachers—John Stipp and Zalia Harbaugh—who had helped me when I had desperately needed advice and direction. I could recall the many activities as well as the numerous agonies of that growing-up period. It also occurred to me that, as a teacher of English and history, I might in some small way help to rebuild and reshape a world in which I had once taught others how to kill with lead, steel, fire, demolition, and judo. These were the reasons I gave my counselor for changing my college objective. I didn't mention my principal hope—that now, perhaps, I could dwell with the spirit eyes that followed me and dared me to justify my continuing existence.

Though I did not comprehend much about educational philosophy at the time, Ohio State's College of Education was still attempting mouth-to-mouth resuscitation over the gasping corpse-to-be called the "progressive experiment." The University High School continued to serve as a combination laboratory and showplace inspired largely by Rousseau's "natural man" and John Dewey's "pragmatic child." My first education courses had the effect of half convincing me that my view of teenagers must be either sadly out of date or badly distorted by my own experience in a traditional school. These courses, in some instances, were being taught by young graduate assistants, Ph.D. candidates who had recently discovered a Lord in Bertrand Russell and who wore their agnosticism like badges proclaiming their faith solely in man. (The same breed of novitiates teach some of these classes today, the only difference being that they have traded Dewey for Sartre.) My worst moments were spent in something called Education 533 and 534 (so bad that they had to assign two numbers to it), in which I learned two valuable lessons: (1) that I did not care to teach in a one-room schoolhouse or in the Girls' Industrial School, to which we took field trips, and (2) that the doughnuts in the snack bar to which we regularly adjourned grew soggy after ten o'clock if it were a humid day.

Fortunately, there was another side to the college coin. Nobody who ever sat in Howard Francis Seely's classes on the teaching of literature and language will find it possible to forget him. For two years I thought I disliked the man intensely, and for nearly twenty years I have felt an ever-increasing respect and gratitude for his impact upon my professional career. Seely was to a prospective English teacher what Parris Island was to a would-be Marine. He made me think and work if only out of a vain desire to prove he was wrong. With a face and voice like actor Everett Sloane's, a perpetual tweed suit, a stride right out of Sousa, and a straight-lipped brittleness that I can compare only with some of the characters created by Clifton Webb, he represented at once the anathema and the greatest blessing of my junior and senior years. He was a conservative in many respects, but always with individuality.

It seemed to me that there was a constant personality clash between us. "It's not fair!" I used to tell my wife as I furiously waved a B or B+ paper. "How can a sapling grow in the shade of a Sequoia?" My wife would smile knowingly, for she understood then as she understands now that the only people who can force angry sounds from me are those for whom I feel a growing affection and sometimes, out of vanity, a reluctant sense of inferiority. But it angered me that he gave me B's and refused to make any allowance for the pressures I felt from my job at the Treasury of the State of Ohio and from my responsibilities as a brand-new father.

Only once did that remarkable granite pose relax in *my* presence. I had taken one of his exams the week before, and, frustrated by constant financial problems at home and difficulties with my job, I had had several drinks and had taken the test in a passionate to-hell-with-it frame of mind. He called me in to talk about the paper.

"Mr. Rousculp, I'd call this product a genuine curiosity. I'm not quite sure what to do about it."

His face was turned away from me, and I could only imagine a triumphant glitter in his eye. The damage was done, and my point-hour average was at his mercy. There was no point in sounding penitent, no advantage to be gained in rehashing my problems, so I told him flatly that I'd been half-stoned when I'd taken his damned test. When he turned around to face me, I was thunderstruck. He was smiling at me with a surprisingly elastic moustache, and I saw for one fleeting instant the man behind the granite. Then the smile was gone again.

"I've decided to ignore this—this abortion. Your other work indicates that you have a good understanding of the course materials. You have it in you to be a fine teacher, but you'll find teaching much harder than my examinations. Good day." And with that crisp benediction, he turned to his papers.

When Howard Seely retired from the classroom some years ago, education suffered a considerable loss, I think. His greatness lay not merely in the superb methodology he taught and not alone in those books of his which have become imperatives in any bibliography of English education. There was a something else that I glimpsed in that old room in Lord Hall and in his Arps Hall office—an enduring professional example, a flesh-and-blood icon of integrity and purpose and strength. If I have in my own small way become a Teacher of English, it is because I belong to a very special breed—those who bear and wear with unutterable pride and gratitude the Seely stamp.

If I have emulated any teacher's classroom manner, it is that of Wilfred Eberhart, Seely's one-time colleague and subsequent head of English education in the college. Wilf helped me to feel literature—to hear in A. E. Housman's poems, for example, my own lament over the passing of youth. In addition, he gave me my basic training in semantics and oral interpretation, and he has over the years encouraged and recommended my efforts as a writer and educator.

Another figure, unnamed here, wielded a very strong influence on my thinking. With a voice like Henry Fonda's, an immaculate appearance, and a relaxed poise not unlike that of a well-known crooner, this professor was a first-rate spellbinder. He was so eloquent and impassioned in his denunciation of the Phonies in education that it took me fifteen years to understand that he was indicting himself along with the others. Today, as then, he maintains a coterie of disciples who do not yet grasp why he is so expert on the psychology of the "Hollow Men."

After having been exposed to these men, I was certain that I was ready to teach. All that I had to do was to become, through mimicry, a composite of these teachers and to take the subject matter of Professors Logan, Hughey, Wilson, Charvat, Altick, Elliott, *et al.* Unhappily, to become a teacher is a not so easily attained goal. It is not that a teaching degree is hard to come by; the degree, itself, is possibly too readily available. There are hundreds of thousands of people who have been granted certificates for teaching, but there are only a few teachers. Many of us go through the motions of teaching, yet so few come even close to satisfying the ideal.

Of professional goals that a man might pursue, to be a teacher is probably the second highest. Only the minister, the soul-worker, has a higher calling. The teacher ministers to the mind, though he may at times reach the spirit. It took me years to realize how overly ambitious I had been in deciding to become a teacher. After nearly two decades of trying to be one, I know that I shall very likely never reach that goal in its fullest sense. Nevertheless, I have no words with which I can communicate the joy, the satisfaction, and the peace of mind that my *trying* has brought to me.

Needless to say, there is an irony in the would-be teacher's situation. Because most teachers have fallen very short of the ideal, Society is inclined to view the efforts of an aspiring teacher with some contempt and considerable curiosity. In some respects, the teacher is even laughable from the materialist's point of view. Society always smiles at those of its members who are impractical enough to dream and to follow a dream. Like the priest, the teacher is an oddity, a contradiction of Society's shabby, shallow values; and it is characteristic of people to find mirth in the face of that which is incongruous, inconceivable, or incomprehensible to them. From Ichabod Crane to Mr. Peepers, men have guffawed perennially at the spectacle of those who presume to teach. A *Mr. Novak* series is far less appealing than an *Up the Down Staircase* to a public conditioned to smile when teaching is mentioned.

Occasionally even I laugh, and I get my biggest laughs on paydays. Sometimes when I get my monthly insult, I go down to the teachers' lounge, and there we all sit down and have a good laugh together. Then the next day, I go back into my classroom and soberly reflect upon the countless rewards of my work which I cannot deposit at the bank but which I owe in part to my family's willingness to deny themselves for my happiness.

I certainly haven't ignited the planet in my attempts to teach, but there have been those now-and-then moments in Room 106 when I have sensed that the mysterious event called learning was taking place. The real teachers—Socrates, Santayana, Arnold, Ascham, Kittredge and Company—would shake their heads over my fumbling, inadequate approach, I know. They would marvel at my errors and deplore some of my techniques, but they could not stop me. Browning's Andrea del Sarto says, "A man's reach should exceed his grasp," and Shakespeare's Polonius advises, "To thine own self be true." Then there are those other voices, torn from shrapnel-ruptured throats—from the pockmarked beach, from out of the sulphurous bowels of ashen hell—who breathe their message: *There were teachers before, yet we are dead.* In an infinitely smaller voice, I can only answer, "Though it is beyond me, it is what I want, and I cannot give up my quest."

One day a very competent young man in my classroom asked me a quite personal question. The remark was made in a friendly, even complimentary spirit. "Mr. Rousculp," he inquired, "why did you become a teacher? You could've been so much more than a teacher." It took me a little while to get over this intended praise; students aren't often so charitable. Finally I responded. "As a matter of fact, John, I honestly believe that I *could* have been anything that I might have wanted to be, except for two things: I'm not a good enough man to speak for God, and the second-best, second-hardest job I know is the one I'm still trying to do."

In this way I came to the chalk dust, and for these reasons I linger in a room where the past intersects the future. Surrounded by the young, I share their spring and their indomitability. What is more, I've talked myself into supposing that some little part of me will travel into the tomorrows I shall never see.

Professor Seely had been right. Nothing I had experienced in college was quite so difficult as the struggle to teach. To begin with, it was one thing to talk about the theoretical paper student and quite a different matter to be confronted by dozens of flesh-and-blood entities with dozens of strikingly individual patterns of thought and behavior.

I had gained some awareness of the theory-reality discrepancy when I had done my student teaching at Columbus Central, the school I had deliberately asked for because I had felt it would be challenging. It was all of that and more. The teacher whose class I had taken over had been badly overloaded, and she had eyed me with the expression of a Custer seeing reinforcements on the way. After handing me a seating chart, a spelling list, and miscellaneous other materials, she had grabbed her bottle of aspirin

The Chalk Begins to Talk

and immediately dematerialized, leaving me on the Little Big Horn with the Sioux.

Many of Central's students were drawn from the chaotic and unfortunate conditions found in any transition area—any section in which run-down homes and apartments coexist with industrial plants. In some ways, however, my own background provided me with some insights into their attitudes and problems. After I had got over my worry that I might, in unguarded moments, flavor my comments with Mother Marine Corps, I began to enjoy these young people. I think I might even have taught them a little something, but they taught me even more.

The first papers which I marked and returned to the class provided a lesson in learning to expect the unexpected. In the upper right-hand corner of a girl's paper, I had written "Date?" where she had neglected to indicate the day on which the assignment had been turned in. On the revised paper returned to me, I found her phone number neatly inscribed under my notation.

One boy—Keith, I think, was his name—was out to make life miserable for me. His manner was always at its worst whenever Seely or Eberhart came out from the University to observe my progress. Finally, in desperation and without much regard to professional ethics, I called my classroom saboteur out into the corridor and spoke to him through my incisors. "I'm going to tell you this just once, so you listen, damn it! If you mess up my grade at the University, I'm going to dribble you down Broad Street and jump-shot you into the river!" I closed the interview with a solid whack across his back. It was the first and only time I ever touched a student in anger, and I was deeply ashamed of the whole business afterwards. But, I must admit, it produced the desired effect. Thereafter we were like Buster Brown and Tige. Not only had I bruised his clavicle, but I had gained a staunch supporter in my classroom.

When I took a job at the high school in Worthington, Ohio, a Columbus suburb, I let myself suppose that here, perhaps, I would find the sort of student that instructors liked to talk about in some of the more ethereal education courses at State. I had wanted a half-time teaching assignment because I planned to spend part of my days in graduate school working on an M.A. in English. So from September till Christmas I carried two morning courses at OSU and made a stab at teaching one class of world history and two sections of sophomore English in the afternoons. After school, I'd go home to tussle with my two-year-old daughter, swallow and try to digest a meal, and then work until after midnight at my desk, both on my own compositions and on those of my students. It was a murderous schedule, and by the time the holidays arrived I was seriously considering dropping out of graduate school.

When Worthington offered full-time employment in January, I accepted and simultaneously discontinued course work at the University. The only reasons that I did not leave Worthington instead were my earlier contractual commitment to stay the year and my continuing need for money. Otherwise, I would cheerfully have left, because the sophomores in my classes had really put me through the mill.

My trouble at Worthington grew mainly out of my failure to establish the proper classroom atmosphere and to maintain a level of discipline in which my students and I could feel comfortable. I was treating them as unreal young people, and they sensed the artificiality of my approach long before I did. I had made the mistake of thinking that these teenagers, most of them from enviable home environments, must be self-disciplined and very different from the students at Central or those with whom I had attended high school. What I tried to do was to be "human," but my definition was faulty, and I merely succeeded in producing the absurd image of a teacher whose limits of tolerance and understanding were anything *but* human. Naturally, my classroom regularly deteriorated into anarchy and riot.

With an added preparation—freshman English—my teaching load in February became such that something had to give. The turning point came one afternoon in a sophomore-English section when I was laboring over some grammatical distinctions. I was still worried about my wife, who had recently suffered a miscarriage, and I had had trouble earlier that day with a girl in study hall. I was also thoroughly exhausted from grading papers that week.

Just about the time that I was groping through the snarl of restrictive and non-restrictive adjective clauses and phrases, about six or seven tête-à-tête's struck up at various points in the room. I raised my voice several decibels and asked for their attention, but as soon as they had glanced my way and reassured themselves that "He really doesn't mean it" they returned to their conversations. About half the class was still trying to hear me, but I had the feeling that soon I would be the only one listening to me. All my instincts cried *Get physical!* though I was just rational enough to know that, if I took hold of a student, I might do him serious damage. Still, my rage and sense of impotence had to explode. I chopped furiously at the desk with my left hand, knocking several books onto the floor, and with my right hand hurled with all my strength the piece of chalk I was holding.

That stick of chalk was poorly directed, thank God, though I don't know that I had any particular target in mind. The whole class must have been sprayed with the chips, however, because it ricocheted off at least three walls. Heads ducked in all directions until the remaining stub finally came to rest in the lap of a sweet little girl who seldom if ever failed to give me her attention. Her name was Ruth, and I couldn't have frightened her more. To say that the class was in a state of shock would be to grossly understate the case. Open-mouthed, wide-eyed, immobilized, they sat in a silence that would have made the faintest peristalsis sound like a cataract.

As for me, I felt weak, completely drained. *My God*, I thought, *did I put down a grenade just to throw chalk at kids?* In the quietest syllables I had uttered all year, I told Ruth that I was sorry, that she had not, after all, been one of the offenders. Then, with no further show of penitence, I went on with the lesson. When the bell had rung and I had dismissed the class, I saw that they glanced at me curiously, as if they had never really seen me before. Their faces were hardly comforting.

I leaned my shoulder against the chalkboard and looked down across the open field toward the river. *I'm not safe in a school*, I considered. *I might have put someone's eye out.* I had wanted to be a teacher. I had wanted them to respect yet like me and, most of all, to learn through me. Where had I gone haywire? I had to talk to someone.

Ray Heischman, my principal, was sitting in his office when I got there. He was a big man in his thirties, his hair receding rapidly like my own. He coached basketball and sold real estate on the side, but he was also a first-rate school administrator. Ray had a streak of Deutschland stubbornness in him, but his teachers could always count on his advice and support, and this professional strength is a cardinal virtue in a principal. In another five years, Heischman would leave education to become a co-manager of a housing-development firm. Eight years later he would die in an automobile accident.

"There's something I'd better tell you," I said. "Just in case you get some phone calls from irate parents."

"Something happen?" Ray looked serious. The prospect of unpleasant phone calls is the scourge of school administration.

"I threw a piece of chalk at my ninth-period class."

"Did it hit anyone?" he asked.

"Yes. Well—not really. It dropped in a girl's lap." He started laughing, and I felt more comfortable somehow.

"You threw it at the whole damned class?"

"Yeah," I said and grinned sheepishly in spite of feeling rather miserable. He continued chuckling.

"Did they deserve it?"

"Some of them did."

"Good! If you need any more chalk, see Mrs. Cox." Another teacher came up to the door then with a handful of eligibility lists. Dow Nelson, the biology and health teacher, also served as Worthington's football coach.

"Everything going well?" Dow asked.

"I just scared hell out of a class," I answered. Ray couldn't resist telling him about my lobbing my chalk like Schoolboy Rowe.

"Looks like he threw some at himself, too," observed Dow. "You've got chalk dust on your shoulder." As I brushed a cloud from the right sleeve of my suit coat, he added, "In this business, you usually wind up with chalk dust on your backside from leaning against the chalk trough."

As I re-entered my classroom, I saw a boy standing by the desk. Behind him I noticed that someone had picked up the books I had knocked to the floor. They were back on the desk, neatly arranged. "I just wanted to apologize, Mr. Rousculp. I was one that was talking today. We've been giving you a hard way in that class, but I don't think we will anymore."

"Just because I got mad—finally blew my top?"

"Not exactly. I mean we didn't think you'd *ever* get sore. I— I'm glad you did, sorta. I guess in a way we even feel more comfortable or better somehow when we know there's some limits in a class."

"Thanks for coming in, Chuck, and—" He lumbered off before I thought of mentioning his very probable assistance in straightening the room. As I gathered papers from the desk, I couldn't help reflecting upon what had at first seemed ironic in his words, yet very reasonable with a bit of thought. Youth wants to find strength in parents and teachers, for youth is as frightened of anarchy as his elders. It was up to me to provide a more reasonable, more lifelike atmosphere in my classroom. Rousseau must be tempered by *Candide*, by some realism. Voltaire might have thrown a whole can of chalk today.

That was the day when I really passed my crisis as an apprentice teacher. Henceforth, my students would see me as a real person— not as a talking mannequin wound up and walking about on educational theory. The student grapevine would begin to work for me. The young would know that there was law as well as liberty in my classroom, and they would expect me to be righteously indignant and outraged when they tried to take advantage of my desire to be a friend as well as a teacher.

All this was still to happen. Meanwhile, I knew only that I could be a better teacher tomorrow, sensed only vaguely that something important had happened that afternoon. I thought again of the expression on Chuck's face as he had said, "I'm glad you did, sorta." Then I thought of another boy—the boy I had been, the boy who had strewn death and destruction in another part of the globe. That boy had secretly wanted greater guidance in his life, had been half afraid of himself before he had become lost. But here was youth rediscovered, or at least I had come closer to understanding it and myself. The chalk dust had a healing quality, perhaps. And, indeed, there *was* chalk dust on my shoulder.

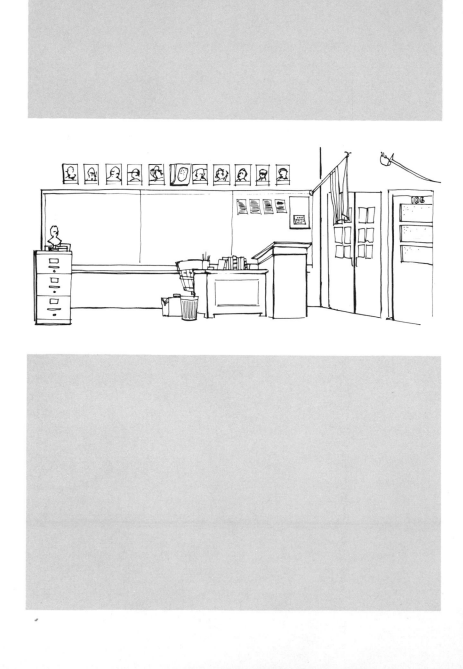

"I remember looking into the room long before I was a Senior. It was not a classroom. Someone lived there. Someone had made that room into a house of writing and creative thinking. Before I was able to enter that room, I could glimpse only the pictures and the shelves of books and the variety of color. To an underclassman that room was adventure and intrigue. I had heard that, to a Senior, the room was a place of 'true' learning."

These words may not carry the stamp of deathless prose, but when slender, blond-haired Betsy wrote them she couldn't have pleased me more. She saw the room exactly as I secretly wished my students to see it. For I have lived there since that portion of the new school was opened, and I have tried very hard to make it "a house of writing and creative thinking."

Room for Improvement

Located in the main building of the high school and opening onto the fifth-of-a-mile corridor that connects the east and west wings, Room 106 is the only piece of Worthington real estate in which I hold any "equity." Since its initial use, the room has housed, along with such distinguished tenants as Chaucer, Shakespeare, Milton, and Keats, over two thousand upperclassmen. Outside 106, passersby are frequently treated to such sights as three witches preparing for an appointment with Macbeth, monologists repeating lines and struggling against imminent nervous breakdowns, and distraught Roderick or Madeleine Ushers half buried in sheaves of make-up work.

The interior of the room offers a somewhat less forbidding, if not very conventional prospect. It does seem, however, to give young people something to talk about. Sometimes students asked to write a descriptive theme in a subjective manner will select the room as their subject. Of course, they don't always see it as the Utopian setting for an academic millennium. As one newly arrived student commented, some find that "the room, like its subject matter, is very nearly, but not quite *square*."

At the front of the room my desk, usually littered with student scribblings, front-office forms, and college applications, was described by one young satirist as "a flat wastebasket." Seldom in the same position for two consecutive days are the lectern, its base showing well-rounded corners because of my leaning and rocking on it, and the stool behind it, which I have not yet learned to use. A few steps away are a table once referred to as "Miscellaneous, supported by four hopeful legs" and two file cabinets in which, one pupil declared, "items are lost in alphabetical order."

On the north side, beneath the only windows in the room, and along the back wall are bookcases in which the volumes suggest both chaotic arrangement and quite omnivorous reading habits. The green-glass chalkboards on the remaining two walls—east and south—usually testify to my not-very-legible chalkmanship.

Thirty-six desk-arm chairs, in six uncertain columns, command most of the floor space in 106. The built-in closet by the door seems to present an open-and-shut case—one door is almost perpetually locked, and the other nearly always neglects its obligation to conceal the disorganization inside. The major physical properties of the room do not, I'm sure, indicate any particular individuality or identity.

The bulletin boards doubtless provide the best clue to the subject matter treated in this room. Above and behind the desk a number of modern British and American authors strike various poses of meditation and quiet confidence. Steinbeck, for instance, is eyeing a cigarette, and Hemingway appears to be about to savor his favorite Bacardi on the table beside him. On the south wall the bulletin boards customarily contain materials pertinent either to the literature and history of England or to facts about the English language and effective usage. The framed pictures on the remaining wall space treat a greater variety of subjects: a steam locomotive, a sailing ship, and a winter landscape from Currier and Ives; a Remington cavalry horse stalked by Remington wolves and a Remington stagecoach pursued by Remington Indians; a fisherman taken from an old steel engraving; Rembrandt's *Man in Armour;* a scene from *Ben Hur;* a portrait of Whitman; a student's ink drawing of some imagery in T. S. Eliot's *The Wasteland,* another's charcoal sketch of Shakespeare, and still another's portrait of Milton's Satan. The air of Americana that some of the pictures exude is enhanced by the southeast corner of 106, where a fifty-star flag extends its bars above the closet and a Civil War saber arcs above the door.

There is an air about the room, but it involves more than molecules of literature, history, art, and patriotism. Somehow there is a very distinct aroma in the place that caresses the nostrils and stimulates flowing tides of saliva and gastric juices. Sometimes a breeze seems to have risen from nowhere, a rustle of calorie-laden oxygen that whispers of onions being peeled, fish being fried, or beans being stirred. The riddle of the olfactory delights that find their way into 106 can be quite readily solved. Some lesser light of the architectural world, with the intellectual incandescence of a tulip bulb, arranged to have the air-intake conduits for 106 placed directly above the ventilator fan for the kitchen below. Some days I don't go to lunch—I've taken on pounds just breathing.

High-school students, being alert and curious creatures, often suppose that there are other, less explainable mysteries about the room. Occasionally they inquire about the sword, and I am naturally eager to point out to them that I did not participate in the Civil War. At times they wonder about the black bust of Goethe, who peers intently at them from the top of a filing cabinet. In rarer instances young people ask about the missing bookend and an obsolete 1959 calendar on the desk. And once in a very great while, a pair of eyes (especially in one of the larger classes) seems to question silently the one desk-arm chair that I do not assign. Most commonly, they probe my reasons for ever becoming a teacher, and I regularly and optimistically assume that they have the kindest motives in doing so.

I do not tell them the full story of the sword, nor am I about to inform them that Goethe has discovered another Faust close by. I will not enlighten them about the delinquent Grecian-urn bookend or the anachronistic calendar, and I sidestep discussing the history of the Chair.

Though I provide several "pat" answers regarding my choice of vocation, I do not feel really competent, myself, to explain entirely the force that brought me to 106. Nor can I completely fathom or adequately describe the something that keeps me here in this place that is only a point of departure for so many others, presumably. "I think you have a love affair going for you in that room," remarked one of my colleagues some years ago. I laughed at the time, but the more thought I gave the statement the less preposterous it seemed. There are very few objects in 106 that I do not readily associate with some movingly dramatic moments out of my teaching yesterdays—the strange and beautiful and inexplicable phenomena of youth as it grows and suffers and learns. In a way I *have* been in love in this room and with this room.

At the risk of sounding like an Edgar Cayce case-study, I must confess that I have this "thing" about places and objects. For many people, the curtain between life and death seems very insubstantial—every day we can see examples of living death and deathless life. If the scientists are right and human beings are bundles of flaking atoms and cells and if the theologists can not settle the issue of what comprises the soul, how can we know that something of the spirit does not attach itself to our surroundings, and to the objects with which we come regularly into contact? I am not a spiritualist—indeed, I know little about such matters— but I have, if it is no more than the product of an active imagination and a strong memory, this feeling that something of the individual's essence remains in a place which he has frequented. Thus, for me at least, the faces and the voices and the hearts are still here in this limbo of lost lessons and late papers: the boy who moulded me into the image of the father he lacked, the girl who in confusion and hurt offered herself to me, the gifted student who turned to theft in desperation and pride, and all the others who have laughed and stumbled through the curious mazes of literature and baffling incongruities of language.

Yet there is a paradox in this room and, I suppose, in the classroom of any other teacher who feels as I do about youth. As a teacher, I must encourage teenagers to put away childish views and to become adult; therefore, any success that I experience must inevitably cause youth to die a little. I have mixed feelings, then, when I see my students purchase new and essential adult understanding at the cost of priceless youth.

Shortly after I had begun teaching, I decided to take a trip back to the high school I had attended. I thought that I might thereby refurbish some hazy recollections of my public-school days and consequently gain a fuller understanding of my own students. I was lost in the corridors of the old building and troubled by the faces that seemed so alien there. When I saw my name on a bronze plaque, it looked like someone else's. No, I couldn't "go back," no matter how hard I tried. After a time, I found a teacher whom I had known, but at first she seemed different—a stranger as she walked toward me. Then her eyes widened in recognition, and they were the eyes I remembered. She spoke my name, and I knew, Tom Wolfe, that you had told only part of the story. Though we can't recapture or relive the past, there are those in whose hearts we never really left Home.

Maybe this thought has led me to rationalize the lingering presence of my past students in Room 106. I will not accept the idea that the room is merely a graveyard for youth, though some of my students might like the comparison. Here, I endeavor to keep alive, at least for myself, those parts of themselves which students leave behind. The unseen citizenry of 106 are a boisterous crew. Sometimes they dream over their books, drop pencils, gaze out the windows, make terrible boners when they recite, and give me withering glances of disgust and the most ridiculous excuses ever invented by the juvenile mind. But I wouldn't have it any other way.

It isn't just that I love my work and that 106 provides a means whereby I can enjoy the curative properties of the chalk dust. I like to think that I grow and improve with my students.

"But I've never had my papers marked like this before," the young man groaned. He had come up to my lectern after class with a blend of panic and shock on his face. "Is my writing really this bad?"

"As a matter of fact, Ken, it's rather good. That's why I put a B— on it."

"But I was getting A's last year, and look at this—it looks like it was bled on." I didn't tell him that, sometimes in the wee hours of the A.M. when I'm red-inking compositions, I feel as if I'm bleeding, myself. I reached for the paper he was holding.

"Maybe you weren't making all these errors last year," I answered, not wishing to sabotage the inexperienced teacher he'd had as a junior. "Look at the misspellings!" I pointed to a half-dozen corrupt forms. "You know better than to make mistakes like these. And see the way your idea jumps around. That's what I mean by 'Lacks coherence.' " I spent several minutes in trying to show him how the piece might have been logically organized. I stopped when his expression of defeat had reached the critical point.

"And I wanted to be a writer some day," he declared with self-scorn and self-commiseration hanging on the words.

"I'd like to be one, too," I said, "but we've both got a lot of work on our hands if we're going to make it."

"You've published some things, haven't you?"

"Not very much. Besides, when I look at them now, they look pretty bad. There's always room for improvement, and that's what you're here for. That's one of the reasons I'm here—to improve, or try to." I handed the paper back.

"So maybe you're not a Hemingway or Thurber—you don't make errors like this."

"Maybe not the same kind, but there's a lot that's wrong with what I do. You mean you think the *big* professionals don't goof? Ever hear of a novel called *Across the River and into the Trees*?

"I don't think so."

"Read it sometime after you've read *For Whom the Bell Tolls*. Even you and I can tell when Hemingway had bad days."

"I'll bet guys like that don't make mistakes with grammar," he returned.

"Look, you mentioned Thurber, and I think he's great, too, but listen to this." I reached to the desk and picked up a volume that I had enjoyed several days before. After turning to a selection called "Snapshot of a Dog," I read a paragraph to Ken. "He's been describing a dog fight, hasn't he? Well, get this next sentence. 'Working their way to the middle of the car tracks, two or three street cars were held up by the fight.' You see the mistake in that?"

He didn't see it right away, and I handed the volume to him. Then his eyes lit up. "Oh, yeah! Dangling modifier, isn't it?"

"Exactly! And making it sound as if those streetcars had to struggle to get to the track is pretty absurd. Thurber's a terrific writer, but sometimes he, too, is funny when he doesn't intend to be. None of us ever gets so good at anything, Ken, but what there's room for improvement." He shook his head a moment, then slipped the marked-up composition into his notebook. He got to the door before he turned with a smile.

"That *room for improvement*—that's a cliché, isn't it?"

For a minute I wanted to defend my phrasing. But I knew that both of us had more to gain the other way. "Yeah, I guess it is," I admitted.

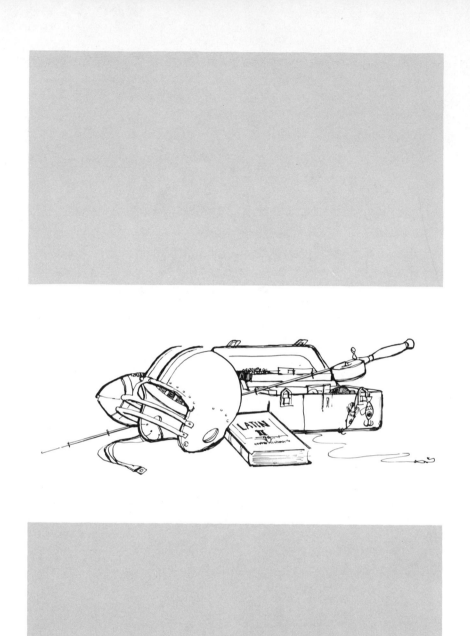

"Dow?" I was still groping through the night-day, sound-silence, life-death of sleeping and waking. *"Dow?"*

"He died last night. Frank called. I—I didn't wake you. I didn't want to—" Alice pressed her hand against my shoulder in the early-morning darkness as somewhere behind my eyes the heart's own projectionist illuminated a massive screen with a parade of images. The pictures kept coming, even after I had struggled to a sitting position and launched myself toward the kitchen and that pulsing, comforting mother's breast of morning called a percolator. But the pictures—

Baccalaureate and two dozen of us—the long-ago faculty of Worthington High—lined up to follow the graduating class. Jeanette Fry looked younger than her years as always. And Dow Nelson was standing beside her in our file of two's. All of us were

The Soul of a School

feeling like animated anachronisms behind the flushed, cap-and-gowned seniors. Suddenly, through the strains of the processional, Dow, his eyes suspiciously aglint, leaned toward Jeanette and me and satirically whispered: "I think I'm going to have a nervous pee."

The two of them—the soul of a school—the essence of Worthington High. How many years had passed since that yesterday, that fragment of potted ferns and choir and clergyman? Jeanette had retired, and Dow had—Dow was—"Turn if off, God damn it!" I blurted. But the frames reeled on, however I might seal my eyelids over the cloud of caffeine and salt that I gripped. The baccalaureate Sunday faded into a PTA Tuesday, and now I was standing with Jeanette and Mrs. Bobrovnikoff in the new high-school gymnasium. ". . . for meritorious and inspired teaching," the speaker was announcing. Now he was handing me a certificate and a check. *This isn't mine*, I thought. *It's really Dow's.* Then I was searching the bleachers, culling out faculty faces, seeking his. He was there, smiling and nodding. The utter humility of the man! Dow must have known what I felt, but he would not agree when I told him afterwards. "You—and Jeanette—"

"You've earned it," he interrupted and slapped my shoulder to change the subject to one of his famous Nelsonville anecdotes.

I couldn't forget—cannot forget. If, indeed, Room 106 became a "room for improvement," Dow and Jeanette made it happen, for they were the pillars that bore the weight and tradition of Worthington High School. I had leaned upon them in my on-the-job training. They had pointed my path through classroom and corridor. Surely the roof must come tumbling down, the walls disintegrate, the school dissolve into nothingness. Or so I thought, but I was still learning . . . learning . . . though they had taught me so much.

A school, I knew, does not exist in an architect's drawings. A school does not proceed from the passing of a bond issue, the taking of bids, the awarding of a contract, the laying of a foundation, the dedicating of the finished work. A school is not a building. It is, instead, made up of the men and women and children who labor and learn within the shell of mortar and brick and glass.

Too often, however, people are inclined to point to the edifice itself and to see it as the total school. All too frequently a community fails to understand that the structure is merely the site of the institution. It is a rare community which fully appreciates that the truly significant school construction is what takes place between and among the people who tenant the physical plant.

So the myth is perpetuated. Realtors take prospective buyers past the beautiful campus and buildings of Worthington High School. Visitors from elsewhere walk the corridors and praise the facilities. New teachers often sign contracts after their tour of the classrooms. Moved by esthetic considerations or the more practical desire for agreeable surroundings, there are those who readily mistake architectural elegance for educational excellence.

Not that Worthington High is mere facade, not that many in the community do not grasp the importance of what goes on behind the sills and porticoes, not that Worthington's teachers compare poorly with those of other schools. My point is simply this: that, while the school is generally first rate with a number of competent people on its staff, the community needs to be better informed and more sharply aware of the true foundation of a school—the career teachers, themselves. Too many academic pyramids have been built to house educational sarcophagi. Public schools should be the birthplace of ideas and sound values, the training ground of dynamic young citizens-to-be. Nowhere in America is it more crucial to find a high morale and an inherent faith in America's future than in our public schools, whose spirit in large part depends upon the public-school teacher.

Worthington has been in some respects fortunate in its professional staff, largely because of its location. Situated as it is, it gains in two significant ways. First, it is quite close to a number of colleges and universities which can keep it supplied with a long list of applicants for teaching jobs. Otterbein College, Capital University, Ohio Wesleyan University, Denison University, and Ohio State are all located within a twenty-mile radius of the suburb. Add to this benefit the attractions of suburban surroundings and the nearness of a great state university for work on advanced degrees, and it is understandable why Worthington should experience no teacher shortage.

Ironically, the proximity of OSU has also worked to the school district's detriment. Many of the novice teachers are women who are marking time in Worthington Schools until their husbands have graduated from law, medicine, and other colleges at State and who, therefore, often leave the system after two, three, or four years. Because teaching skills, like those of any other work, grow with experience and because it normally takes a half-dozen years for a new teacher to begin to get on his feet, the loss of these fledglings to the school (and community) economy is staggering. The departing teachers might be compared to journeymen who take the benefits of their apprenticeship out of the firm and often take it to another employer. It has been customary for Worthington to lose, on the average, 25 to 30% of its teachers annually—a substantial loss to its taxpayers.

After all, if a beginning teacher of no experience is paid approximately $6000 and after three years the teacher leaves, the community loses an $18,000 investment, and this is hardly good school economy. The Ohio Education Association's research has indicated for many years that, among the state's exempted-village schools, Worthington has ranked near the top in teacher training (degrees and graduate work) but near the bottom in teacher experience. Thus, despite the plenitude of teacher prospects, our community suffers. Not just Worthington, but communities across the land should further study this problem of teacher-turnover.

Some communities lose their career teachers because of a set of school policies which have been established with one major objective—to prevent the development of a strong teacher's organization—despite the reverse effect which such policies frequently engender. Replete with clichés and double talk, school officials in these communities will often insist that they appreciate their career teachers, but will rationalize teacher turnover by arguing that they don't want teachers who wish to *retire* in their systems. They are using *retire* in a special sense implying that experience has some deadening effect, but curiously they would have it apply only to public-school teachers, and not to those other professions of which some of them are members. Such officials, along with their supporters, are more destructive of public education than any other factor in America.

Turnover naturally guarantees a weakened teachers' organization and seems to assure a board of education and its administrators that the professional voice in its schools will be stilled— that school officials can pursue a monolithic, arbitrary course without fear of teacher dissent. Officials who wish such an outcome will inevitably begin to talk about the desirability of a merit-pay system which will reward "outstanding" teachers, thereby cutting down turnover. The truth is that merit pay, as it is usually administered, has the net effect of putting teachers even more completely at the mercy of officials who don't want anyone to rock the boat—to question their policies or decisions. Merit pay is not new at all—policies regarding "promotions" in schools, as well as in business, are frequently suspect.

Fortunately, communities across the country are beginning to abandon this myopic philosophy which protects the weak, short-term, wholly dollar-motivated teacher and which prevents its corps of career professionals from protecting and ensuring stronger teachers. I trust that no such cynicism or despotism will ever put in an appearance at Worthington, but the continuing exodus of teachers with developing skills demands solutions here and elsewhere.

Of course, there are some who would make a career of teaching who should never have entered the field in the beginning. Any profession has its misfits. I can imagine no fate worse than having to work with young people if I did not really like them. For the young know right away those classrooms in which they run a poor second to the teacher's first love—subject matter. And in such cases, youngsters rebel and retaliate, understandably.

Classrooms in which subject matter is taught to the exclusion of pupils may be a product of those colleges and universities so thoroughly concerned with their faculties' research and publication that they permit little time or incentive for teaching. In other instances, it is merely a matter of the wires being down. There are still too many people about who assume that teaching has everything to do with content and little to do with the teacher's personality and ability to communicate. Ohio State's arts college, long at war with the contentless courses conducted by some instructors in the education college, suffers from its serious need of more scholar-writers like John H. Wilson and Richard D. Altick, brilliant researchers who can also speak compellingly and excitingly. At all levels of education except, possibly, elementary schools, where it is practically impossible to ignore the students, there are teachers who have abdicated their responsibility to communicate. Graduate-school seminars, in which the emphasis is upon individual work, have too often found the professor serving as no more than an academic ornament and distributor of bibliographies on an M.A. or Ph.D. assembly line where the production slogan runs "You stay in your carrel, and I'll stay in mine, and never the twain shall meet." Nothing in the definition of *seminar* excludes sessions for the exchange of ideas and for illumination by the professor.

Clearly, education is at present confronted with its own automation problem—teaching machines, TV, more and more audio-visual equipment, etc.—which threaten, if misused, to reduce teacher-student communication even more drastically in classrooms everywhere. As this communication is lost, the function of that other requirement in the humanities will dwindle—our perception of other human beings and their individual identities and feelings.

Ask any man, and he will remember at least one teacher for whom he retains a strong dislike. Most often the teacher he recalls with such animosity was one who failed to perceive his students as young persons with a right to be treated fairly. Even when a teacher's perception improves, he must more or less live with his early mistakes. I have known some potentially strong teachers whose original shortcomings were never forgiven by their students and against whom the "grapevine" worked unfairly and unfavorably, very often because the teachers allowed these early experiences to embitter them. Though children invent nicknames and are sometimes amused by their teachers' idiosyncrasies, young people do not base their reactions to teachers upon superficial factors. Physique, complexion, health, age—rarely will such aspects prevent youngsters from responding favorably to a teacher who does not himself allow these circumstances to affect his relationship with his charges.

What is it, then, that makes a teacher? I was still puzzling over the question, though Jeanette and Dow had shared their wisdom for a decade and a half. Suddenly, I was glad that the pictures still came. Retirement? Death? No, my colleagues were there beside me, and I reached out to them, seeing them as I had first seen them.

A slightly built dark-haired woman of 35, Jeanette Fry had been at the school for only nine years, but she had become in that time a legend throughout the school and the surrounding area. I saw right away that, when she spoke, other teachers listened— out of respect and affectionate regard. Keen-eyed, intellectually alert, Miss Fry was a very vibrant personality, intensely human, altogether genuine, and sometimes embarrassingly direct. People said to me, "You always know where she stands."

When I started full-day teaching, I had to share her room in the old two-story structure which was then the high school. In those days there was no teachers' lounge, and the boiler room was too far away for a smoke between classes. If ever I needed an occasional cigarette, it was during that first year, so I had to resort to grabbing a now-and-then-puff-or-two in the large, high-ceilinged storage closet just inside the room. I kept an ash tray on a high shelf, and I could slide open the door, step in, light up, take several drags, and exhale ceilingward. I never considered that anyone would be the wiser. I knew the fire laws prohibited it, but it seemed such a small crime ranged alongside my other transgressions.

One day I had just finished my nicotine interlude when Miss Fry came into the room to prepare for the French class soon to arrive. She looked as if she had something to say, and I hurriedly cleaned up her desk, which I had left in a great clutter. Just as I was leaving, she said, "Say, I wonder whether you'd mind not smoking in here. Now, I'll tell you why I ask. My students know that I smoke outside the school, and I'm afraid they'll think I'm smoking in here as well." For a moment I felt rather as if I were one of her students being chastised. Then my good sense made me realize that I had put her on something of a spot. I told her I understood. Besides, the boiler room wasn't nearly as far away as I had supposed.

Students of mine who also attended Jeanette's Latin and French classes said, "When she teaches you, you've been taught." I used to feel a sharp pang of envy at the praise they gave her, but, because I wanted to be a good teacher, I went to her on numerous occasions for help. She was my sourcebook for formal grammar—something they didn't teach in college—and a ready reference for discipline problems.

In truth, Miss Fry was the school's expert on discipline. She was what the education theorists call an authoritarian, and she managed her classes like a first sergeant. Her teaching methods were always the old, time-tested ones—she had always felt a thorough dislike for so-called progressive education and the pedagogical pabulum served up by permissive teachers. Miss Fry practiced her calling with fairness, absolute impartiality, utter self-confidence, and the belief that, as life contains rules and deadlines, the best classroom would provide the same. If there was any element of fear in her classroom, it was that sort of fear which can be a very healthful influence in training youth. As one of her students put it, the greatest lesson she taught was responsibility. "If you hadn't done your work, you caught hell," he told me some years later on the OSU campus.

Jeanette was an expert at showmanship. When a class had obviously not studied, she would put on a display of pyrotechnics that could transform a homecoming queen or a football halfback into a blubbering wreck. One day I asked a student who was frantically preparing an assignment for her why he was in such a quivering panic. He looked up at me with haunted eyes and bleated, "She got so mad at me yesterday I was afraid she'd hurt herself pounding on the desk."

Year after year I saw her former students, some of whom had grumbled the loudest, come back to seek out the woman who had taught them discipline better than many of their parents and to thank her for that and other lessons. All over the country there must be people in every walk of life who remember her with gratitude. *"Amo, amas, amat, Miss Fry,"* breathed the whole school when, after thirty-five years of professional striving, she retired in June of 1965.

Now, nearly six months later, Dow. . . . No, it was really 1949 again, and I saw the picture of a man bending his broad shoulders over the circles and arrows of football strategy in the fall, and on quiet spring evenings sliding the battered tackle box under one arm and grinning his path down to the bank of the Olentangy—across the field which would one day bear his name.

I remembered the man who had been my friend and advisor when I was groping about and throwing chalk in my first ludicrous passes at teaching. If Jeanette had shown me the need for discipline, Dow had helped me to recognize the need for a sense of humor in my work. And the two of them were *dedication* defined.

A year before I came upon the Worthington scene, Dow had suffered a heart attack of the worst sort. At that time, his father, a physician, had frankly told Dow that victims of such attacks had, on the average, about fourteen years remaining to them, provided that they learned to relax and to brush off tension. When Dow returned to the rigors of the classroom and coaching, he had to live in the knowledge that he might never see his daughter (seven years old at the time) graduate from high school, that he might indeed be struck down at any moment. Yet he took time to listen to my problems and to tell anecdotes that enlivened my day and lightened my anxieties.

A superb coach, Dow turned out two more undefeated teams before he was appointed to the newly created position of athletic director and no longer piloted the football squads. As a teacher, he organized a health-education program that was widely praised. So well known and respected was he that, at the time of his death, he was serving as the secretary of the Ohio Athletic Directors' Association. As a man, Dow had an extraordinary compassion for others.

Sometimes when he told stories about people who were hurt by life, he'd laugh, but not in the usual hearty way that he responded to humor. After a while, I had begun to hear in that special way of laughing Nelson's manner of fighting tears. Now the picture was talking once more, and I listened to his account of a Negro boy who had been subjected to a merciless kicking and beating during the pile-ups in a football game:

44

"I took him home that night after the game. He was crying—the poor kid hurt all over, and his face was really banged up. I wanted to explain to his parents what had happened, but I couldn't even explain it to myself. And Pete kept asking, 'Why did they do that to me, Mr. Nelson?' I think his folks understood, but how do you explain that kind of ignorance and hate to a kid?"

Little wonder that Nelson's athletes and students looked to him as a second father and a model for manhood. Even though the man was only ten years my senior, I must admit that I had felt similarly—so much so that I used to worry whenever he spoke at functions or assemblies, for I could hear the tension well up in his voice.

Several weeks before he died, he must have known that death was on the way. I found out later that, as the pains increased in tempo and severity, he had simply resorted to using more of the nitroglycerine and digitalis he carried with him. Another man would never have attempted to attend and address the gathering at the football banquet on that November night, but almost as if he were taking this last chance to say some things to young people that needed saying, the old Dow Nelson returned for a few splendid minutes.

They say the tension left his voice, that he was magnificent as he told his experiences and love for the sport and as he strove to explain to those boys why their poor win-loss record comprised a winning season. Almost in the middle of a sentence, the fatal attack came. His face turned ashen. "I'd better sit down," he said. He was helped across the corridor to a table in another room, but the ambulance which arrived shortly took him to the hospital in needless haste.

These things I learned at school that November morning, and I walked to the door of his room. And he was there with me. It was only 1955, and he was pointing to a small, elderly man who was wandering down the long corridor of the newly built high school in the manner of Holmes's "Last Leaf." We watched him as he peered from side to side into the doors of classrooms like some lost soul. "Retired," Dow explained. "Must be a kind of masochism. Poor devil can't stay away. I'd a hell of a sight rather be dead than to outlive my productive years and come back to see the thing done by someone else—the thing I never actually wanted to stop doing."

Then, several years later, I was trying one day to put together my own philosophy for teaching and living (for they had begun

to amount to the same thing), and I had just written these words—
"the only things worth living for are the only things worth dying
for." I was sitting there and wondering whether I should invert my
equation when Nelson entered the room. When I showed him
the words, he quoted a passage from Erich Fromm which I had
never heard before and which ran something like this: "Man's
great mistake is that he loves things and uses people when he
should use things and love people." The morning after his death,
I heard him say it again. He was looking out the window when
he repeated the words, and a minute later he was telling me a
very funny story, but I knew that he had just revealed the key to
his life. He believed those words and spent himself translating
his belief into action.

The pillars gone? I understood all at once why the roof had not
come tumbling down. It could not, because what Dow and Jeanette
left to the school was the more enduring fabric of the spirit. They
were—and they remain—the soul of a school, and, whether I
stand in the lobby to look at the Hall of Fame portrait of Miss Fry
or move along the sideline to follow the gridiron action at Nelson
Field, I am warmed and heartened by the memory of their friendship, their professional example, and their lasting gifts.

"How do you keep from getting too closely involved with your students?" the student teacher asked me. "Can you like students— I mean really feel close to them—and still be completely professional?" I knew what was possibly troubling him. One of the senior girls had been spending quite a lot of time at his desk. He was barely of voting age and single, and she was beginning to communicate more than an interest in literature. Out of deference to his feelings, I did not make any reference to the girl directly, but I talked with him quite a while on the question he had raised.

"To tell the truth," I told him, "I don't have a good answer— provided, of course, that you're talking about *all* your students and not just *one*. I guess I've given up looking for a solution."

In any profession, I suppose, the problem of relationships between practitioner and the practiced-upon is bound to figure, but

Out of Time, Out of Place

the public-school teacher's circumstances are such that, generally speaking, the issue is much more important and additionally complicated. The teacher's relationships are obviously going to be quite different. He works with young people who spend more time with him than they pass with anyone else, with the exception of their parents and closest friends. The teacher is ethically bound to evaluate his students' work and progress as fairly as possible. If a teacher is genuinely interested in and concerned for the young people in his classroom, then he must inevitably develop sympathies, empathies, and affections. If he can properly divide this compassion or love among all of his pupils, he can maintain a constructive relationship. If he cannot, then in one way or another he's "got trouble right here in River City."

Is it possible for a teacher to grow inordinately fond of a class, to reach such a point in his closeness to them that he is being unprofessional? I don't know. Sometimes I wonder whether my reluctance to see them leave 106 reflects upon my professional character. Yet I cannot subdue these feelings about them and I have given up trying.

My fundamental approach to people, young or old, might not please Parson Peale because it requires the power of negative thinking. Briefly, I hold that any other human being is potentially capable of becoming as great a rascal as I am. I see man as being 95% animal and 5% soul. (Some may quarrel with the ratio I have fixed, but I will insist that the animal is most often in ascendancy, in both adults and children.) I am also in agreement with Jonathan Swift's notion that man possesses an inexhaustible supply of vices, which take up a large share of his time. Taken as a philosophy, these views bestow three very great benefits: (1) I am never disappointed in people, (2) every good thing that I find in people comes as a pleasant surprise, a bonus, and (3) having likened people to myself, I find that I must like them, even if I am sometimes unhappy with their acts. My outlook is similar to but not quite the same as the exhortation, "Hate the sin and love the sinner"—on occasion, like William Blake, I love even the sin, though possibly because it gives me some comfort in my own culpability.

Because I like my students and very much wish to be liked by them, I searched for some years for a methodology that would make my role as a teacher more effective, yet less disagreeable. I finally found the secret in a poem by Alexander Pope:

> *Men must be taught as if you taught them not,*
> *And things unknown proposed as things forgot.*

I must have looked at that couplet dozens of times without pulling it out of its context and seeing the brilliant flash of universal truth in it. Though I have not as yet discovered how to teach so as never to make my students painfully aware of what I am seeking to do, I have discovered some ways of pulling off the trick.

It is possible, for example, for me to hear in Pope's epigram my principal teaching objectives in one of the assignments which I make annually in Room 106. No single piece of work that they do for me has greater value or brings my students closer to me as persons. Every November I require my teenagers to turn in auto-biographies. By subterfuge similar at least to what Pope had in mind, I am pointing them toward a variety of self-instruction through which they can better come to grips with "things unknown" (themselves and the possible future) by an examination of "things forgot" or half-forgotten (their past).

By that time of the year, I have usually succeeded in proving my personal interest in them, and we have worked with literature and composition sufficiently for them to be aware of the kinds of devices and approaches they may employ in their writing. Customarily, I explain to them that, before they can hope to know others, they should take a good, honest look at themselves: "What am I really like?" "How did I get this way?" "Where do I go from here?" or "What do I do about me?" In other words, I urge them to do an intellectual memoir, not merely a succession of dates, places, and anecdotes, but self-probing, purposeful introspection.

I wish them to have complete freedom of expression in the paper. Therefore, I tell them that, while I intend neither to hope for nor to insist upon my personal intrusion into their private lives, what they have to say about themselves and others will be treated in the strictest professional confidence. Finally, I ask that, when they have something unpleasant to say about someone I might know in the school, they use substitute names or otherwise disguise the identity.

Most of my writing assignments involve short, expository themes, but the autobiographies often run to considerable lengths. They have ranged from four to 151 pages during the many years in which I have required them. The average autobiography takes almost an hour to read and mark, and this means that every November I spend some one hundred hours of my out-of-school time in evaluating this one assignment. At least once during the marking of the papers, I wonder why I chose to teach English, but when the work is over I have a much greater awareness of my students and a somewhat closer relationship with them than most teachers enjoy. The information my young people provide in these papers remains helpful to me throughout the rest of their time with me. I have a clearer picture of their interests, their experiences, their feelings, and their ambitions. I have noted, too, that they do some of their best writing on this assignment. After all, they know the subject better than any other—it is one dear to their hearts.

For the student, work on an autobiography can be both a traumatic and therapeutic experience, but the end product is, I think, a much greater self-understanding. They burrow into their lives with surprising thoroughness and often express themselves with shocking candor on those subjects which are central to life but which public education has often been fearful of treating—politics, race, religion, sex, etc. I have wondered at times whether some of my young writers have not been just waiting for someone to come along and listen to them. The paper gives them a chance to "let go," to speak their minds fully. Though there are always some whose papers show inhibition and shallowness, others have treated me almost as a father-confessor and have poured out their hearts in recalling tragedies and expressing hurts and fears.

Of course, there is ordinarily a parent who comes by in the hope that he might read his son's or daughter's autobiography. Parents understand most often when I tell them that I cannot let them do so. When it is apparent to me in a student's memoir that he needs help and advice, I approach the student with suggestions as to who might be of assistance. If the problem is such that I can be of aid, then I arrange a session in which we can sit and talk it out. Often my closing comments on the papers themselves run to letter length.

I know that an autobiography assignment is not a new method among English teachers. Chances are that others have found, as I have, some of the most candid reminiscences and gripping drama in their classroom experience through reading such themes. I laugh at their humorous accounts, share in their triumphs, enjoy their satire, and often find myself comparing my own youth with theirs.

I find much happiness in the reading, but then there is that other side of human experience—frightening, confusing, twisted, bizarre, and sinister. Suburbia's youth have no immunity to the sicknesses which beset mankind. Hear them cry out:

My father hates me and I hate him. He wanted me to be a big deal athlete like he was. He can't seem to understand that he and I are different.

♦　♦　♦

When the Traveler arrived home one day after school, her mother was nowhere to be found. Later, still wondering where her mother could be, the Traveler went into the garage for something. When she opened the door, she found her mother there, hanging from a piece of clothesline.

*One night early in my freshman year I went on a hay-
ride one October night. I was thrilled when a senior boy
I knew in the band became interested in me. Several
other couples were wrapped in blankets and so I didn't
object when he pulled a blanket over us. Later I told my
parents and they insisted on having me examined. I'll
never forgive them.*

♦ ♦ ♦

If I date a girl I take her out for just one thing.

♦ ♦ ♦

*When my parents saw that I was in a car with three
boys and that one of them was a Negro, they started out
with "What will the neighbors say?" I never knew how
prejudiced they were. I just couldn't believe my ears.
I ran out of the house. I had to get away from them. I
was gone for hours, just walking.*

♦ ♦ ♦

*Then I saw the truth, that my mother and step-father
were a couple of swindlers living it high, following the
new oil fields and keeping their eye open for suckers.*

♦ ♦ ♦

*Russian planes flew over the German ship evacuating us
from Riga. The whole ship shook with the explosions of
the bombs. My mother was holding my baby brother, but
we had to jump into the water.*

♦ ♦ ♦

*I wanted to die. I kept swallowing the pills and after a
little while I fell asleep.*

♦ ♦ ♦

*That evening my father called the family together into
the dining room and told us what the doctor had said.
He explained that he was going to die—that he had four
or five months left at most. He asked us not to feel sad,
but to make his remaining time a time of smiles and
help him be strong.*

♦ ♦ ♦

*I never know what I'll find when I get home. Last week
my mother was all boozed up and fell backward on the
stairsteps. When I came home from school she was lying there, out cold with the back of her head bleeding.*

Before much of the summer had passed by, I realized that my Uncle was sick. I kept avoiding him, but one day he came into the room and tried to force me to have sexual intercourse with him.

♦ ♦ ♦

One time when I was about seven years old I was playing with matches in a backyard with my playmate. We accidentally started a fire in some boxes. My stepmother came out and saw it and told me she was going to call the fire department and they would come and lock me up. Then she spanked me and locked me in the closet. I begged and pleaded for her to unlock the door because I was still scared of the dark, but she didn't come for a long time. . . . My second grade in school was very unhappy. I started my stuttering that year and other kids made fun.

♦ ♦ ♦

The American people are weak because they let democracy prevent the nation from being led by the truly capable people—the natural leaders. America has even permitted Jews in the Supreme Court and Negroes in Congress.

♦ ♦ ♦

If my father is an example of Christianity, then I want no part of it. I listen to his sermons and wonder how he can be such a hypocrite.

♦ ♦ ♦

Regardless of what the doctor says, I believe Mommie when she says she is sick and needs me there with her. I know I miss a lot of school, but I owe it to Mommie.

♦ ♦ ♦

In the barn across from the stables the crowd has a little room fixed up real nice so that we can go there and drink beer and take girls sometimes. It makes it nice.

♦ ♦ ♦

He said you could always tell from the sound of the gun where the bullet was. He was laughing when he put the gun to his head and pulled the trigger. Then there was a deafening noise. And then he was laying there, shaking all over, and I screamed and ran. Not for help. I just had to get away from it. It was horrible.

These are the voices of *suburban* high-school seniors, those who supposedly "have it made," who have sometimes been more deeply scarred by life than we may imagine. Their autobiographical efforts have forced me to take a long look not only at their individual environments but at the total nature of the community in which they live. My earliest view of the place had been secondhand and slightly prejudiced:

"Ever hear of a place called Worthington?" I asked a co-worker in the warrant room of the State Treasury one summer morning in 1949. I had just finished talking on the phone to Dr. Eberhart, who had asked me whether I was interested in a teaching job there. It was rather muggy in the basement of the State House where we were quartered, and my colleague had just concluded another unsuccessful effort to explain to one of the women employees the function of the thermostat control on the air-conditioner. He looked at me through the fumes and conjunctivitis of the bad morning-after he was suffering.

"F'Chris'sake, you don't know where Worthington is?" he asked in amazement.

"I've never even *heard* of the place," I said. "Where is it, anyway? I have to see the school superintendent there tomorrow."

"Straight up High Street. Y' can't miss it—unless you're drivin' too fast."

"What's it like there? What kind of place is it?"

"Jesus Christ," he sighed, intoning his customary morning devotional over his adding machine. Then he gazed at me blearily. "I think I spent two weeks there one night."

This brief dialogue, through which I was first introduced to Worthington, illustrates two facts about the town: (1) that all Central Ohioans are expected to be familiar with this suburb and (2) that Worthington was, at that time at least, a comparatively quiet, rather small village. She was still the child of the Old Northwest, her New Connecticut dream hardly disturbed by the Victorian gingerbread and the approaching clamor of something called the Twentieth Century Unlimited.

Worthington is one of those remarkable little communities of Ohio and the Middle West in which the *status quo* used to be marketed like any other nineteenth-century antique. In fact, it required more than 150 years for the village to become a city. Located some ten miles north of where the sluggish Olentangy River collides with the scented Scioto, the town is typical in some ways of the modern complexity called Suburbia. Here, in 1803, the Griswolds, the Kilbournes, and their fellow investors from Connecticut found an agreeable little rise in the landscape and began to build their homes and to fill them with the laughter of children. Probably none of these migrant New Englanders could have imagined then that Route 23 would one day see fit to intersect indecorously in their very midst with Route 161 and that only a few miles away an upstart neighbor would expand into the metropolitan capital of Ohio with a population pushing 1,000,000.

To their credit, however, it should be pointed out that the founders of Worthington were sufficiently interested in education to set aside a sizable tract of land for the support of the school. Running from Evening Street west to the Olentangy, this area is now the site for the "East Annex" of the high school (formerly the high school), the new Evening Street Elementary School, the senior high school with its science and physical-education areas, the community swimming pool, and Nelson Field. Worthington has profited from the wisdom of its founders in this respect, but ignored the Yankee foresight in another, very crucial matter. James Kilbourne, Orange Johnson, and others had realized that communities prosper according to their revenues, and the pioneers set about to develop industries. Only after Columbus had very nearly surrounded the town and annexed potential commercial locations did some influential community leaders wake up to the truth. Today, therefore, Worthington's residential-property owners carry a fantastic (in terms of Central Ohio) tax load already, and their school and public-service needs continue to call for additional taxes.

The Worthington of today is more than a suburb; in reality, it is a state of mind, a social opportunity, and a battleground. Here the lower-middle class and the middle-middle class, in their quest for status and success, bring their families into open conflict with the insecurely entrenched upper-middle class. Here, the politician, the educator, the social worker, the up-and-coming or retired business executive, the land proprietor, the chronic clubwoman—in short, the enlightened and the comfortable—can build their homes and rear their young well out of view of the "sordidness and squalor" of Columbus' "inner city."

In recent years more and more skilled tradesmen and small businessmen have moved into the school district. For some of these people, the principal worth of Worthington lies in opportunities for the right social and business contacts, the quaint warmed-over New England atmosphere, and its almost exclusively residential character. Still others have come because they have been told of Worthington's interest in and tradition of fine schools.

Admittedly, it is quite unfair to generalize about any population area. If many of the people of Worthington seem to chase some elusive vision of social elevation, no less may be said of many other human beings. A considerable segment of the townspeople—artisans and white-collar workers—are quite ordinary in their wants, and doubtless most of them can see at close range that the town is something less than the Utopian mirage that it was from a distance. Yet, if they recognize some drawbacks in their new environment, they seldom voice their feelings. Except for occasional squabbles over "preserving the colonial atmosphere"—sometimes this means allowing anachronistic and decaying architectural remains to offend the eye—and zoning laws, they rarely find issues worth fighting over.

The struggle for social status, however, is a ceaseless, uncompromising one, and there is little peace for the suburbanite. Two decades ago, a half-dozen families were the Destinies of the community. Then the newly monied built around the town and after an all-out battle eventually achieved, if not mastery, at least equality with the village leaders. The result involved a temporary pact between the traditional provincialism and conservatism on one hand and the power of the wallet on the other. Unhappily for those who resisted change, once this bargain had been made, the town would never be quite the same again. The New England village inevitably had to become the modern suburb.

Nevertheless, the name of Worthington continues to carry a particular magic for many people in the capital city. They hear in the word the sound of upper-class substance and solidity, and they eagerly drive north on Sunday afternoons to inspect high-priced lots and dwellings. Yet there is far less wealth than show of prosperity in Worthington. Wealth is, of course, a relative term and the truly wealthy do not reside here. Indeed, the biggest part of the financial well-being in and around the town is only the product of postwar self-improvement and the higher standard of living throughout America.

The cost of the intra-middle-class war is heavy and disheartening, too. Worthington unquestionably has more than its share of divorce, alcoholism, and financial insecurity. The absurdly inflationary prices of houses on Mortgage Row and Inheritance Drive contribute to the problem, without a doubt. A study of heart disease and nervous disorders in the area might conceivably present shocking revelations. In addition, the feinting and jabbing of the socially sensitive does unassessable damage to the youngsters of such a community. When 98% of my twelfth-grade students at Worthington High declare in a survey (taken over a three-year period) that their classmates place much or some emphasis on socioeconomic factors in selecting friends, it is only reasonable to assume that either a distorted sense of values, a considerable social insecurity, or a combination of both is affecting these young people.

Interestingly enough, astute real-estate salesmen often point out the schools as being one of the strongest factors in the appeal of this area to prospective buyers. Of course, the schools are Worthington's in name only; actually, the town shares its control with the outlying population in a fairly extensive district in which there is an increasing economic and cultural heterogeneity. Though the realtors are the school's best press agents (their advertisements almost without exception refer to the quality of education in Worthington), there is little question but that the school is quite valuable here. In the midst of the social upheaval around it, the school provides the only major meeting ground and the outstanding common interest of the community. Here the psychological injuries sustained by the young may be partially repaired.

The student autobiographies indicate that Worthington has its share of mixed-up youngsters. While many of our youth have a material edge over teenagers elsewhere, they nevertheless constitute a very real challenge as young suburbans with their own peculiar problems. Suburbs breed forces every bit as destructive as those at work in crowded, smoke-fouled urban centers. If we have juvenile delinquency here—and we do—it is generally of a more sophisticated, less violent, seldom publicized variety. For want of a better label, I often refer to our local problem-youth as "white-collar delinquents."

I have found one great advantage in my work at Worthington. Most of my students like school and are eager to learn. They have been conditioned by their parents and their community to understand the importance of education, and in most cases they work quite hard for me. Being absorbed by my subject and by the presence of questioning minds, I am perhaps remiss in my duties at times—I probably do not concern myself sufficiently with objecting to unorthodox apparel or other superficial matters. I am much more concerned with the minds, the people behind the facade. Teaching is somehow more meaningful, more enjoyable when you lose things but find humanity in the process.

I sit alone with their autobiographies at the school or in my study at home, and I listen to these Worthington students tell their stories. Through the faulty grammar and mechanics there rings an eloquence and something else—a spirit of fellowship. Sometimes I write comic parodies to the verse they include, occasionally I scribble questions in the margins in order to make them consider the logic of their comments, and often I jot sympathetic statements or try to advise them about some matter. In the midst of marking an autobiography, I may even indulge myself in personal reminiscing.

In further testimony that most of my seniors take this assignment very seriously, they often make references to the papers afterwards. Sometimes, later in the year or even years after they have graduated, students will write epilogues or letters to me to bring me up to date on their lives. Regularly, too, I hear of former students of mine—some one hundred of them have taught English —who are requiring their students to write autobiographies.

Some observers might say that I should concentrate more upon my subject matter and less upon my students and their environment. The only answer I have is the one I gave my student teacher —that I could not be happy in teaching without the relationship I have with my seniors. If this feature of my work detracts from my professional posture or character, then so be it. Perhaps it is a matter of semantics. "I am involved in mankind," wrote John Donne. How can it be otherwise for a teacher?

I'll call him Doug for two reasons—to cut down on pronouns and to emphasize his special significance among the alumni of 106. Doug was not a star in Worthington's academic firmament. He was only a fairly good student. As an athlete, he never served as a captain or top scorer. In his classrooms he frequently found himself completely at odds with his teachers, and in the halls totally out of step with the other students. Without intending any pun, I can't help noting that the position he played on Worthington's varsity football squad—he was a defensive back—best summarizes his personality during the first several months of his stay at Worthington. Back of all his outward animosity and pugnaciousness, he was on the defensive. When I was beginning to feel comfortable with the chalk dust on my shoulder, Doug was beginning to writhe under the two-by-four he carried around on his.

The Windsor Knot

Like me, Doug had seen his parents separated and divorced when he was only ten or eleven. He, too, had spent the major portion of his childhood in an urban zoo prowled by uncaged predators, the sort of environment in which a boy learns to use fists and knees rather than to find out about music and art and what they can provide for the human spirit. Then his mother had remarried, and overnight he was uprooted and brought to Worthington, where an entirely different pattern of living flourished.

As a transplant, Doug would have made Luther Burbank throw in the trowel. The boy fought with his stepfather, his teammates, his teachers, and himself. Stocky, well shouldered, quick, and strong, he had at least a fair chance of winning any purely physical contest, but he lost the fight with himself every time. In effect, then, he was a chronic loser by the time he sauntered under the sword into Room 106.

On the day before the official opening of school that fall, I had seen his name on my roster. Having heard about him, I had methodically set up my seating chart in advance so that he was well removed from the window and effectively surrounded by four comparatively quiet, studious, long-faced, uncommonly sweet but undiverting girls whom I had taught in junior English the year before. In that way I subjected him to one of the worst kinds of solitary confinement ever suffered by young manhood. Though I had never seen the boy, I had conjured up an image of what he must look like, based upon the stories I had heard from other teachers. Let me say that I try always to avoid prejudicial attitudes which might affect my work in the school, but this fellow's reputation had so preceded him that he became a classic exception. I was sure that he must look like an unphotogenic gargoyle, that for a face he must wear a split-level sneer.

I rarely look at faces as I call the roll and seat students on the first day. My whole *modus operandi* is to establish at least a mild degree of shock and to bring the summer to a precipitant, jarring, nerve-shattering halt. For that reason I make it a practice to have a seating arrangement prepared and to have duplicated copies of the daily assignments for the full year ready for distribution at that initial session. Actually, my English program is somewhat more open to later modification than this procedure suggests, but the first day of school should not find any teacher emphasizing his flexibility.

After my third-period class had settled in their seats, I glanced reluctantly toward the chair to which I had assigned Doug. Instead of the genetic throwback which I had half expected to see, I found a fine-featured face with hazel eyes, the slightest suggestion of beard around the chin, an unsmiling mouth, and set jaws. That he was taking my measure was fully apparent, but ten to fifteen other pairs of eyes were similarly engaged. Others, already familiar with my first-day peculiarities, were soberly awaiting the next order of business.

Once I had issued the textbooks, handed out the assignment sheets and book lists, and previewed the year's work, I had a little time left over for my first try at getting new faces and names memorized. In that process of studying countenances and repeating names, I made every effort not to show special concern over Doug's presence. Every other face would grin or show some friendly acknowledgment when I called its name. His face remained immobile, his eyes seeming to reflect a mixture of hostility, contempt, and finger-drumming curiosity. When the bell rang, I watched him rise with an exaggerated ennui and make his exit with the slow, stiff-legged, rocking stride that I associate with the Varsity Syndrome.

I don't wish to leave the impression that my work permits me to make a case study or special project of every person in my classroom. Doug was only one of one hundred thirty-five students in 106 that year, and every one of them had particular problems and a right to a fair share of my time. Still, I couldn't help seeing Doug as a special challenge, observing him closely, watching his responses to subject matter, and cataloging his ostensible reactions to me and to his classmates.

For the first several weeks, Doug never spoke voluntarily. Nevertheless, when called upon, he regularly surprised me with the quality of his recitation. He was obviously studying, and his insight into Chaucer and Shakespeare was strong, especially where an understanding of characters was concerned. His comments were always brief; I could see that he felt discomfort when reciting. Almost always he would look around self-consciously at his classmates when he replied to a question. Written composition constituted his biggest difficulty. When I read his first theme, I felt like Champollion contemplating the writings on the Rosetta Stone. It was evident, though, that Doug was becoming interested in literature.

A somewhat unexpected metamorphosis occurred just after the Thanksgiving holiday. The rather mousy little girl who sat to the left of Doug arrived one morning without her glasses and with something different about her hair. In addition, she was wearing a bright emerald-green sweater in such a way that she had soon energized Phil, the most comatose of the senior male animals.

Before the bell I saw her talking animatedly to Doug, whose expression announced that he had never seen her before. During the class I noted that he was having great trouble concentrating on *Gulliver's Travels*. Several times I saw him glance appreciatively at the new and engaging creature sitting beside him. The Age of Reason was no match for a green sweater and—now I understood what had happened to the glasses—new green eyes.

Sandy (that was the name she began putting on her papers instead of the old *Sandra*) and Doug began dating that week, I learned in the teachers' lunchroom. This new development seemed a very happy one in the beginning, but there was a gleam in Sandy's contact lenses that promised no good for a young man in the throes of first love. Doug's grades didn't tailspin until Sandy began searching new horizons. And inevitably she had to try her new wings. After all, she was Eve's sister—her little sister, I'll concede—and she was attracting the attention of some other senior boys. I was grateful that she waited until after Doug had given his monologue before she dated one of the others. Then all of Doug's background boiled over. He had, as I have noted, grown up in surroundings where feelings can quickly and violently erupt, and soon he was back in the principal's office, having law and order explained to him. He drew a three-day suspension for fighting with the boy who had dated Sandy.

When he came back, he was his old surly self, had little to say in class, and once more walked the corridors alone. Sandy, meanwhile, was adding new conquests, and Doug watched in mute misery her continuing social successes. He was carrying a weak-C average when my concern about him led me to call him in after school.

"I've read your autobiography, Doug. It really doesn't do you justice." He merely looked at me and shrugged. "You've got a good head, and I know you feel strongly about things, but you really keep it bottled up, don't you? In your autobiography, anyway." My last several words were intended to twist the knife, and the smoldering in his eyes finally got to his voice.

"What could I write that *you'd* be interested in? What could I say that you'd understand?"

"You mean you figure you're so unique, so special that nobody's ever had your troubles before?"

"They've got it made—all of them. Clothes, cars, big college plans—"

"Oh, you must have it rough," I interrupted. I was going to say something about the $50,000 hovel his stepfather owned, but then I realized it might sound like low-income teacher talk. "You're not going to college, then?"

"Not if I have to on my stepfather's money." He said *stepfather* as if it were the most repulsive word around.

"I don't understand. According to your autobiography, there isn't any trouble at home now."

"There wasn't. Not until I got kicked out of classes. He blew his top and I blew mine. I'm not asking him for anything from here on out." His whole manner reminded me of someone I had known too well, a boy who had hurt others, however innocent and well meaning, just to strike out at a world in which he had been torn with a grief that seemed past healing. I hated the memory of that boy, or at least that side of him that had wrought havoc in so many lives. I did not want this boy to follow the unhallowed, unhappy paths I had trod. I shook my head and glared at Doug.

"And you sit there and tell me somebody else has it made. Do you know how I had it made at your age? Listen to me, Doug. My father left home the same way yours did. I watched my mother live in loneliness for seven years, faithful to a man who had no intention of coming back. When I was a senior in high school, I was working half-days at a locomotive works and helping to pay off accumulated bills. And let me tell you something else, you poor abused kid. I turned down a four-year scholarship because I was stupid enough to suppose I knew all I needed to know and because I was too proud to take help from my father's family. And after that, I watched a lot of kids who never had a fraction of your advantages wallow in their own blood. You think you've got a monopoly on the world's troubles? You've got a corner on the stupidity market. My God, boy, you've got nothing but cream— pure cream!"

"But you—you don't look like––" he began lamely.

"I don't look and sound like I came from the wrong side of a steel and railroad town? That's what you're saying?" My own heat subsided some, then. I hadn't meant to give him my autobiography. I hadn't intended to refer to the man who remained a boy's hero, however tarnished, or to the woman whose love and faith and utter selflessness had kept together a home for two sons. I hadn't expected to froth at the mouth at him. "I suppose I don't —and there's one clue in that for you. You don't have to talk and act like an animal all your life. But there's only one way that'll happen—education! And if you don't get as much as you can, you're a damned fool." He stared at me for a minute or two in silence. "That'll end my after-school noises, Doug. I guess it's more than I wanted to say. And I wouldn't have said that much or said it in that way if I weren't interested in what you do with yourself. I'll see you tomorrow, third period." He looked at me curiously, rose slowly, and shuffled to the door.

"One more thing, Doug. It's none of my business, but, if I were you, I'd play it cool with the young lady."

"Who? Sandy?" Once more he looked surprised.

"I'd let her know that she's not exactly indispensable."

"But she's the only one that—that—"

"Yeah, and she *knows* it—believe me, she *knows* it." I turned to the gradebook on my desk as his footsteps scuffed their slow-time down the corridor.

From that day on, Doug saw me in a somewhat different light, I think, and his work improved at an astounding rate. He had a B average for the semester—not a strong B but good enough to strengthen his chance for an athletic scholarship. His other teachers began to make encouraging remarks about him. After the second semester had gotten underway, I discovered that he had already dated two other seniors and a pretty little junior. Rumor had it that Sandy was greener eyed than ever when the junior showed up at school in Doug's letter sweater. In class Sandy was certainly showing renewed interest in him, but his reaction to her indicated that the sometime romance in 106 was altogether extinct. I usually observe such affairs with disinterested amusement, but I couldn't help finding poetic justice here.

Apart from his work in class, Doug made no concessions to me at all—not until the evening he was to attend a sports banquet at which he was to be honored. That night I had returned to my room to get some materials in order and to run off a test for the following day. I was at the desk, sorting odds and ends, when I caught a glimpse of someone standing a step or two outside the door. Then I saw it was he and wondered how long he'd been there in the corridor. He was wearing a light-gray suit, and his shirt collar hung open.

"Well," I asked lightly, "what're *you* doing out there?"

"I—I thought maybe you were busy." He shifted awkwardly as he spoke.

"C'mon in, Doug. I can take a break." Then I saw that he was holding something. Whatever it was had once been a necktie, but now it looked like a strand of crepe paper left over from last Halloween. I recognized his problem even before he had spelled it out.

"Can you—well, would you show me how t' tie this? The way you tie yours."

"Sure. Be glad to." Some of the misery left his face as he handed it to me. "But you know what I think? I think you've put this tie through quite an ordeal."

He laughed. "Yeah, it looks pretty bad at that. I guess I was as rough on it as it was on me."

"Wait a minute." I walked to the built-in cabinet next to the door and looked into the side which is rarely closed. Here I have a combination bookcase, clothes press, and prop room. I found what I was looking for, a comparatively new necktie. "How about this? It ought to go all right with that gray."

"Yeah, but you shouldn't—"

"Doug, my family has this thing with ties. Whenever they run out of things to do, they trot out and buy me another tie. I think they're harboring a secret desire to see me strangle myself." I handed him the tie, and I began to use his as a demonstrator. "Which do you like, four-in-hand or Windsor?"

"I dunno."

"I use a Windsor." Actually, tying a necktie is a much harder process for me when I have to think about it, but I finally succeeded in showing him how. He mimicked the several flips and adjustments and then buttoned his collar and slipped the knot into place. I pointed him to the cabinet door with its small mirror, where he examined the result and grinned. From downstairs came the sounds of others arriving for the banquet in the cafeteria.

"Thanks a lot," he exclaimed warmly.

"Any time, Doug." I slipped off my neck the stained, droopy tie he had brought. "You'd better take this along."

"No, it's had it, but I'll bring yours back tomorrow."

"No sweat," I said in his vernacular. "You keep it. It'll just litter my cabinet."

After he had gone, I closed the door to 106 and went back to the job on my desk. I didn't get much work done, though. I sat there, looking at the empty chairs and thinking about the role I had just played. I remembered another Doug, the boy who had missed his signals and turned out to be the daughter I love. No, I would never have the son I had wanted once, yet I have had, in a way, many sons in my time. And just now I had gained another. Another young man had joined my growing family, not because I had explained to him the satire in *The Canterbury Tales*, not because I would show him how to avoid dangling modifiers by steering away from passive-voice verbs, but because a teacher, even an undistinguished English teacher, deals in much more than subject matter. If a classroom is to be a benign influence upon humanity, then more than the mind must be nourished there—the human heart and spirit must grow a little there.

The last time I saw Doug was the day after commencement. I was in my room giving the place a last-minute glance before going to the office and checking out for the summer. He came in briskly, and I reached to shake his hand and congratulate him on his alumnihood. He started to say something, then looked down at his feet. When he looked up, his eyes were brimming. I had to do something to keep from getting somewhat sloppy, myself, so I brought my other hand across and clapped the back of the one I still gripped. "Thanks for everything," he said. There had been more in that knot than a tie.

The rest of Doug's story has so far been a happy one. He got his athletic scholarship, arrived at an understanding with his stepfather, and a few years ago took his law degree. I had a package from him just after he married. In it I found a necktie and a letter in which he paid me many compliments with such sincerity that I still reread it occasionally when my morale is lowered by disappointments or trials in my teacher existence. "I want to be a man like you," he wrote. I read that sentence and think to myself *I want to be the man you describe, son.* Then I put the letter back into the folder with something that resembles a strand of crepe paper left over from last Halloween.

... THE ACCUSED SHALL ENJOY THE RIGHT . . . TO BE INFORMED OF THE NATURE AND CAUSE OF THE ACCUSATION; TO BE CONFRONTED WITH THE WITNESSES AGAINST HIM. . . .

These phrases will have a familiar sonorousness for most Americans. They are drawn from Amendment VI in our Federal Constitution. Of course, they specifically have to do with the protection of the citizen's rights in courtroom trials which involve criminal cases. But many Americans would argue that, in principle, such rights should be recognized and upheld by any public officer whose duties include a quasi-judicial function. Unfortunately, the law does not always provide a recourse to slander and a guarantee of justice.

I am pleased to say that, at the present time, a citizen who wishes to register a complaint against a teacher in Worthington

The Trial of a Teacher

High School will be heard—but he will also be required to confront the teacher he accuses, if pressing for action against the teacher. This was Principal Bill Lane's personal policy—a reasonable, professional approach to such matters—one still followed by the school. In the same way, a teacher who brings forth a charge against a student must stand ready, if the circumstances warrant, to appear, with any witnesses involved, before the student and his parents.

Lane formulated his policy after he had had several years' experience with chronic agitators who wished to remain anonymous as well as venomous. It came to a head one day when someone in the community phoned that a teacher on the staff was not properly gesticulating and articulating the Pledge of Allegiance to the flag at the beginnings of school assemblies.

And it was true. The teacher, a friend of mine, held that the Pledge was an empty lip service for many people—a superficiality to which he would not subscribe. I personally disagree with my friend on this issue. When I pledge allegiance, I voice my loyalty to certain ideals which, for me, the nation's colors represent. I am not shouting, "My country, right or wrong." Nor am I, like uniformed convention drunks, unreeling toilet paper from hotel windows and shooting squirt guns at little old ladies under hotel marquees. Yet my friend's right to turn his back on symbols is a part of what I pledge my belief in. Moreover, though he remains quiet and undemonstrative, he believes as earnestly in freedom and democracy as I do. My friend would be damned reliable company in a foxhole, I suspect—a whole lot better than those perennial drum-beaters who disappear at the first sign of blood.

Besides, my fellow teacher was an agnostic, and the *under God* addition to the Pledge makes it virtually impossible for him to utter conscientiously the full statement. I wonder how many agnostics or atheists publicly make liars of themselves in pronouncing their allegiance. We have put many loyal citizens into a bind by inserting that phrase. It is not, therefore, mere anti-symbolism that prevents my friend from taking loyalty oaths. Actually, though he might not admit it, he is moved by emblems as much as any of us, though such outward show carries different associations for him.

Without digressing further, let me say that, upon this teacher's request, the principal asked the parent to come into the office with his grievance and his innuendoes. Lane was just as weary as many teachers everywhere are of the critics who like to hide behind telephones, Kaffeeklatsch circles, and Number Three tees. I have forgotten the outcome in this instance, except that the teacher remained for another year of non-pledging before taking an assistantship at OSU. It was not at all difficult for him to sign a loyalty oath at the University.

This is a case in which the schoolteacher was heard and the charge against him brought forth by the accuser in the teacher's presence. Though hardly a cause célèbre, this case demonstrates the correct role of an administrator as an arbiter and as a professional leader. Bill Lane had learned, just as I had, that the school critics and teacher-baiters in a community are going to be heard one way or another and that it is always better to go to the source and to air the matter as quickly as possible. We had learned this lesson together in the ordeal of Harriet Somers.

Many of the people who had important roles in the Somers drama are dead, have left Worthington, or remember it now with vague distaste as something better left alone or forgotten. More than a dozen years have passed since that very fine, but unfortunate woman figured in a controversy which left her dreadfully ill, yet indirectly led to somewhat improved conditions by scaring the teacher-baiters themselves. Opposing loyalties and views divided the entire community. The whole school system was shaken to its several foundations. New friendships developed, but enmities set in everywhere. The expanding circle of antagonisms marked the last sad throes in the saga of a hamlet that had to become a city. Though Harriet was badly hurt by the whole ugly business, I know that she would be among the first to say, "Let us forgive and learn from this." It is in that spirit that I undertake to tell this story.

Even now it would be so easy for me to set my file aside and pretend these events never happened. To do so, however, would be to deal in untruth. My own part in the Somers case seriously affected my thinking and my career in the chalk dust. Most important, however, is my obligation to my profession to present as objectively as I can a narrative which probably has had its counterpart in every local school district in the country. The greatest problem is in getting to the facts, for in such episodes there is usually as much conjecture as fact available. Here some of the truth may have died with a disease-stricken girl, a principal turned realtor, a woman killed on the Ohio Turnpike, and a boy whose plane crashed. Some of the truth may have been lost through distortion and soothing rationalization.

That I lack the whole truth, I very much regret, but that is precisely the point I wish to stress in my criticism of present statutory law. The account that follows is not intended to represent an attack upon teachers, administrators, board members, or community. As human beings, most of the persons treated have been (and remain) friends of mine. As a community, Worthington is neither worse nor better than any other population center of similar history and like composition. My quarrel is with the law, and I will always oppose any purposeless and fundamentally evil policy or rule which has the effect of forcing me to choose between friends.

The story began, no doubt, when Mrs. Somers started teaching at the high school some years ago. She was a long-time citizen of Old Worthington—the wife of a well-known dentist, a leading figure in the town's vaunted Garden Club, a member of the local Players' Club. She was a tall, vivacious woman who took much pleasure in working with young people. She was highly qualified for teaching speech and drama. Gifted and thoroughly trained, she had taught years before in the neighboring town of Westerville. Now that her children were in high school, she determined to resume her work in the classroom. Like every other teacher, she found it was a task to begin or to resume teaching. As any other staff member does, she made mistakes. Nevertheless, she was enthusiastic, tractable, and pleasant to work with. When my seniors were preparing an original commencement production, she cheerfully gave of her time and skill to help me stage the necessary historical tableaux.

Her willingness to help out may have been a factor that contributed to her eventual problem. For Harriet the school day never ended at four o'clock—her play rehearsals, cast parties, and get-togethers with young people took up many of her evenings. I hate to admit it, but my profession is so rife with clock-watchers that the really enthusiastic teacher often incurs some suspicion. Harriet liked inviting the high-school staff to her house as well as having students in. No doubt she talked about her school work to people around the town—perhaps too spiritedly for some, maybe unwisely to others. However that may be, she probably stimulated jealousy among some mothers and fathers who envied her close relationship with the youngsters in the high school.

I heard the first ugly, snide remarks about Harriet shortly after she and several other faculty members had performed in the school's annual variety show. She had done an impersonation of Sophie Tucker, and, though it was her spirit of fun and the specific request of her colleagues that led her to do it, it gave her critics something to sneer at.

Not one, but dozens of lessons for teachers may be gained from Harriet's experience. She was unwise in her variety-show act, but she had the added disadvantage of her beautiful and talented daughter in the freshman class at Worthington High. That class would be long remembered as one of the most competitive ever to graduate from Worthington. Their rivalry extended to all things, including the scramble among the girls in that group to date junior and senior boys. If I had it in my power to institute just one rule in the high school, I would make it impossible for freshman girls to attend such events as junior-senior proms, and I would discourage as much as possible the dating of senior boys by ninth-grade girls.

So lethal was the competition for status in that class that daily some of the girls were in tears. As seniors, three years later, they still carried the scars of the largely parent-prompted struggle. Bonnie, Harriet's daughter, was often hurt by her classmates, too. On several occasions Mrs. Somers was forced into the injudicious dual role of mother and teacher. When by force of natural talent Bonnie made opportunities for herself, there were some who gossiped that Harriet's presence in the high school gave the girl unfair advantages. The town tongues began to wag, and the wags began to tongue the malicious sort of tripe so often current in little communities and among little people. What I heard was enough to convince me that my daughter should never attend any school at which I taught. It works out satisfactorily for some, but the dangers are ever present.

The foulest mouth in the community belonged to Nate McKenzie, an overbearing ass who liked to play rough-and-tough big brother to the high-school students who visited his home. McKenzie had much success in bullying and bulldozing his way around the town until the community got tired of it. He was in his influential heyday during the trial of Harriet Somers. He found his big opportunity soon enough. If his attacks on a woman sound unmanly, it must be kept in mind that McKenzie was in reality the big boy he pretended to be. I can forgive even McKenzie, though Heaven would find me more convincing if he had several teeth lodged in his larynx. I know that there must have been good things about him—I didn't know him well enough to say what they were. I was subsequently pleased to see that his children had not inherited his unpleasant traits.

If my memory is trustworthy, the next major event in the Somers chronicle occurred two years after Harriet started teaching at Worthington, when she was directing the senior-class play in the fall. After one of the rehearsals, or possibly a cast party, one of the freshman girls declared that a senior boy had attempted to rape her when he took her home from Mrs. Somers' house. Whether there was any truth to her story, I cannot say. The girl was pretty, petite, and perhaps imaginative; the boy possibly made a well-defined pass at her. It is not important now as to what occurred between them. What is significant is that McKenzie and several people under his influence used this event to suggest, with a chivalrous show of protecting the girl's name, that the Somers residence was not the best place for youngsters to congregate and added some subtle insinuations about Harriet and her daughter. McKenzie was the sort that would have accused Hilton's Mr. Chips of homosexual leanings.

I had little in common with Harriet except that she taught two or three sections of English in addition to speech. No two teachers use exactly the same *modus operandi*, and we were probably miles apart in our methodology. Nominally, I was chairman of the English department, and she frequently came to me with questions about materials and approaches to the subject matter. When the anti-Somers phone calls began tying up the superintendent's and principal's time, they naturally took steps to observe her work and to make recommendations to her. Principal Ray Heischman made several personal observations in her classroom and was satisfied that Mrs. Somers had made the suggested adjustments or improvements. He talked to me one day about her work and said that she was coming along very nicely. It was just about that time that Nate McKenzie was heard bragging publicly, "I'm going to have that Somers woman's job. See if I don't!"

That same spring I was busy with twentieth-century British authors, a commencement script, and another job which I had reluctantly assumed in September—the presidency of the Worthington Education Association. The WEA had been formed two years earlier and was rapidly becoming a laughing proposition among the teachers. I had helped draw up the bylaws of the organization, but in its very constitution the movement was not working.

I might add, parenthetically, that I enjoy too much the work of a teacher to spend any of my time in conducting or suffering worthless meetings. I let the organization nominate and elect me only after I had told them I would depend upon their support in my program. I tried to strengthen the organization wherever I could. In this work I was fortunate in having a strong executive council. Bill Lane, who was then teaching math and physics in the high school, represented that building on the council. The Association's vice-president, Christ George, was a superb teacher of proud Greek ancestry, strong in principle and willing to fight for what he believed in. The rest of the council, too, were of that militant, dedicated variety that make for a strong teachers' association. When the crisis came, however, we discovered that our howitzers were resting on the quicksand of Ohio law.

I was leaving the school one night in April when two teachers brought me my first real inkling of trouble. Harriet Somers, they said, was being fired because of idle town gossip. "The WEA should try to help her," one of them exclaimed. Then they gave me that Well-you're-the-president-what-are-you-going-to-do-about-it? look. During the next two days the whole school was buzzing, students included. Another teacher came to me. It was a question of teacher morale, he said. Something should be done. If, indeed, a small group of agitators were behind it, an undesirable precedent was being set. If the town crucified one of its own, what would they do to an out-of-towner like him? He left no question in my mind that some of the staff were waiting to see what I would do, if anything.

Ray Heischman was stacking the student schedule requests for the following year when I walked into his office after school on Friday. I didn't really know how he stood on the issue of Mrs. Somers' contract renewal. It crossed my mind that he might have changed his views about her progress. I should have known better—once Ray made up his mind about a thing, he rarely gave way. He motioned to the heaps of forms before him. "Look at 'em," he said. "I wouldn't be surprised if we have a 1500 enrollment in another ten years."

I shook my head appreciatively, then got to the point. "Ray, wasn't Somers' contract renewed?" He looked up steadily at me for a minute, and I could see that he was smoldering.

"No," he said, "and if your WEA is worth a pot to whistle in, it'll ask why—it'll ask the Board."

"Didn't they say?"

"By law, they don't have to. It's only when a teacher has tenure that they have to state reasons. You know that."

"Yes, I do," I returned, "but I thought Somers had her tenure. She's taught before."

"Not here and not consecutively."

"Did you recommend her for rehiring?"

"Yes, I did."

"Don't they customarily act according to the administrator's suggestion?"

"Yes," he said, chewing the word. Outside the door his secretary appeared. "Be with you in a minute, Margaret."

"Look, Ray, don't you have some idea, confidentially, of why she's being fired?" He exploded then, as he piped several surnames, spiced with invective, of people in the community who, he felt, had been crying their dissatisfaction to the Board instead of him. He was still fuming as I left his office.

There was no time for a council meeting, certainly no chance for a full-scale WEA meeting. I went home to a weekend of sheer hell in which I had no choice but to act unilaterally and solo. As a teacher, I knew my sympathies clearly lay with Somers, Heischman, and my fellow professionals. I had a tenure contract, but I knew that I nevertheless had to lay my position at Worthington High on the line. Things were beginning to go well for me in my work. I had already developed a satisfactory working relationship with my students and with the other teachers. I had no designs on administrative work, which some people choose to call promotions. I had taken my master's degree in English. I have never really thought of my profession as being vertically structured, except where quality is concerned. All I really wanted to do was to teach, to close my classroom door and to work with the young people they sent to 106. But I couldn't do that now. As president—or was it fall guy?—of an education association with only the feeblest heartbeat and the most rudimentary program, I must take a position.

I didn't sleep much that Friday night. I had a letter to write—to the Board of Education. In the ninth and final draft, it read:

```
The Worthington Board of Education,
Worthington Schools,
Worthington, Ohio

Attention: Superintendent of Schools

Gentlemen:

    (1) Because a number of her colleagues
        have expressed surprise and shock
        at the dismissal of Mrs. Harriet
        Somers,
    (2) since these same fellow teachers
        have seen abundant evidence of the
        high standards which have charac-
        terized her work in our midst,
```

(3) insofar as Mrs. Somers' immediate superior has found no occasion to question her teaching competence and professional character,

(4) inasmuch as the dismissal of any administrator or teacher, under circumstances which are not entirely clear to our organization, could conceivably prove destructive to the general morale and to the attainment of our mutual goals, and

(5) in view of the fact that a genuinely professional group has a responsibility in getting all the facts before drawing any conclusions or formulating any attitudes,

we wish to extend an invitation to any and every member of the Worthington Board of Education to discuss with the Worthington Education Association's Executive Council the principal points and their ramifications in the case involving Mrs. Somers. The Council will convene at 3:50 P.M. on Monday, May 3, in the high-school library.

While the members of the Worthington Education Association do not question the authority of the Board to employ and to dismiss as it sees fit, a constructive and informative discussion of this case will do much to preserve our unity of purpose in these days of school expansion issues, annexation issues, and explosive educational controversy.

THE WORTHINGTON EDUCATION ASSN.

Once I had the letter written, I couldn't simply set it on the desk and wait till Monday. As a teacher's correspondence with a board of education properly goes through the office of his superintendent, I decided to take it to him on Saturday afternoon. Understandably, I was concerned with his reaction. Though he and I held some professional differences of opinion, I had had a satisfactory teacher-administrator relationship with him.

He wasn't at his home in Worthington when I arrived, so I waited for a time. Before long he drove up, and, after we had exchanged greetings and some small talk, I handed him the letter. He read it through and looked at me, then glanced over it again. Afterwards, he took a long breath and rubbed at a piece of tar on my new Chevy. He asked me then whether I realized all the possible outcomes of my letter.

"I have no choice," I replied. "I'm not acting as an individual in this. If you think I'm enjoying this job, you're dead wrong." He told me that he'd see that the Board got the letter, and I left.

Back home, I plopped myself into the front-porch glider and sat brooding over matters as they stood. My wife wasn't long in reading the signs. Nor was she long in asking what was on my mind. "All right, what is it now?" she said as she eased into the glider.

"Alice, you'd better know that my days at Worthington may be numbered."

"Is it about Mrs. Somers?"

"Yes, I took a letter to the Board over to the superintendent."

"Do you think you did the right thing?"

"I know I did. I had no choice."

"Then there's no reason to be bothered by it." It was as simple as that, from her point of view. I mentioned a name, that of a Worthington teacher who was several years younger than I.

"Now he would never have written a letter or taken such a position. And from the world's point of view, he'll get ahead."

"But you're something he'll never be," she countered.

"Like what, for instance?"

"An honest-to-God man."

There are, it is true, so many people who live in fear. The islands had filled me with so much fear that that emotion was exhausted in me. Except for my loved ones, I don't suppose that I can ever feel true fear again, not that perpetual half-panic that keeps people cowering and defensive. Ever since the war I had felt like a condemned man with a stay of execution. Since then, every day of my life has been a dividend. Maybe that's why I like getting up early in the morning—to see whether still another bonus is waiting for me.

I realized that the only source of real concern I felt now had to do with my pleasant relationship with others—the people I worked with and for. On Monday I would find out very quickly where I stood with them. For once, I had put myself in the position of expecting other people to do the right thing. I was wide open for disappointment, I speculated. I had in this instance abandoned my rule for happiness—the power of negative thinking.

After telling Ray about my letter, I asked him to call a special staff meeting in Room 106. The announcement sounded over the PA system, and within ten minutes the high-school staff of approximately twenty-five had gathered in my classroom. Harriet did not attend; Ray had suggested that she not come, for he had serious doubts about whether the meeting would be free of differences in opinion. The other teachers must have known that something was in the air. They were unusually quiet as they sat there.

Ray turned the meeting over to me, then sat down by a window. I told them what had happened—what facts were known, what facts were lacking, what I had done, and what the letter said. "Now, I've crawled way out on a limb because I believed I had to. I can't guarantee how strong that limb is, but there's plenty of room on it. The WEA didn't compose the letter. The Executive Council didn't write it. I did. But I'm in hopes you'll stand up and be counted as supporting that letter and that point of view."

Jeanette Fry was the first to speak. "I move that we unanimously support Mr. Rousculp *and* the letter," she said as firmly as she might have given us an assignment in Latin vocabulary. I was so touched by her endorsement that I never knew who seconded her motion. Two minutes later the meeting adjourned in unanimous support of the position stated in the letter. It was the first and only time that I can remember the high-school staff's ever taking a single and unqualified stand on so serious an issue.

When the students outside the room entered for their first-period class, I knew that they had more than a faint idea of what had been transpiring. The rugged young fullback of Dow Nelson's last undefeated squad came to my lectern. "We know what's going on, Mr. Rousculp, and we're on your side."

"Sturgal," I told him, "I appreciate your feelings, but I can't ethically talk to you about it. It's too bad you people have to know about it at all." I didn't really know exactly how ethics fit into the situation, but it seemed wrong that students, whose minds should be on other things, should be drawn into any quarrel of their elders.

Later that same day I saw Harriet and explained to her that the WEA would do what it could for her, though it was questionable whether we could change the circumstances. There were tears in her eyes. At least, she said, she felt less alone. Shortly after I had left her classroom, I encountered the single disappointment of the day. Another teacher, a fine physical specimen of a man, stopped me in the hall. "Look," he squirmed, "I voted for the motion this morning, but I thought I'd better tell you something. If it comes down to possibly losing my job, you won't be able to count on me." He wasn't looking me in the eyes, and I was glad—I didn't want to see the shame on his face. I prefer to think that it was indebtedness and problems at home that made him do the only crawfishing I heard from the staff members.

The vice-president of the Board came to meet with the WEA Executive Council sometime in May. With the high-school mandate, Bill Lane took probably the firmest position of anyone present. Still, the only result was an indication from the Board's representative that he would report to his group the request from the Council for a hearing. It was, of course, comforting to know that every building representative on the Council had instructions from his constituents to support the high-school position. There was no need to call a general meeting of the WEA.

In the meantime, the uproar continued to spread in the community. People on the streets and in the bank would ask me about it and couldn't understand my declining to comment. My phone began to ring more frequently. First, I spoke with a man who led a citizens' group supporting Harriet; then Columbus *Dispatch* and *Citizen* reporters got on the line. Where they had got their fragmentary information, I couldn't say, but I refused to talk about the case. I was convinced that Mrs. Somers' best chance for reinstatement would come with a minimum of publicity. Perhaps I was wrong. I didn't know—and I still don't.

The public hearing was finally held, shortly after school had closed for the summer. I went with Christ George, then president-elect of the WEA, and Bob Drury, the Ohio Education Association's legal counsel. The three of us sat together on one side of the quadrangularly arranged tables. The atmosphere was charged with emotion, as I had expected. On one side of the room sat several dozen citizens backing Harriet's cause. Directly across from me were the clerk of the Board, Harriet's husband (she was not there), the superintendent, and Heischman. To my left sat the members of the Board. There was no smiling in the room. Faces would crack occasionally in mock cordiality, but no one felt easy. The room was a place of unrelieved, short-fused, edge-of-the-chair tempers.

I looked at the Board. No doubt, under the circumstances, they had been in informal, executive session sometime before the hearing. Their faces were noncommittal, though. Five of them—ordinary, friendly, well-meaning people working at a nonpaying, often thankless job of legislating the financial affairs and governing policies of a school district. I had already taught two of their children, and in the years ahead I would work with another ten youngsters from their families. The Board had made a decision involving a teacher, probably not fully aware of its potential impact upon the school and the town. Why? They hadn't said, and the law did not require them to do so.

Is it possible that in an issue there can be one wrong side and two right sides, equally valid? To this day, I remain loyal to Harriet Somers. Yet I was undoubtedly too hasty in my judgment of other people involved. I know that it takes guts and a willingness to serve a community for a person to run for a school-board office. God knows, there's little prestige in the job and a lot of oversized headaches. Rumor had it that one of these people was ready to resign. I watched them. Five faces to study, five heads bent over an agenda for a special hearing, five judges who must live with whatever grew out of this tempest.

Would they change their minds? Usually for a board of education to do so is to leave itself vulnerable to pressure groups which take heart from one such backing-down. For a board of education to reverse itself is to incur public suspicion that elected representatives have acted hastily in one instance, so perhaps in others. Nevertheless, I believed that, if they had yielded to the blow-hard-and-hot McKenzie element, the opposite faction and conscience would give the Board some second thoughts. Perhaps I was ignoring a fundamental truth in moral dilemmas—that what spells RIGHT in one mind may represent an oversimplification in another's thinking.

At that time, my knowledge of the Board members was quite limited. Number One had a sound reputation in his profession, and many of the townspeople saw him as the watchdog of funds for public education. A dozen years later I would mourn the death of his gallant son in the Viet Nam conflict. Two was, I had learned, a college professor with a leave of absence for work with the State of Ohio. Widely respected, he was known for his breadth of interests and eminent qualifications for service to public schools. Number Three, associated with OSU, was a strong, far-seeing exponent of Worthington's becoming a city and annexing certain of the school-community area which Columbus was threatening to absorb. Number Four was the wife of a prominent attorney, and Five, the proprietor of a retail furniture store in Columbus. These two I knew least of all. But I couldn't study them further.

The president, Number One, was opening the meeting. He would call upon me very soon to present the WEA brief. When he did so, I set forth the Association's position as stated in my letter to them. I ended my statement with this inquiry: If a teacher satisfied his administrator and was subsequently dismissed, how should other teachers on a school staff be guided?

The rest of that hearing is somewhat clouded in my recollection. I do remember Heischman's speaking his point of view and some of Christ George's comments. There was one heated exchange between Harriet's husband and two of the Board members. The meeting adjourned with the Board's assurance that they would take "under advisement" the reports of those who had spoken.

And that was the end of it—so far as official Board action was concerned. Harriet was not rehired. It was with little comfort that I received a note a few days afterwards assuring me that "the Board has the highest respect for you and the manner which you presented the WEA case." Nor did Harriet's letter of appreciation to me make me feel any better about the outcome. It tore at me, that letter. It made me question whether I had, indeed, done everything I could do in her behalf.

Though I appreciated her "thank-you" for the little I had done, her words carried the sound of one whose spirit has been broken, whose humility is more than the heart should have to bear. *Please let me teach again* I heard in those sentences, and I wondered whether I could ever be brought to that low estate.

Why Harriet Somers was not rehired, I may never know. Did the Board have information upon which they felt they were properly proceeding? Had the Board felt that even gossip which they recognized as false had done sufficient damage to her image that restoring her job would be bad for the school and possibly worse for Harriet? I am convinced now that the Board exercised their prerogative of silence in the knowledge that an explanation might have brought lawsuits, not merely from Harriet but from the McKenzie faction as well. It is possible that their original action stemmed from a flood of hearsay, the very presence of which they saw as potentially damaging to the school.

Regrettably, I can not know *all* the facts. Yet I have sought to know them. When the WEA requested a hearing on the Somers case, the organization was seeking the *whole* truth, the exact reasons for the teacher's dismissal—not simply in her interests, but for the greater purpose of removing all questions, for the good of the schools. I firmly believe that public education should, in every respect, be a matter of public record. If the teacher is, as I hold, the absolute crux or hub of a school system, then a board's not renewing *any* teacher's contract should be accompanied by a full report of the board's personnel committee, supported by the principal's and superintendent's testimony, as to *why*—this information to be made public at the request of the teacher or his professional organization. The law, particularly as it involves non-tenured teachers, clearly needs revision to eliminate once and for all the possibility of unfair indictment of not merely teachers but boards of education, too.

The aftermath of the Somers' incident merely added to the tragedy. Harriet became ill and was bedfast for quite a time. Though Christ did much to keep the Association strong, it became, after his departure from Worthington, a voiceless coffee-and-doughnuts, inservice educational joke. It would remain so for many years to come. Morale in the high school floundered the following fall, and with Ray's later resignation teacher spirit hit an all-time low. Not until Bill Lane was appointed principal did something akin to the earlier professional sense of well-being develop once more.

Whenever I take a stand on an issue, I am emotionally involved. I have never been a graceful loser—it's not in my nature to be. During those years I went back into my classroom, convinced that I had succeeded at doing little but to make people distrustful of me. I closed the door of 106 and concentrated on doing the best job I could to develop my own English program. For a time I talked about job offers at several schools, and I even sat down with an insurance-company executive who tried to lure me into that field. What kept me in 106 was the young people in my classes. They began to treat me with an affection and respect that I hardly knew a teacher could enjoy.

That growing closeness with my students was only one benefit that I derived from the Somers affair. There were others. Nobody who was associated with her misfortune could fail to grow wiser. Teachers, Board, principal, superintendent, community—we are all much more enlightened today. Worthington has become a city—or, at least, part of a city complex. Had Ray lived, he would have seen his prediction come true—a 1500-student enrollment in the high school by 1964. And I doubt that there will ever be another incident like that involving Harriet Somers, at least not in Worthington.

Of course, there will always be the gossip-mongers. After a long, embarrassed silence, Nate McKenzie began again, not long ago—his target, a football coach with an unfortunate win-loss record. Though McKenzie and his ilk are done in Worthington, they can still be found poisoning other communities. Many American teachers still suffer at their hands.

When private individuals are slandered, the misfortune is usually restricted to the victim and his family. On the other hand, the subtle and insidious attacks launched against one who teaches can create much greater tragedy, with implications for a whole community. In my opinion, the law that permits or demands a judicial camouflage of teacher-baiters is wrong. Someone says, "Yes, but you're trying to draw an analogy between the question of retaining a job and the matter of imprisonment or capital punishment when you talk about the right of being confronted by accusers or witnesses." For me, however, the analogy is fundamentally valid. Teaching, from my point of view, is a way of life. If they were to take Room 106 away from me, they would take away a considerable part of my life. Perhaps Harriet Somers felt the same way. I will always believe that, in the trial of a teacher, there must be the opportunity for the defendant to meet his accusers or critics and to defend himself from calumny.

"But how can a *teacher* act like that?" the girl asked me. The high-school senior was troubled because a man who had taught her the previous year and who had represented manly perfection in her eyes was now involved in a divorce suit and subject therefore to the most absurd gossip.

"Like what?" I inquired. The man she referred to was a friend of mine, a competent and promising young addition to the school staff.

"You know—divorce and all that." I don't ordinarily discuss other staff members with students, but this young lady and I spoke together often and I felt, too, some need to defend my good friend.

"I know about the divorce, but I don't know anything at all about 'all that,' " I returned.

His Eye Was on the Pigeon

"Well, even divorce," she insisted.

"Divorce isn't an unusual thing among people, Sherri. I don't have to tell you that."

"Yes, but a *teacher!*" she cried.

"Are you implying that teachers are different from other people?" I asked.

"Well, they should be models for living—examples to their students."

"Do you mean models or wax dummies?"

"You know what I mean, Mr. Rousculp."

"I know you're putting teachers into a category that would deny them the privilege of acting like human beings. You're suggesting that teachers are islands set off from the rest of the species."

"I heard you say once that you feel like an island sometimes," she answered.

"Yes, but that's mostly in the classroom. Outside the school, you'd be surprised how the ships come and go." My figure of speech didn't do much for her, and she returned to the more concrete subject.

"I guess I did think Mr. Durkin was something special," she conceded sadly.

"You mean that now he isn't?"

"Well, I thought he was a tower of strength, I guess. Now, to hear some people talk—" She broke off and looked at me, knowing that I probably wouldn't appreciate the rumors she had heard.

"Don't listen to them, Sherri. Some of those who are sounding off are possibly miserable themselves and have to find pleasure or relieve their own frustrations by saying ugly things about others."

"You still like Mr. Durkin, don't you?"

"Of course I do. He's still the same person he was last week, or last year, fundamentally. I'm sorry about his marriage going bust, but I know he was brought up in a broken home himself and doesn't view divorce lightly."

For a moment or two Sherri picked at the dog-eared cover of a paperback book she was holding. When she looked up at me again, I could see a trace of moistness about her eyelashes.

"I suppose I had a schoolgirl crush on him. That's silly, isn't it?" she said in a half-questioning manner.

"Oh, I'd be the last to say that. I seriously considered kidnapping the beautiful woman who taught speech in my high school. Every day I'd sit in her class feeling as if she were a Sabine gal and I were a young Roman." She laughed at my reminiscence.

"It is silly, though, idealizing someone like that."

"No," I asserted, "I think it's very nice. But it's better to love people knowing that they are, after all, people-people, not half-people. And you know what? I think you *did* know that he's 100% human being. I'd bet that this business about his divorce bothers you mainly because it reminds you that he's married."

She looked serious over that remark. "Come to think of it, I never really have thought of him as being married. Maybe you're right. Oh, but that sounds—well, awful."

"Because you maybe didn't want to think of him as a married man? Why so awful? It would have spoiled your crush, wouldn't it? And a crush—so long as it's no more than that—is a very beautiful, worthwhile thing."

"But it's not the same now. And it hurts for a little while, getting over a crush. It makes you find out things about yourself. It's like—well, sorta like finding out your father sleeps with your mother and that they're like everyone else." She looked embarrassed then. "That's awful too, isn't it?"

"I'm not sure about what *that* refers to in your sentence, but I think this may be one of those days when nothing seems exactly right to you." She was straightening out the curl in the paperback cover once more. "You know, Sherri, you haven't learned to accept people for what they are. So far as I know, Mr. Durkin is above blame, but suppose for a moment that he were actually in the wrong. Would you turn right around and condemn him? If people never did wrong things in life, how would we ever appreciate those times when they do nice things? If we love those who never seem anything but deserving, what is so great about our love? If we love people who have no capacity for sin, what's so great about their possibly loving us? You have to be a little cynical about people to find happiness in life, I think."

"Now, that's your old power of negative thinking. You mentioned that in class one day."

"Well, it works for me, anyhow."

"I don't understand how you can expect the worst of people and still be happy. Why not look on the bright side and be hopeful?"

"Oh, I'm always hopeful," I explained, "but I'm not about to be dependent upon anyone until I just have to be. To fully depend upon others is the way to disappointment and pain, I think. I've learned to love people even knowing that at any minute they may do something that hurts me or completely offends my own notions of what's right and wrong. I think I've even learned to like them better because they're that way."

"Have you always felt like that?"

"Oh, no. It took a lot of lessons to get the point across to me. Once in a while I still slip up and get hurt a little. Any time I forget and begin to see people in an unreal, half-true manner, I can expect sooner or later a several-hundred-thousand-volt jolt. Life is a big hot wire and it isn't very well insulated. If you take hold of it—really hang onto it—you're bound to feel the current. It may not always hurt, but it will always shake you up. That being the case, you can do just two things. Stay away from life, the way a lot of people do, or wear your own insulation, as I do unless I forget."

"I can't imagine your ever getting shaken up. You always look so calm."

"Little do you know," I told her. But she was begging for an example, and I couldn't resist telling her a little anecdote about a summer's day and a traffic snarl, many years ago.

Not many things in this world can make me swear with gusto, but on that day in August three things conspired to bring out the worst of my invective. To start with, the heat and humidity were insufferable—it was one of those gasping, soggy, oppressive, no-relief-in-sight-ha-ha-says-the-weatherman days. My muttered epithets had offended my wife long before I managed to back the car out of the driveway. Because my reverse gear had gone out two days earlier, I had to park on the incline in my drive and depend upon gravity to get the car into the street. As I might have expected, there was less gravity that day, so I had to take part of the curb with me when we started forward.

Nor did the driving add comfort. Even at forty miles an hour, the breeze could not absorb my perspiration. What little air came into the front seat merely drove the rivulets across my forehead and into my eyes.

But the weather wasn't the only circumstance coloring my speech. Another source of my agitation was that we were late for an appointment. We were due at the bank where we had applied for a loan—such activities are bound to figure in a young schoolteacher's time. I despise being late, but there we were, a half-hour's drive from a bank that would close in half an hour, my wife not speaking to me, and I with my jaws putting a strain on my fillings and my eyes stonily fixed on the road ahead. Then it happened—Joy Number Three. The Great American Traffic Jam.

Where I would normally have made a right turn, I had to bring the car to a maddening idle, losing the advantage of a green light. The intersection of Fifth Avenue and Leonard was clogged with bumper-to-bumper motorists, every one of them in need of a Bayer-break. To my right, I could see what appeared to be the genesis of the tie-up. An auto of ancient vintage, only slightly older than my own, was apparently stalled under the railroad bridge. There the vehicle perched precisely over the line dividing the two narrow westbound lanes.

On such occasions my wife invariably says something like "Now, don't get all upset—we'll get there on time." She has faith in the flexibility of time, and, oddly enough, the hours often seem to stretch and contract according to her wishes, but too frequently right down to the second. I don't like to arrive at my destinations too early, but operating on the margin of a few clock ticks does things to my nervous system. Her customary remark came, however, just as I was about to deliver an impromptu harangue on the perversity of traffic. I bit off the first syllable, leaned forward slowly to peel the back of my shirt from the plastic seat cover, and tugged briefly at the Windsor knot in the striped noodle I was wearing.

Still, I had to make sounds of some sort, especially after I had broiled my elbow on the window frame of the car door. I spoke slowly, enunciating with great care and inflecting my words with a lilting quality: "To—him—who—in—the—love—of—nature—holds—communion—with—her—visible—forms—she—speaks—a—various—language." Meanwhile, there was a "various" language originating with the troglodytic figure who was straddling a foreign sports car directly in front of me. The creativity and imagery in his commentary on the traffic bottleneck made my recitation of Bryant's "Thanatopsis" pallid and unnecessary. I leaned back against the seat with a muffled splash and relaxed somewhat as he expressed many of my own sentiments with marvelous diction. From time to time he punctuated his Anglo-Saxon with a gunning of his motor.

It was in doing so that Beowulf really sabotaged himself—and helped me out at the same time. His motor died, and just at that moment the traffic in the righthand lane began to move. There was barely enough space for me to turn right and to ease past him, and I jubilantly accelerated to two miles per hour with all my valve lifters chirping loudly. "Now, see?" said my wife with irritating serenity.

But our troubles were certainly not over. There was a truck preceding me, and getting around the old green Whatisitmobile posed quite a problem for the truck driver. Again I braked my Chevy to a standstill and sat breathing deeply the exhilarating diesel fumes of a bus in the left lane. I took advantage of the pause to shake one of my feet so that the perspiration might pass around the ankle obstructing its flow. Behind me a chorus of horns announced that Beowulf was endearing himself to his fellow motorists. Then, just as my mental radiator was about to boil over once more, I saw something which somehow altered the whole afternoon's experience.

He was crippled, one leg missing from the knee down, and he was hanging onto a single crutch and bending over something at the base of the concrete bridge support separating the eastbound and westbound lanes. From the look of him, I judged that he must reside in the neighborhood around the underpass—an area where the houses, if you could call them houses, would have provided great copy for the Kremlin's propagandists. Suddenly, I saw a blue-gray flurry beside the man's foot and realized what he was doing there.

It was a pigeon that flopped grotesquely about in the dust. One of its wings was obviously broken and trailed awkwardly to one side as the bird hobbled back and forth just beyond the man's reach. I understood now why there was no honking of horns beneath the bridge. As the old Samaritan strained to rescue that crumpled, dirty-feathered creature, I felt my wife's hand on my shoulder. I turned to her and saw her pretty eyes intent upon the drama before us. Then I glanced at the mirrored face of the truck driver, at the profile of the bus driver, at the eyes of several of his passengers who, having risen from their seats, were peering silently and fixedly at the shaded scene.

I think it was the late Gilbert K. Chesterton who once said that the most remarkable thing about coincidences and miracles is that they *do* happen. As the cripple of one species reached for the cripple of another, as life touched life and lifted it from the dust, a sense of beauty and well-being must have touched the heart of everyone in that motorized audience. When the man turned, his bearded face seemed transfixed with empathy and compassion. With one hand he cradled the bird lovingly against the soiled T-shirt he wore, and, completely absorbed with his feathered bundle, he moved slowly around the truck and out of sight.

The image gone, I turned again to my wife. There was the suggestion of tears in her eyes and voice as she softly repeated, *"To him who in the love of nature holds communion with her visible forms, she speaks a various language."* The way she spoke the verses would have pleased the poet, I know. Nor did she say them to remind me of my earlier traffic tantrum, but only because the words were so singularly appropriate.

How the pigeon came to be there, how the man was able to operate the old green car, I do not know. I remember only that, during and immediately after the tableau I had witnessed, the heat seemed less stifling, the time less urgent, the traffic less annoying, my life less harried. My wife and I didn't make it to the bank on time, but young schoolteachers and their families are inured to sandwich-filled weekends. Moreover, I didn't swear once during the rest of the day.

Sometimes I have wished that there were no postscript to this account, but there was a sequel—one that taught me much about life. I told Sherri about how, for a long time, I carried back of my eyes the image of the one-legged man and his act of mercy. He was a source of inspiration, of hope for the world. In his begrimed T-shirt and scraggly beard, he assumed the character and appearance of some latter-day Walt Whitman. Sometimes, too, I'd associate him with the crippled lighthouse keeper who cares for the injured bird in Paul Gallico's moving story entitled *The Snow Goose*.

It was on a winter night of the following year that I next saw my Birdman of Leonard Avenue, and I was surprised by the difference between the mental image and the man himself. I had just picked up my wife at the hospital where she was working. I discovered on the way home that I was out of cigarettes, so I stopped in front of a little neighborhood bar located five or six blocks from the underpass where the bird had been rescued. As I have already indicated, this area of the city belonged to (or was rented by) the indigent and unfortunate, and the bar, exterior and interior, reflected its socioeconomic setting.

There were only three or four patrons sitting along the badly eroded counter. Because I had to wait until the bartender got around to giving me the necessary change for the cigarette-vending machine, I had an opportunity to see how the other twenty percent drink. I didn't recognize the one-legged man at first—he was dressed differently, as the season required. His mien was considerably different, too, for he was grinning broadly at a younger man beside him. I think I saw the crutch leaning in the shadow of the bar before I saw the stub of upper leg and the face with the twelve-o'clock shadow. That the man was well into his cups was not offensive to me. There is little that I can't overlook in a person who possesses an innate kindliness and a deep respect for life.

I left as soon as I had my cigarettes. I wanted to speak to him, to tell him that I had seen and remembered his generous act, but I didn't like leaving my wife alone in the car. "Guess who I just saw," I said when we were nearly to the bridge. She looked at me indulgently. "A long-lost girlfriend?" she asked, too tired from the day's work to appreciate guessing games.

"Our friend with the pigeon. *You* remember." She did, indeed, and during the remainder of the drive home we reminisced over the events of that summer day and the man's impact upon us.

For several months I made it a habit to stop at the little bar at least once or twice a week, but I never again caught sight of the old fellow. I finally determined to ask the bartender whether the Man with the Crutch had been in the place recently. But I'm glad now that I didn't tell the story about the bird. Something made me feel that night that I might learn more by asking a casual question without any preface.

The bartender knew right away the subject of my inquiry and talked about him enthusiastically:

"Oh, you mean old Fred! No, I haven't seen him in five, six weeks. Never f'get the ol' fella, though. He used t' say he had a real love f'r jist two things in life—good beer an' creamed pigeon on toast."

For a minute I thought Sherri was going to be sick. "Oh, Mr. Rousculp, that's simply terrible. Oh-h-h!" she exclaimed.

"I felt the same way at first," I replied. "The trouble was I wasn't accepting life—I was hanging onto a pretty little illusion about the old man. Now, I can understand him better."

"Understand him! Oh, how can you say that? That horrible old man!"

"Isn't it just possible, Sherri, that an old man, maybe down on his luck, might be hungry? Do you know that they still eat doves regularly down in the hill country? Even on some aristocratic tables. As you grow older, you'll discover that human beings can feel hungers that you never knew existed."

"I suppose you're right, but—"

"And, Sherri, you'll even learn that it's possible for any person to be so hungry for human understanding and affection that he's willing to shock and offend others in his reaching for it."

She was quiet for a minute, then spoke with a slight hesitancy. "You mean someone like—like Mr. Durkin?"

"Y-e-e-e-s," I said slowly, putting on a thoughtful expression, then feigning some surprise at this application of my statement. "Even Mr. Durkin, I suppose." But I couldn't conceal the slight convulsion at the corner of my mouth. She saw that I was grinning inside at the way my trap had sprung.

"Oh, Mr. Rousculp!" she exploded, her hands on her hips. "You are the most exasperating person I've ever been around. A person asks you a question, and you make her answer it. Sometimes you make me feel as if I'm talking to myself."

"Now, can I help it, Sherri, if you're smarter than you think?" I asked her with a still-innocent face. Then we both broke up. We laughed so heartily that a curious faculty member appeared in the doorway of Room 106.

"Okay, you two, let the rest of us in on the gag," demanded the math teacher.

"You're already in on it," I said and winked at Sherri.

"What's that?" asked my colleague, very puzzled.

"Life," said Sherri and winked back at me.

"What do you think of our commencement programs?" I was somewhat relieved to hear Ray Heischman come up with this question in the principal's office one winter day in 1953. A few minutes earlier I had been searching my mind to recall something I might have been throwing besides an occasional mean glance. Still I didn't know how to answer him, and I wouldn't have felt relieved at all had I known where the conversation was to lead.

"Fine," I said, and then I saw him wince. "Well—uh—they're about as good as anyone else's, aren't they?"

"That's what I thought you'd say. Did you enjoy our commencement last June?"

"Does anybody like commencements?"

"That's really what *I'm* asking." He looked at me intently for a moment, then grinned. "It's no wonder people cry at graduations— my God, they're bored to tears."

Their Own Commencement

I had to agree. Always the same potted ferns, formal introductions, trite platitudes, seemingly endless marchings-up-and-down-again, and wet handshakes—the great American graduation exercise! "Yes, it's too bad they can't do something to make them more meaningful."

"*We can.* Ever consider having some of your English students write a commencement program of their own?"

That's how it all started—a complex but exciting and rewarding experience of my teaching career started as simply as that. I promised Ray I would give it a try if the students were willing, and as I left he was arranging an appointment with the class officers.

That year the students of Worthington were just as busy as the rest of Ohio in celebrating the sesquicentennial of Buckeye statehood. As a matter of fact, they were perhaps a trifle busier because the founding of the town itself extends back to 1803 and because the town and school were commemorating both events. As it turned out, however, tradition was not to be the only keynote of the students' activities. The Senior Class of 1953 agreed with Ray that the graduation ritual needed overhauling. They wanted to undertake some pioneering of their own, to make a "production" of their commencement exercises, and to abandon the conventional ordeal with its often-uninspired speeches and its squirming, perspiring audience.

Before long the students had approached me for my assistance. They wanted me to select and advise a committee capable of planning and writing a commencement script with a sesquicentennial theme—one which recognized both Worthington's and Ohio's anniversary. I had already committed myself in my conversation with Ray, and I accepted the honor with about the same enthusiasm that marked my "volunteering" in the Marines. If my reluctance in the matter ran counter to the ideals of Education 533 and 534, remember tolerantly that English teachers are known for the heaps of papers on their desks—and the stack on mine was reaching an impressive altitude. Moreover, spring would soon be breathing on our necks, and the project that they had in mind would have to battle time all the way.

On the other hand, I had some truly fine student writers that year, and I selected seven responsible and creative seniors from my twelfth-year section. My first meeting with them was full of surprises; they turned out to be seven fully charged mental batteries, fairly loaded with ideas. The following weeks found us prying into fragmentary histories of Worthington, interviewing the town's oldest citizens, listening to Ohio music, wrecking the local librarian's peace of mind, and keeping the file-cabinet rollers in the superintendent's office in perpetual motion.

Each of the seven writers was responsible for approximately one-seventh of the 150-year period. Within his time division, he was responsible for local, state, and national events of importance. For example, the student whose responsibility included the events of the 1850's had to take into account Ohioan Salmon P. Chase's reaction to Henry Clay's "Omnibus Bill," Ohio's response to *Uncle Tom's Cabin,* and the activities of the Underground Railroad in Worthington. These facts had then to be forged into forceful, interesting, coherent sentences. The research and actual writing had not progressed far before we saw that we were compiling a brief history of our own school, as well.

Meanwhile, I had "conned" the vocal-music teacher into organizing a senior chorus and trying out the old Ohio songs that the committee had suggested. She reported tremendous effort and interest in the choral work. For young people, innovation and variety are the salt-and-pepper of school life—and they were proving it once more.

Several steps remained. The disjointed manuscript would have to be put together with appropriate transitional paragraphs and sentences. Once unified and revised, it would provide the basic narrative. A student narrator had to be selected. Tableaux would have to be organized, cast, and costumed in order to depict various events alluded to by the narrative, and this addition required help from the dramatics teacher. The art teacher assisted a subcommittee in the preparation of silk-screened programs.

When, after three rehearsals, the seniors took their annual trip to Washington and New York, I was seriously concerned about the effect of interrupted practices. It was needless worry—on buses, trains, and boats the seniors sang the music and practiced lines and cues of their own volition.

There was time for just two more rehearsals after their return; and, if anything, the students were even more enthusiastic. On the appointed night, they filed into the old elementary-school auditorium and gave their commencement audience a delightful shock and a welcome relief from the ordinary. The Class of 1953 gave "their very own" graduation program—not one packaged for them by their faculty and administrators.

One hitch could have developed at the conclusion of the program. How could the audience be kept busy while the students formed in the corridors for their formal processional? The superintendent had planned for the time space, and he took this opportunity to introduce and to present certificates to the surviving graduates of 1903. Later he thanked the many other alumni who had traveled from all parts of the country at the invitation of the graduating class. Then a brief, formal program followed, in which a board member spoke a few words and diplomas were awarded. A group of young people had shown their elders that they could fashion something new out of the past.

It wasn't until the following year that I realized the full significance of what had been done. Succeeding classes would hardly be disposed to return to the old "put 'em t' sleep 'r keep 'em miserable" commencement. Our students would want not only their "own" graduations but better and better programs. It didn't take very much reflection for me to see the uppercase letters on the bulkhead. The Class of 1954 soon confirmed my suspicion by asking for a commencement play. I acquiesced, but with one reservation—this time we would do the writing in the English sections.

The system that I developed that year I followed, with some minor changes, through the remaining years of our experiment. The senior-English students were divided, during the early part of the second semester, into five commencement-manuscript groups. I took complete responsibility for this division in order to eliminate any possible inequities in "choosing up sides." Each group was organized to include a heterogeneity of necessary skills —each group had, in its membership, people with ideas and originality, students who wrote effectively, and pupils with training in typing, shorthand, art, mechanical drawing, and vocal and instrumental music. At its first meeting, each group elected its own chairman, and—hardly a miracle—the typist volunteered to do the typing, the industrial-arts student agreed to do the designing of the stage and set, the shorthand expert accepted the task of note-taking . . . for guidance is always most effective *when the guided knoweth not*. The groups were given separate meeting places for their work after we had, in the regular class meetings, laid some groundwork on possible themes.

After their first small-group discussions, they came back all fired up and—I must confess—began to kindle my own imagination and hopes. Without exception, the groups wanted to do a sort of "class autobiography," a recapitulation of their twelve years together. One group was even toying with a title, *The Road of the Past.* "But," objected another group, "aren't our parents concerned about our future, too?" A compromise was arranged; the theme would be "The Past and Its Probable Relationship to Our Future." One very capable young lady, who later joined the editorial staff of a newspaper, suggested another title—*Highway 54*—for she liked the road metaphor, yet wanted it to suggest the year of graduation. Though she had never been especially popular with her classmates, she was the heroine of the moment, and the classes voted unanimously for this title. They were jubilant despite my comment that they needed a script to go with their title. Oh, they would take care of that "little problem" in no time at all, they assured me.

I had somewhat begrudgingly allotted three and one-half weeks for the project—quite a bit, in view of all that must be done academically in senior English. The third week found me fretting as I moved from one group to another each day, taking attendance and offering comments. My panic grew as I listened to group reports. Other teachers inquired about what was taking place in Room 106, and I doggedly explained to them that I hadn't *really* become a "progressive educator" and that whatever was going on would be over in a few days.

It was on a Friday afternoon that I was handed the first drafts of the group manuscripts. The two days that followed comprised a kind of literary "lost weekend," in which I paced back and forth over five imaginary stages and mentally listened to the lines in five grossly different versions of this class autobiography. To be sure, each of the scripts manifested some strong points. In one or two the dialogue was excellent; in another the function of a speaking chorus was commendable; in yet another the song parodies and stage design were effective and original.

At no previous point in my teaching had the question "Where do I go from here?" troubled me more. The only hope, it seemed, lay in a compromise among the writing groups. If they could only be talked into developing a "hybrid" manuscript out of the five, it would be possible to incorporate into a finished work the better portions of each. A compromise was not easy to manage, however. Each of the groups was acting as if it had just created the "great American commencement program"; the *esprit de corps* within each group was unbelievable. Nevertheless, after considerable debate, the English sections agreed to select certain elements in each of the scripts and to work together on a final revision and adaptation.

The reworking of the scripts into a finished product did, in all truthfulness, demand more time than I would have preferred. Still, we were able to turn the last several pages over to the mimeographers on the deadline date.

The actual stage production of *Highway 54* was undertaken shortly thereafter by the senior class, of whom nearly 100% participated in the presentation. Seniors who had elected twelfth-year English and who had had a hand in the preparation of the script were proud of the excitement with which their classmates accepted and rehearsed the program. The eleven hundred people who attended commencement that year were delighted with the entirely original production.

For both audience and graduating class, there was greater meaning and additional drama in such a program. Two large maps, representing the Past and the Future respectively, were mounted on the sides of the scaffold stage erected in the new gymnasium. The map of the Past indicated the various and (in some cases) remote origins of the class members. The map of the Future suggested the areas of the world that were the destinations of individuals in the group. Two speaking choruses—the Past and the Future again—told the story of the group's past, the possibilities for their future, and the dramatic happenings of the twelve years (miles) through which the school had brought them to their many-directioned division in the highway. The stage was utilized to present tableaux depicting school experiences. While choral speaking accounted for much of the dialogue, individual voices were frequently heard; and both choruses from time to time sang selected songs and song-fragments. The story itself emphasized the fun they had had together, the serious problems of growing up, the difficult learning tasks, their mutual sorrows (including those which grew out of the death of a classmate), and their hopes for their tomorrows.

The Worthington commencement story did not end in 1954. Through six more years, senior students continued to write and produce commencement plays, and in each succeeding product the story line and staging were more fully developed and more polished. In 1955, for instance, the English classes managed to fashion a fantasy with at least a rudimentary plot called *Hall of Echoes*. The theme suggested that a class never truly leaves a high school, but remains in the form of a spirit that reflects the individuality of a class. Twenty years after graduation, the Class of 1955 were still there to observe the growth of the school and to watch a custodian rummaging through souvenirs of their school days. This program was so successful and so readily adaptable to other schools that at least three other high schools have written for copies and permission to produce it for their own graduations.

In 1956, an even more highly developed situation-play entitled *The Magic of Time* found a responsive audience. Enhanced by costuming and several parodies of Rodgers and Hammerstein, the production contained a theme appropriate to commencement—

the ability of today's graduates to measure up to the responsibilities of citizenship. A synopsis of the action runs as follows:

Three Seniors (representing all of the Class of 1956) fall asleep on the pedestal of the Statue of Liberty during their trip to New York. In their dream they are scolded by Liberty, who declares that they can hardly be expected to cope with the challenges of the modern world. By way of reinforcing her argument, she calls on Father Time to turn back the clock and to show the Seniors the great Americans of the Past—Columbus, Roger Williams, Ben Franklin, Thomas Jefferson, Abraham Lincoln, and Will Rogers— each of whom represents a particular American trait. These figures appear in characteristic poses while a speaking chorus called "Moments" describes their personalities and contributions. The character "Moment to Remember" comes to the rescue of the disheartened Seniors and the discouraged Liberty and presents, with Father Time's help, a series of scenes of school experience which suggest that the Class have been prepared to meet their obligations as young Americans. These scenes are punctuated by musical selections from the singing Chorus designated "Chimes." Finally, as the Seniors and Liberty find their problems resolved, the character "Big Moment"—the moment of graduation—announces his arrival.

I began to view my work with the commencement programs as something comparatively unique in secondary education. The long hours I had to spend annually in studying manuscripts and directing productions never became drudgery. I shared with my students the enormous gratification of seeing our work brought to fruition, to life upon a stage.

The mass-writing experiment, as I came to call it, would probably have continued had not several problems arisen. Beginning in 1959, senior English became a required subject, and this very desirable curricular development inevitably led to an increased number of group manuscripts, necessarily longer plays, and finally to senior sections who, having been assigned to another teacher, would not be able to participate in the writing. Then, too, the lack of adequate auditorium facilities defeated us. The gymnasium bleachers bred stiff necks and grid-lined posteriors, the building was very poorly ventilated, and our audiences (drawing visitors from around the state) grew in excess of two thousand.

During the 1960 play, our last, every breath of air I took had been in several other lungs. In this setting we could not avoid creating some of the same physical discomfort that conventional commencement programs hold. Packed as it was, the place was a cauldron. The microphones notwithstanding, stage voices were lost in the rustling of a perspiring crowd, listless children wanting drinks of water, the sound of ineffectual fans, and the soggy air. It was another Black Hole of Calcutta.

I was convinced that weeks of work had gone unappreciated, and some of my seniors felt much the same. The next morning I told the principal that, until we had an auditorium, I was unwilling to continue the commencement experiment. Of course, I knew that it meant the death knell for the annual project because Worthington's continuing need for classrooms seemed to rule out the possibility of our ever getting a new auditorium.

I didn't want to stop this work—it meant a great deal to me and to my students. I thought that I was contributing something worthwhile to the school in my efforts, and I liked thinking so. I did continue for several more years in the classroom writing of senior-day plays, but Worthington returned to conventional graduation format the following June.

There were many moments of irony that next spring. One day I heard an underclassman say, "I heard they're going to do something *new* for graduation. They're going to do like Upper Arlington and have a speaker come in and talk to the seniors." I was bending over the water fountain and very nearly strangled. As I helped line the seniors up for their processional that year, I missed the frantic last-minute questions of the student director, the scurrying of the property man, the excitement of actors poised behind a curtain. Later, as I stood watching the recessional move slowly off the athletic field, another teacher exclaimed, "It makes quite a beautiful sight, seeing them go over the hill and seem to disappear like that, doesn't it?" "Yes," I lied. I felt like a cheat—maybe I should have tried to give this class a play, even outside, daring it to rain. I looked at my comrade. It probably never occurred to him that I would be anything but relieved to give up the commencement plays and the work involved. I decided that there must be something cockeyed in my makeup. I'd never honestly been able to enjoy seeing my seniors leave. Now the last of the blue gowns and the white were passing from sight. Beautiful? Perhaps.

I used to flatter myself that I could perform wonders in Room 106. It was a delightful fantasy to suppose, for a short while, that I was God's gift to the classroom. Now I know better. I possess certain strengths in my background and memory, but I have troubling limitations as a teacher, too. I see now that something else is at work for me in that room—the fundamental need of every human being for love and compassion and, most of all, an image of flesh and blood, an anthropomorphic something whose ear is available to our confidences.

They bring their innermost secrets—their shames, their triumphs. They do not wait for or limit themselves to autobiographies. They are waiting at my desk when I enter the room in the morning. They come to me between classes and after school. They ask for counsel, for small talk, in time of crisis, in time of

The Father-Image

happiness. There is not time to listen to all of them, yet I cannot send them away.

I am not alone in this. Every one of us who teaches must experience some of it, this cry from the young for wisdom and strength that, most often, we ourselves lack. But I can not say, "I am busy. I can do nothing for you. Go see somebody else." Some of them have bestowed the ultimate compliment upon me by believing that I am something extraordinary among people. But most of them have not draped an illusive mantle about my shoulders nor seen me as some super-being. The great majority want only someone who will listen, someone who will seem to understand when they speak, another human being who will serve as a sounding board. And I do not send them away. I can not do so because I remember a time when I was in need of such a person and could not find him.

After I had turned fourteen, my relatives became troubled about my soul. I had been reared in the Lutheran church. The year my parents separated, I had been taking my catechism lessons faithfully. I worked hard enough at it to graduate summa cum laude. I worked hard at school, too. I think that, perhaps, I was motivated by the notion that my father's departure was a renunciation of me—that possibly I was lacking as a son. I remember that, at my confirmation, I was the only kid in the class without a suit. I wore a black sweater instead of a coat. My mother's pride was so bothered that she went into debt to get me a suit the following week. But I stopped going to church regularly at the age of fourteen.

When I broke with the church, I did not stop believing in God— I simply reached the conclusion that all the praying in the world would not bring my father back. Moreover, I was half convinced that there was some sort of curse on my family *"unto the third and fourth generations"* (divorces went back two generations on my father's side and one on my mother's). If I couldn't fight it, I should accept it.

I promptly did so. Where sex is a part-time fascination for most young people, it became a full-time adventure for me. Where many teenagers strive for independence, I went one step further, into a voluntary spiritual isolation. At least two of my teachers sought to help, but I blocked their efforts after a time. There was no one for me to talk to, no one to whom I could comfortably turn. I could not find an image to substitute for the man who was my father. Still, in some inexplicable way, I found a kind of happiness— mainly, I think, because I was striving to emulate my father.

As I recall, my brother and I had been the envy of our neighborhood, largely because we had *him* for a father. Some boys had bikes before we did, some had bigger homes, and a few possessed unthinkably expensive toys, even during those Depression years, but my brother and I had *him*. When work got better for him, he brought home the first electric train in the block, and he was on his knees beside the track as often as we were. I remember, too, the lead soldiers that I used to play with. There was one whose uniform I could not identify and I remember asking him about it. "That's a Marine," he said. "I'd put him out front." I must have remembered the tone of his voice very well.

My father was a Pied Piper of sorts. In my mind's eye, I can still see the neighborhood boys crowding around when my father was home. They would edge into the circle with great-eyed wonder to hear him talk, to watch him fire an old muzzle-loader on the Fourth of July, to see him unloading or cleaning pheasants or bass on our back porch, to ask questions as he oiled or assembled his favorite rifle. For other boys it was a privilege to be in his presence—and my little brother and I felt much the same.

I don't think he ever struck me more than two or three times, and I really deserved it then, if not for a specific reason then on general principles. He taught me to defend myself but never to bully. One day when several boys had chased me home with little clubs, he made me go out of the house with a bigger club and see how the other side could run. After I had received a spanking in the first grade for fighting on the school grounds, my father called my first-grade teacher and complained, "I taught this boy to take his part, and I don't want it whipped out of him." He didn't like violence but he couldn't tolerate appeasement, either. The infrequent physical punishment he meted out to his sons was a waste of energy—a frown from him was the worst punishment of all.

What was he like, this father-image of my youth? In those years, before the circumstances and illnesses of his life had shrunk the sinews of his body, he stood just under six feet, though there was something in the look of him that made taller men seem to shrink in his presence. He was, at all odds, a man's man—masculinity personified. Dad was a handsome person, serious faced, lean of body, squarely shouldered, and intent in his feelings. He had the face of actor Paul Lukas and the manner of Errol Flynn.

I have never known anyone who disliked my father. His dry wit, his way of listening to others, his individuality, that intentness about the eyes—even those moments when he seemed to withdraw into himself and to partake of some half-forgotten sadness—attracted people to him. Even after he had made his mistakes, I never heard anyone speak ill of him.

He had known an unhappy childhood. At the time of his own parents' separation, his mother had become so absorbed in self-pity that for years my father had to depend upon an aunt to look after him. Like many boys of that time, he quit school too soon, after the eighth grade, and, after working at various short-term jobs, he became a machinist. He married my mother very early in 1923, when he was twenty-one and she, eighteen. They were two babes in the woods of the Roaring Twenties, starting from scratch in search for some security in their lives.

My birth in December of that year was probably the worst thing that could have happened to them. I say this because my father was still, in many respects, a boy in spirit. In addition, my mother, who as a child had lacked the parental love and protection she had needed, tried to compensate by devoting too much of her attention and love to me and to my brother, born four years later. If my parents had been inwardly as independent and secure as they seemed to others, perhaps their marriage might have succeeded. Unfortunately, the tragedies of their childhood and the financial stress of their early years together inevitably brought their separation.

Of course, my father's "adventures" were the immediate cause of the broken home. There was a time when I could not comprehend his actions. I have lived too long now not to understand and to forgive him, for he and I have had much in common despite the miles and years between us. When he left home, he was running away not from his family alone, but from himself, his childhood, his sense of inadequacy and guilt. Even when he was not sure how he could feed himself, he was addressing little money orders to my mother from different parts of the country. Back in my neighborhood, when other boys would ask about my father, my brother and I never had to defend him, because for our friends, as for us, the hero remained the hero even with some rust on his armor. Nor did the years ever alter that image.

During those years, my father turned to the one source of solace he could depend upon in life—nature. He had always been an avid sportsman—the crack marksman, the skilled angler—but I can remember those times when he would prop the rifle against the tree or ignore the setline and turn simply to enjoy the air, the color, the multitudinous sounds of furred and feathered life. There was much of the man called Thoreau in my father, and more than a little Byron, too.

I don't think he ever read these authors, but he knew Tennyson. I came downstairs one Sunday morning, just late enough not to have to go to Sunday school, and found him reading, of all things, poetry. My elementary teachers had already cultivated a strong distaste in me for verse, my worst travail having been to recite "Abou Ben Adhem" without having the faintest idea of what Leigh Hunt meant. Suddenly, there was my father, reading something called *The Idylls of the King*. I was a long time in understanding this strange facet of his interests.

After a while I came to realize that he regretted not having continued his schooling. He often said to me that people should get as much education as they can. He hated his own limitations, and he overcame many of these by private reading. Still, I recall a textbook on mathematics in our old library case that I would see him frowning over. There were things in that book he couldn't grasp, simply because he needed more formal education.

Admittedly, he was bound by much of the bigotry of his family and his era. That was a period in America when everyone was looking for someone to blame the Depression on, and the hate-peddlers really had an easy time of it. Sometimes in his frustration my father would vent anti-Jewish, anti-Catholic, and anti-Negro feelings, but he never subscribed to what was going on in Germany and elsewhere. Once, while I was overseas, he wrote in a letter, "Only God and Joe Stalin know what this war is all about." Though he doubtless overlooked some significant causes, there was an element of prophecy in his words.

I can see my father more clearly today, but before I enlisted I understood him no better than myself. Moved by William Blake's phrasing, I put all my hurt and arrogance and misanthropy into an autobiographical potpourri called *In the Forest of the Night or Eighteen Shadows* and plunged headlong into a thoroughly dissolute and destructive existence. So my relatives became even more worried about my spiritual well-being.

When I applied for enlistment, some of the family may even have breathed a sigh of relief. As my entrance into the Corps was held up by somewhat embarrassing circumstances, the family once more had reason for distress. It was my aunt who arranged for me to take communion before my passage to Parris Island. I would not have gone to the church except for my mother's sake. I couldn't say *no* to her. I had hurt her too much already.

I stood in the church at two o'clock, waiting for the minister to arrive. Peter Steindorf, the pastor, was the same gaunt, somber-faced preacher partly because of whom I had left the church several years before. When, as a Hi-Y president, I had arranged to include a Jewish rabbi among a series of speakers for my organization, Steindorf had called to take me to task. The Hi-Y was affiliated with the Young Men's *Christian* Association, and my action was shocking, he had charged. Steindorf offended my concept of a Christian. But I had come to the church for my mother and my aunt, not for their pastor.

When Steindorf came in, he was dragging little Peter, his son, who was leaving for the Navy. Someone in the family had thought it would be nice if young Peter and I were to share in this private communion service. God will recall with me that that communion service was a dud so far as my soul-cleansing was concerned.

"Our Lord Jesus Christ, in the night in which he was betrayed—" repeated the old man, looking down at his kneeling son. All the time, I kept thinking: *Even here, the cards are stacked. Pete has two fathers here. I've got just one.* "Take, eat; this is My Body—" the elder Steindorf intoned, and I felt the wafer stick to the roof of my mouth. It was just as well—my throat was past swallowing.

"Drink ye all of it—" the pastor was saying now, and I thought: *Yes, I will drink, all right. When I get out of here, Oh, how I will drink.* Somehow I got the wine down, but it was a sacrilege, every trickle. I rose and tried to be gracious in excusing myself. As I left, I saw old Steindorf put his hand on his son's shoulder, and I hated that old man because he had tears in his eyes. I was still seeing the tender look on his face when I got to the bar, four blocks away.

After my stay in the non-Pacific Ocean and my discharge at the Great Lakes Naval Training Station, I went to my hometown to see my mother. She had remarried during the war, and I was happy to see that at last she was making another life for herself. I stayed there about a week, then took a train to Baltimore to visit my father. He and I had a wonderful time together for a week, trying seafood and antipastos, seeing stage shows, drinking beer. Those things which I had not understood about him were no longer mysteries. We were enough alike to be—but it remained for him to say it.

We had just come back from enjoying ourselves at Benjamin's, one of the better bars in the bayshore section of the city. We began to talk about the lost years. I remember thinking, *It's funny, but I feel none of the hurt—it's gone, all gone.* It was . . . until he turned to me and said, "You know, you don't seem like a son to me. You've always seemed more like a brother." He meant to acknowledge my manhood, my coming of age, my seeming maturity, and the things we had in common. Yet, suddenly the years welled back, and unuttered words were caught in my throat: *But I wanted to be a son to you.*

I didn't get much sleep that night. I lay and tossed with a new awareness that I had never really "lost" my father. He had walked with me every step of my life. He was not the prosaic, run-of-the-mill father of the movie and radio families, nor was he like the other fathers in my block. Despite his flaws, he had been much more than these. I had not needed him to fill a chair at father-and-son banquets. I had drawn a strength from that empty place at the table to counteract the weakness it produced simultaneously.

Now I knew why children loved him. He was young hearted. He was still driven by the unquenchable desire to see the other side of the mountain, to plant flowers along the highway (as he did many times along the Pennsylvania Turnpike), to try the stream farther down, to climb the unscalable escarpment. Perhaps the young would one day crowd around me. No, I would never be without my father. He was in my walk, my voice, my eyes.

I realized in Baltimore that, had my father been there for me to talk to during those years in which I had to learn everything the hard way, very little would have been different for me. Talking to him would have been very much like talking to myself.

Still, even if that youthful perspective was part of my inheritance, in certain respects I was even older than he. There was a bit of gray in his hair and moustache, but there was a grayness of the beachhead in my life. The vicissitudes of war had aged me in a way that he would never know. Like him I loved the woods and streams, though the joy had gone out of hunting when the "game" had begun to fire back at me.

I went back to my church that Christmas, not because I had been trained as a Lutheran—I would never fit perfectly into that denomination again. I went because I had had that last communion there—that miscarriage of bread and wine in which I had been too much absorbed with the sight of another father and son to grasp how much I had been blessed by my own earthly father. If the cards had been stacked, they had been arranged in my favor. Whatever my father's faults, he was never the hypocrite. When I finally bowed my head to ask for absolution, I did so with sincerity and a new and precious wisdom.

The boy, trembling in the wake of his first romance, brings his dilemma to me in 106: "We're in love, but I know we've each got four years of college ahead of us. Now we've reached the place where we both want sexual relations. I've held off about as long as I can, and she stopped saying *no* last night. What would you do?" I do not tell him what I would have done at his age—that would not be helpful to him. I cannot send him to a guidance counselor because he wants to talk to me. Although I know that what I say to him will possibly be of little value, anyway, I give him my best advice. I may flavor it with my own diction out of fun, but he knows what I mean. "If you're as bright as I think you are, my friend, you will keep your reproductive members securely ensconced in your BVD's."

A girl comes to me. She is still in the shadow of her parents' divorce and her mother's remarriage: "I hate my real father—I can't help it. I can't stand being around him." I tell her the story of my own father, whose feet were of the same clay. "Don't hate him," I tell her. "He lives now in his own private little hell of self-indictment, or if he doesn't yet he will some day. Forgive him. It may not be easy, but when you're farther along in years and have seen more of life, you'll know him better. Come back in ten years and tell me if you've ever met a saint."

"What about Augustine?" she counters with a quip. She is strong in church training, though.

"You mean you've never heard of his famous prayer as a young man?"

"No."

"It was John Donne's, too. It goes: 'Give me chastity, oh Lord, but not just yet,' " I recite. She is laughing when she leaves. And she later writes this in a note:

> I really have appreciated all the advice you have given me, and the masculine image you have provided. I think every girl needs this image in order to choose a mate. I hope that Rusty will acquire some of your personality traits because, in my opinion, you have all the qualities I would like in a husband.
>
> I feel closer to you than any man I know, probably because you are the first teacher to whom I

*have revealed my real self. I feel
that this experience was worthwhile,
because you likewise showed
me a part of your personality that
I'm sure some students never see.*

These are the words of a girl who hated her father, and I have become his substitute. She has yet to forgive him for his affairs with other women. That she should choose me as a model makes me both proud and humble. For I know something that she doesn't know—that the father-image she admires is fundamentally the image of my father.

On the American educational front, no current practice reflects more futility and produces greater frustration than that wonderful resolver of student schedule conflicts euphemistically labeled "study hall." Of course, the outstanding value of a study hall is that usually it can accommodate, at any given hour, a large number of beings that are not scheduled to be in classrooms. A study hall, in theory, is an academic watering-trough, replenished by a Pierian spring, to which herds of students are daily led. Because many of them either lack thirst or find the water unpalatable, study halls customarily fall into two categories—the Heidelberg and the Lidice—the classification depending chiefly upon the temperament and background of the "trail boss."

The Heidelberg is managed by a personality that must draw upon the natural passions of a P. T. Barnum, an Olsen and John-

The Big Cage Called a "Study Hall"

son, and a Ben Grauer observing Times Square on New Year's Eve. Everyone in the manager's ken is either an Allen and Rossi, a manic-elated, or a smiling spectator. There is a festive holiday air about the place, though some individuals turn from the excesses of the fiesta to enjoy brief siestas. There is no time in a Heidelberg to contemplate the world's sorrows. This is a Mudville in which Casey, leading the league in RBI, clears the bases daily and twice per doubleheader.

In the study hall a la Lidice, the fuehrer is either Heinrich Himmler or Ilsa Koch. On the face of this *erzieher* is a grimace suggesting impacted wisdom teeth, ingrown toenails, and hemorrhoids. A brooding silence permeates Lidice as the Argus-eyed leader patrols the living dead propped at their desk-arm chairs. Lidice is a ghost town without a ghost of a smile, a gesture of warmth, or a tumbleweed of chance. Any sign of life among the mannequins here leads instantly to the *gauleiter's* crematorial frown—or worse. Outside Lidice there are horrid rumors about what the master's briefcase is made of and about what he carries inside it.

I will admit to some exaggeration in these descriptions, but the fact remains that study halls contain either the atmosphere of the circus or the pall of the cemetery. The fundamental reason is the nature of young people. Like their elders they either enjoy a respite from their labors or find it hard to work when someone close by is not.

A contributing factor in studyless study halls is the novice teacher's lack of preparation for such a job. Nowhere in my training for secondary education did I hear that first mention of study halls. Though some schools have been able to rid themselves of the old-fashioned study hall, most beginning teachers will find that their job assignments include some study-hall supervision. On their first day they blithely stroll to a designated room where study will presumably happen and where they are astounded to find that it does not. In a study hall the typical beginning teacher has the naïveté of a Marie Antoinette discussing the French peasant's diet.

Heidelberg Hall is most often seen in the care of an inexperienced monitor or of a veteran who doesn't particularly give a damn because he feels that he cannot count on administrative support for his disciplinary procedures. My own early ineffectiveness in study-hall management stemmed from the same source as my classroom failure—an unrealistic view of young people. In fact, it took me a full year to understand that a quiet study hall requires Himmler at the helm. Even then, I learned that there are many students who merely stare without interest or comprehension at textbook pages, create the cars of tomorrow on notebook pages, or spend their time waiting for restroom passes.

My first study hall was a badly lit, drab-looking room packed beyond its capacity with sophomores, juniors, and seniors, all of whose expressions seemed to say of me "Is he for real?" Merely to turn my back was to invite a tumult of conversation. Trying to isolate and discourage such disturbances was rather like trying to plug a countless number of holes in the dyke with one finger.

One day in December, the star of the varsity basketball team, whom I will call Homo Globulus Gigantis, had the temerity to challenge me when I told him to cease and desist from flapping his big mandibles. He actually rose from his seat to insist that he hadn't been talking. Of course, I couldn't prove that he had been, but I did know that he had been mouthing gutteral noises which he *intended* as communication. It was one of the half-dozen times in my entire teaching experience to date when I found it necessary to take a student to the principal. Ray Heischman, who was the Glob's coach as well as my principal, explained to the big forward that, unless he developed respectfulness, his star status would shrink from nova on the floor to orange-colored dwarf on the bench. (Ray taught physics and some astronomy, too.) Thereafter, Glob was quiet and contented himself by sullenly glowering at me through the period. By the time the basketball season was over, he was finished doing anything but sitting.

In my second campaign of study-halling, I was much improved. During the subsequent years I even developed a very nearly foolproof system—except for an occasional fool, that is. I endeavored to limit restroom passes to one per sex—in those days I could always tell one from the other—and I established an effective means of preventing idle chit-chat among my charges. Moreover, I stubbornly held to the standard definition of *study* in running a study hall.

I was much more successful in limiting the boys to one pass than in restricting the girls. To begin with, I really don't like to have people asking me whether they can go to the restroom. Occasionally one finds an exhibitionism of sorts in people, especially girls. I distinctly recall one young lady who used to march to the desk for the pass in the manner of someone auditioning. Then, too, girls have the knack of contorting their faces so as to imply that, at any minute, they may urinate with abandon.

Males, I think, are more embarrassed by and less demonstrative in their need for such facilities. Some, I suspect, even believe between trips that they are above such animalism. Therefore, I could discourage the misuse of the boys' pass much more easily. One day when several boys dashed sportingly to get the pass, I said loudly enough that all could hear: "All right, back to your seats. If you're in that big a hurry, you'll never make it, anyway." It turned out to be worth the gamble. Most of the boys stopped watching for the pass to be returned.

In eliminating the clandestine conversations in my study hall, I followed this procedure: Upon the first offense, I issued a warning to the culprit and explained the shape of things to come should he not mend his ways. If he violated the rule a second time, I required him to write 5000 words on a subject of my choosing and to turn it in to me within three days. If he failed to comply, I shipped him to the office with a recommendation that the principal expel him from school for three days. Such expulsion would mean that the offender would draw F's on all work done in his classes while he was out of school. This punishment may sound harsh, but I had learned only too well that if one study-hall talker is not dealt with firmly the monitor soon has fifty of them on his hands. Moreover, in following this procedure, I let the chips fall where they might. If my grandmother had been in my study hall and had spoken twice without permission, Grandma would have had her arthritis aggravated by writer's cramp.

Seeing is believing, and several youngsters had to see of course whether I really meant it. To the principal's credit, he expelled the first two students whom I sent with that recommendation. Afterwards, only Miss Fry had a quieter study hall than mine.

My no-talking rule thoroughly rankled some people, in and out of the school. Judy, a very pretty sophomore, was mainly interested in attracting boys, so she talked to them whenever possible. Actually, her reasoning was bad—she could have done much better by being quiet, for her conversation was no asset at all. When I assigned the writing penalty, Judy was very angry with me. Next day, she brought a note in which Mama expressed her unhappiness with me. According to Judy's mother, "Judy does not have time to do this work as she needs all her spare time for study." I replied, "I fully agree that Judy needs all her spare time for study. The purpose of this assignment is to make it clear to Judy that my study hall *is* spare time for study. Unless the required work is in my hands by the day after tomorrow and is in Judy's own handwriting, I shall request that she be expelled. In such a case, perhaps you can temporarily improve upon my efforts to discipline her use of spare time." The mother, I learned later, had written her note without a full awareness of Judy's loquacity.

Even in the most orderly study hall, there are those times in which the atmosphere can be ruined. In one instance, I wanted to arrange a conference in order to help a student of mine who was also in my study hall. She was sitting with her back toward me, and I couldn't gain her attention. The room was as serene as a mausoleum, and I endeavored to step as softly as possible till I reached her chair. I leaned easily over her shoulder, and with my first whispered syllable she leaped from her seat and emitted a deafening scream. I don't know what she was thinking about or whether she had been hearing any of Joan of Arc's voices. I only know that I had badly terrified her, and that the piercing outcry had frightened the rest of us. The study hall was a shambles the rest of the period, everybody laughing with relief.

Teachers don't help one another's study halls. They come in looking for students, for information, and for small talk ranging from the last staff meeting to the opening Series game. The worst distraction ever caused by a teacher in one of my study halls came from Jack. He was a highly nervous young man who was in his first year of teaching and who left during the Christmas holidays to join the Army. Much of his trepidation grew out of his effect upon the girls in his classes. Apparently they found this clean-cut, unmarried fellow of twenty-one absolutely irresistible. One of the junior girls whose libido was obviously and completely out of control had an especially mad "crush" on Jack. When he tried to reroute her energies, she came up with a novel attention-getting device.

I was standing in my study hall when I heard the door squeak open slightly and saw his sallow face peer round it. He motioned furtively for me to come. Had I known the sensation that his appearance would create, I would have stepped outside to talk to him. Unfortunately, I swung the door open wide. The additional squeaking caused most of the heads in the room to turn to the spectacle there. Jack's eyes were mainly whites as he pointed to his collar, where all that remained of his red tie was a knot with several threads hanging from it. "Look!" he intoned in a low, frantic voice. "What would *you* do?"

My first thought was to tell him that, in a like situation, I'd take the tie back to the store and complain. Still, I had never seen a tie disintegrate in quite that way. "What happened?" I asked, casting an evil countenance toward the craning necks in the room.

His eyes rolled as his voice took on a rising inflection. "She did it! I was leaning over the desk, and she took a pair of scissors and —look!—she just cut it off!"

"Who's she?"

"That idiot, Margaret Ann—she's the one! I tell you that girl's not right!" he shouted in his tenor pitch. My study hall roared.

Jack would have joined the French Foreign Legion to get out of Worthington. He had lots of ties, but Margaret Ann's principal objective had nothing to do with haberdashery.

Girls are the chronic note-passers in study halls, and most often their subjects wear trousers. To discourage this diversion, the teacher must watch hands and circulate regularly around the room. One morning I found out that even an old married man of thirty can activate a schoolgirl's endocrines. While this discovery was not without a certain flattery, the note-writing involved did nevertheless interfere with the study process. Two girls—a junior and a senior—were busily working with a shorthand assignment, it appeared. But their occasional glances in my direction and their covert smiles over their work hinted at some sort of collusion.

It was time for one of my tours about the aisles, so I took a circuitous route that soon brought me to stand behind them. Clearly, they did not know I was so close or they had faith in my inability to read the Gregg forms, for they made no effort to conceal their handiwork. The characters they had scrawled were of an exaggerated size so that they could see and enjoy each other's replies more readily. Having had two courses in that system of shorthand, I read portions of their notes with ease. The senior girl's observations focused upon my vest, shoulders, and—she had to invent her own form for it—my moustache. It was the junior's statements that indicated greater precocity. For example:

Her notes made some of the most exhilarating shorthand I had ever seen, and with some embarrassment I broke off reading and retreated to the back of the room to "reorganize my troops." There I made two copies of the following note in my best shorthand:

> Dear Joan and Marcia:
>
> Your notes about me are quite interesting and heart warming. They are also a form of talking— which is against the law in here. Need I say more?

I dropped these on their desk arms, and a few seconds later the crimson glow of their cheeks brightened the study-hall time and the remainder of my day.

The monitor of a study hall cannot afford to have a friend in the room. He must be charged with venom and constitutionally poised to strike without rattling. The sense of aloneness that a teacher lives with a large share of the time is even more poignant when he is assigned to such duty.

In my judgment, to fill a room with senior-high students and to say to them "Now you must study" is absurd. Some senior-high people still need playgrounds and supervised recesses. It would be much more practicable and realistic to assert "Here you *may* study, provided that you do not abuse the privilege of the room." The only other sensible alternative, as I see it, is the graded study hall—which issues reports to parents on the individual student's use of study-hall time.

Meanwhile, the only study hall in which anyone studies requires an inflexible disciplinarian. I know that when students leave a study hall of mine some of them are sufficiently full of pent-up orneriness to become real discipline problems elsewhere. Yet I know that Heidelberg Hall produces even less study and sets up many more students for trouble. Either kind of study hall can add to a school's discipline headaches.

It has been my good fortune to escape study-hall duty for the past several years. I have been doing lunch-hour hall duty, instead. The school has hired some non-teaching personnel for the largest study hall in the building, and this step has been helpful, at least to a few teachers. I have heard it said that, if a school wishes to get rid of a teacher whose tenure-law protection makes dismissal otherwise impossible, the best way is to assign him to day-long study-hall duty. Nobody could stand up under such a trial and remain rational.

"May God forgive me. My baby—I've killed my baby!" In terrible grief and despair, the woman half fell to the floor, where she knelt beneath the burden of her guilt. Her child, born with gruesome deformities produced by the thalidomide drug, was dead at the mother's own hands. Around her some twelve hundred witnesses listened to her confession. They sat muted and misty eyed, forgetting that they watched this scene from the bleachers of Worthington's high-school gymnasium. The "mother" was an attractive seventeen-year-old Negro girl whose work as a monologist in Room 106 had led to her being asked to perform before the student body. Barbara's monologue treating an issue that was current and controversial left her audience in emotional exhaustion, and the student whose performance followed hers worked under a considerable handicap.

The Chalkboard Set

The genesis of senior-English monologues at Worthington High came in the fall of 1953. Our classroom writing of commencement plays would demand that my students have additional practice in visualizing settings, in preparing manuscripts that incorporated pantomime and stage directions, and in creating characters with believable, meaningful lines. Before my seniors turned to dialogue, monologue work seemed to provide a logical stepping-stone. I believed, also, that such experience could provide students with a much clearer notion of the challenges faced by the playwrights whose works they studied—Shaw, Barrie, Sheridan, and Shakespeare.

Yet, when I first assigned the monologues, I did so experimentally and with some doubt. Certainly the expenditure of at least a week of class time on such a project required sacrificing some other course content or activity at a calculated risk. I didn't really consider, then, that this type of assignment fits perfectly into Alexander Pope's formula of teaching "as if you taught them not." I knew only that, if the monologues were successful, they would interrelate beautifully with other phases of the program in 106.

Looking back across more than fifteen years and 1500 senior monologues, I still feel surprise over the immediate and continuing success of this assignment. Most of that success I must credit to the highly articulate and creative nature of 'my students, to their competitive drive, and to Mr. Durante's thesis that everybody wants to get into the act. The teacher's role is clearly minimized in such an activity—his task is merely to explain the assignment, to imply that standards are high, to advise students needing assistance, to schedule the presentations, and to evaluate the individual outcomes. A student can feel, therefore, that his accomplishment in the work is almost entirely his own.

Early in November, when my students are completing their autobiographies, I hand them a sheet of instructions relating to monologues. Annually they produce a gasp identical to that of their predecessors, momentarily exchange frantic buzzings, then bend their pupil pupils to the specifications, which read as follows:

ORIGINAL MONOLOGUE REQUIREMENT

1. Create a character, preferably one whose traits are quite different from your own. Your treatment of this character may be sympathetic, satirical, or entirely objective.

2. Select a situation in which to place your monologue character. Try to develop a set of circumstances in which the character will reveal himself to the fullest possible extent, insofar as his traits and attitudes are concerned.

3. Prepare a monologue in which you include appropriate pantomime, voice, and props. In props and costuming (when these are involved), always let simplicity and ingenuity be your aim. Your monologue may include lines addressed to imaginary persons involved in the situation, or it may simply concern the revelation of thoughts as in the case of soliloquies. Your work should be sufficiently developed to insure a length of 4-6 minutes.

4. Present the monologue before the class.
   To create a greater illusion of reality and
   a smoother presentation, you should avoid the
   use of notes. You may wish to preface your
   monologue with a brief explanation of character and situation or setting; such intro-
   ductory remarks are entirely optional, depending upon the needs of the monologues. Once
   you have begun the monologue proper, you
   should seek to remain in character throughout
   your presentation. Strive to be as convincing as possible.

5. On the day your presentation is scheduled,
   provide the teacher with a neat, legible version of your monologue, typed or in ink.
   This manuscript should follow all the regular
   style requirements in its format and organization.

6. Provision will be made for each student to
   sign in advance for the particular day on
   which his monologue will be given. Once the
   student has been scheduled, the monologue
   calendar will be viewed as inflexible, except
   for absences growing out of illnesses and
   other excusable reasons. Your failure to be
   present and prepared on the appointed day
   works an imposition upon the class.

7. Hard work on your part will result in a
   highly constructive, but equally enjoyable
   week of monologues. As in the past, some of
   this year's monologues will undoubtedly be
   presented before the entire student body.

Though most of the students affect an apocalyptic doom in their
first reaction to these instructions, they nevertheless respond posi-
tively to the challenge. I have carefully conditioned them to accept my view that they are only "glorified juniors" until they have
weathered several classroom cataclysms, among them the monologues. If they were stimulated by every assignment as they are
by this one, my efforts to teach would be eminently successful.
Other teachers tell me that some students begin to anticipate the
twelfth-grade monologues as early as their sophomore year.

As soon as the class has finished reading the directions, individuals begin to quake and question. The following transcript of
a tape-recorded session in 106 will reveal some of the usual anxiety and commotion:

TEACHER: . . . *because some of you may be wondering about the same things. Jim?*

STUDENT: *It doesn't explain on the sheet what you mean by* Original.

TEACHER: *Two things. It means, first of all, that the work should originate mainly with you. Sometimes, though, we use the word to mean "inventive" or "fresh," and I don't doubt that every one of you will find some idea or "gimmick" that will be of your own invention. Uhh —Dick?*

STUDENT: *Is there really anything that hasn't been done before —I mean original, in that sense?*

TEACHER: *Someone has said, "There's really nothing new under the sun," but I think he must have been a miserable, pessimistic fellow. Dick, every time a new pair of eyes is born into this world, I like to think that a slightly different way of looking at things has been born at the same time. Why, the world is constantly seeing new things . . . changes. Look at space flight, cybernation—I think you've read about that in American government—and television.* (AFTER A PAUSE) *Yes?*

STUDENT: *The sheet says we have to do a character that's different from us. Won't that be harder, Mr. Rousculp?*

TEACHER: *Not necessarily. As a matter of fact most of you will find it much* easier. (SEVERAL STUDENTS MAKE SKEP-TICAL SOUNDS.) *Let me tell you why, Ken. To begin with, everyone of us occasionally enjoys pretending he's someone else—someone different. Every one of us has a little "ham" in him, even though most of us do our acting privately, like Walter Mitty. And—*

STUDENT: (INTERRUPTING) *But we have to act these characters out, in front of the class. Won't it be easier if we do teenagers like ourselves?*

TEACHER: *But don't we ever become a little bored with ourselves? And are we really inventing or* creating *if we're just acting our own roles? There's something else, too— how many of you expect to feel somewhat uncomfortable when you're giving your monologues before the group?*

STUDENT: Uncomfortable? *Ha! Someone will have to carry me in and out that day.* (OTHERS LAUGH NERVOUSLY AND SOUND AGREEMENT.)

STUDENT: *Mr. Rousculp, I just can't act.*

STUDENT: *I'll forget my lines, for sure.*

STUDENT: *I think I'm going to be sick.*

TEACHER: *Hey, now, hold on!—you're not being completely honest. What's the <u>real</u> reason for the discomfort most of us feel when we're doing this sort of thing?* (PAUSE) *Then <u>I'll</u> tell <u>you</u>. I'll say it because you don't like to admit it, at least publicly—you're mainly scared of one another, afraid of what the others will think of you. You're apprehensive because when you're up here giving your monologue you're going to see all sorts of expressions on faces out there, and every one of them will seem to be measuring or criticizing you. And that's <u>why</u> I don't want <u>you</u> up here— I want the <u>character you've created</u>. The point is this: If you can become another person in another situation, if you can project yourself into another life for the space of five minutes and do it convincingly, we'll forget all about you and we'll be watching someone completely new to us. The senior named Janet Bennett or Dick Shoemaker will have lost identity—ceased to exist—for a few short minutes. Do you see the <u>method</u> in my madness?*

STUDENT: *I'll have ceased to exist, all right.*

STUDENT: *It sounds like schizophrenia, Mr. Rousculp.*

STUDENT: *I'll still be nervous.*

TEACHER: *Of course you will. The best communication of any sort requires tension. I wouldn't give a plug nickel for any speaker or actor who doesn't feel that inner tension. But this way, you see, you can concentrate that tension on casting off inhibitions and self-consciousness. If you become the character, if you "think" the character, nobody's going to be watching you—everyone will be watching the personality you've manufactured.*

STUDENT: *I don't understand this part on props and costumes.*

TEACHER: *The main thing is not to go overboard on them, Betty. If you lean too heavily on these, you may neglect becoming the character. Any of the furniture in this room will be at your disposal. You have to be very careful of what you use in serious monologues, however, because any incongruous object may break up the illusion of reality that you're trying to create.*

STUDENT: *How much costuming can we use?*

TEACHER: *I'll be glad to give individual advice where props and costuming are concerned. Just remember that the really competent actor can build his own set, erect his own theater, assume whatever guise he wishes— and he can do all this on a completely bare stage and without the help of a costumer.*

STUDENT: *What if you don't have any ideas for a monologue character? They never did anything like this at the school I came from. I don't think I ever saw one.*

TEACHER: *Chances are you've seen them on TV, Lois. But I'm sure that many of us feel much the same as you do right now. You've—all of you—got a tough job ahead. You've got to serve not only as your own actor but as your own writer, director, and stage manager, too. So let's talk about it. Where do writers get their ideas, Bob?*

STUDENT: *From experience?*

TEACHER: *Right. Sometimes, anyway. Any other sources, Bobbie?*

STUDENT: *By watching people, maybe.*

TEACHER: *All right, we've got experience and observation. Isn't there another, very important factor? Warren?*

STUDENT: *Imagination. Like the Romantic poets we were talking about.*

TEACHER: *Exactly. So you might begin by asking yourself, "What do I imagine to be the most tragic or humorous or curious or repulsive sort of person to be like—not counting my English teacher, of course?" Then you might wonder, "What is the most amusing, moving, ah, frightening, or disgusting situation that I can imagine?" Before you're done writing your monologue, you'll probably have included materials that spring from all three sources—experience, observation, and imagination. Carol?*

STUDENT: *Does a monologue have to be all serious or humorous?*

TEACHER: *It's usually best to work for a single effect—that is, to keep the tone or mood consistent. A change of mood is hard to pull off.*

STUDENT: *Shakespeare did it in "Macbeth."*

TEACHER: *Where, Steve?*

STUDENT: *You know. In the—uh—the porter scene. Where he's drunk.*

TEACHER: *Right. But do you see a difference between that and a monologue?*

STUDENT: *You mean because Shakespeare switched characters?*

TEACHER: *Sure. It would have been impossible, wouldn't it, for Macbeth to be very humorous at that point?*

STUDENT: *I see what you mean.*

TEACHER: *No, it's usually difficult in five minutes time to change the mood drastically when only one characterization is involved. It can be done, though, if you're actor enough. I remember Dave Budbill's monologue some years ago, for example. It began with a stereotyped expectant father in a hospital waiting room. Very humorous at the beginning—right up to the point at which the nurse informed him that his wife had died in childbirth. Dave managed, somehow, to make the transition, and the monologue was quite moving as the father talked to the newborn child on the other side of the nursery window. I remember another monologue, too, in which . . . .*

"All the room's a stage, a chalkboard set," wrote one of my students in describing the monologues in Room 106. It was his way of noting that very few objects in the room have not been utilized as stage properties by my seniors. My lectern has served as a TV set, a bargain counter, and part of a space capsule. The table has passed for a bed, a playpen, a row of bassinets, and Santa's sleigh. From my file cabinets have come imaginary cakes and pies, electronic devices, top-secret plans, and dental records. The built-in closet has functioned as a safe, a submarine hatch, and a bar. Just when I am certain that nothing new can be made of 106 and its furnishings, some innovator puts in an appearance.

The monologue manuscript that I require from each student is the only paper that I do not return. I use it, of course, as one of the dozen factors in grading this assignment, but my principal reason for keeping it is, I suppose, my desire to keep something of my students in my files. The cabinets fairly bulge, even without this accumulation, but so many of these scripts hold memories, important to me, of students for whom the monologue was a crisis, a milestone of sorts. Then, too, I have developed an anthology of student monologues which properly credits the work of my student performers. There have been many deserving of a wider audience.

The range of their subject matter is unbelievably broad, and their polish puts some of the professionals to shame. Satire never possessed a keener edge than when Ira's senior citizen, after complaining of speeding teenage motorists on his street, is outraged by the new **DRIVE SLOW** sign in front of his house which detracts from the appearance of his property. Dean's rabid Ku Klux Klansman, attempting to attract recruits and being mobbed by an unsympathetic audience, is equally effective in its attack upon racial intolerance and demagoguery. When Roy presented his caricature of a Boy Scout sophisticatedly showing off his cigarette smoking before some Cub Scouts, this monologist probably did more to make a laughing stock of teenage smokers than a hundred teachers or surgeons-general can do to discourage young people from taking up the habit. One of the monologue "classics" is Bill's uproarious satire on a used-car "bargain" with its manually operated windshield wiper and non-existent brakes.

None of the monologues ever created more laughter than Caroline's wide-eyed psychopath who, threatening suicide on the window ledge of a tall building, begins to amuse himself by spitting on the pedestrians below. Still another very funny monologue features Janet's well-meaning but behind-the-times mother who, concerned about her daughter's dating, begins a mother-daughter talk by discussing the sex habits of the neighbor's dog.

Many of my students have turned to serious drama in this assignment. Strong in its use of symbolism and unique in its employment of verse form, Kathy's monologue presents a caterpillar which, after being bound in its cocoon in a world of death, finds its rebirth or redemption in a butterfly existence. Ginger's work treats a small girl in a concentration camp where her parents have been executed. Judy's monologue character is an older sister who reads a Western adventure to her little brother who lies critically ill in a hospital ward. Receiving no response to a question, she at first supposes that he has fallen asleep, then realizes that the boy has died. A very competent young actress with a good bit of stage and television experience behind her, Marianne has portrayed a little girl visiting her kitten's grave and explaining to a passerby her simple faith in a heaven with mice and catnip.

At the end of a monologue day, I am utterly depleted, having frequently run the gamut of emotions while watching my amateur performers. Sometimes, of course, there are weaker products, but in large part my seniors do a splendid job. Those who overemphasize situation at the expense of character are always a small minority, and seldom do the students depend excessively upon dress or props. Though they are competitive, they strive to help one another by being good audiences. At the outset, I tell them that "we are all in the same boat, however leaky it may be." They seem to agree, and they encourage and applaud each performer as he earns his senior standing in Room 106.

I often point to one monologue as representing the very best monologue of all. Its secret, I think, is in its universality which was enhanced by the superb acting of the monologist. Ron, a young fellow with a very masculine personality, depicted a small boy searching for his dog. After some wandering about and calling his pet, the boy finds the animal lying quite still along the side of a road. Having had no firsthand experience with death, the boy tries to revive his friend, but with no success. Then he remembers someone's having described death to him. With growing awareness of his loss, he kneels before his canine comrade and voices his grief and desolation in the eloquence that only a child possesses.

Ron is the only young man that I have ever seen produce real tears. I saw him do that monologue four times, and each time I saw the tears roll down his cheeks and splash on the floor. What is more, among his audiences I never saw a dry-eyed face.

Naturally enough, not all my seniors are topflight actors, but most of them are good enough to impress their classmates. Some of them find in their monologue experience their first real opportunity to gain recognition and applause from their schoolmates. Recently I saw two students, new to Worthington and nearly frightened out of their wits by the assignment, manage to find the courage to present their work. In each instance, when they were finished, I knew that they would never again walk the corridors alone. When they had resumed their seats, other students leaned to congratulate them and to let them know that they "belonged."

The senior monologues are not merely another assignment. At Worthington they have become a tradition, a proving-ground, a common experience which can draw students together. In the long run, they make Room 106 a friendlier place. In any fifty-five minutes of monologues, my students may be moved from hilarity to tears. A classroom in which youth has experienced such emotional catharses can never again become merely another classroom.

"Gee," said one girl after she had given her performance, "I was never so scared in my life. But now—now I almost wish we had to do another."

In the main ballroom of the Columbus Plaza, the annual senior banquet was about to get under way. As Alice and I threaded our way to our seats, two girls came running up. They pointed to the front wall, where two large caricatures hung above the speakers' table. "Do you recognize the picture on the left?" asked Sue, the first to reach us. I looked and saw something that incorporated my nose, moustache, flattened ears, and nearly nude forehead.

"Why, it looks like the devil," I said with a show of indignation.

"We thought so, too," said the other girl. "And, you know, ever since we worked with *Paradise Lost,* every time Susie and I look at you, we think you look more and more like Milton's Satan."

"Thanks," I grinned at them. As they disappeared into the blur of party dresses and dinner jackets, my wife turned to me.

"Was that supposed to be a compliment?"

The Devil's Advocate

"It might have been. Besides, in my work, you don't dare worry too much about how you look to them." From our table I squinted again at the caricature. Alongside it, the representation of another teacher looked plumply cherubic, more so because of the way the artist had multiplied the chins. The boy who had perpetrated this fiendish sketch of me was the younger of two gifted brothers. The older one had furnished Room 106 with his painting of Milton's Satan, in which he had tried to catch the spirit of the fallen archangel during his apostrophe to the sun in Book IV of the poem. I began to wonder whether I had established a permanent Satanic image for that family.

Students might readily see something of the Arch-Antagonist in every teacher, especially in an English teacher. Hadn't Satan dealt in the Knowledge of Good and Evil? Hadn't Blake's "Tiger" shocked them by suggesting the coexistence of Evil and Good through a single Sponsor? Didn't the literature my students studied with me focus upon human morality and experience more than anything else? And how many times had I played the Devil's Advocate in my classroom, purposely aligning myself with unpopular viewpoints, seemingly defending attitudes which are alien to my true feelings, in order to tease young people into argument and to get them to think. Perhaps the several infernos of my past show in my eyes at times. I had to admit that I regularly gave my students a certain amount of Hell on their compositions, too.

Even my visits to the most diabolic place in the high school probably made me suspect. I am sure that the throngs of young people who daily pass the door of the little 9' x 14' room called the Men's Lounge see it as belonging not only in the West Wing, but East of Eden as well. Many of them no doubt imagine it to be a retreat of intellectual incubi who are momentarily resting and reporting their impregnation of young minds with worldliness. The air outside the door hints at the smoky region, the fire and brimstone, inside. Sometimes, faintly audible references to the Creator emanate from that place as demons enter or depart, and many a student probably supposes that unhallowed proceedings take place in that part of the building. When male graduates return and are invited into the lounge, they always enter with expectant eyes and are disappointed to find that it is only a drab little room.

Within, the several pieces of Danish-modern furniture customarily look as if Leif Ericson had slept here. The fragrance of live cigarettes and pipes, strong coffee, dead ashes, and chemistry teacher Nick Hainen's orange peelings commingles with simultaneous dialogues to produce an eighteenth-century coffeehouse atmosphere. The walls usually testify to one teacher's subscription to *Playboy,* and most often cartoons, news clippings on teacher salaries, faculty verse, and other odds and ends are affixed to the plaster with masking tape. The small round coffee table is littered by the end of the day with crumbs, newspapers, and John Hammill's feet. The single work table—a stock door with a spar finish and wrought-iron legs—is always heaped with pedagogical debris. To grade papers at the table requires, first of all, five minutes spent in rearranging that rubble, emptying an ashtray, and blocking out the interesting sounds made by other teachers.

It is these voices that make the West-Wing Men's Lounge the liveliest, yet most scholarly cubicle in the high school. The topics treated here range from the fallacies of dialectical materialism to the water level in the toilet (which one braggart constantly complains is too high). Much of the conversation in the lounge is valuable in toughening the skin or deadening the personal sensitivities of novitiates on the staff or oldtimers who are still vulnerable to jests directed their way. Simply to enter the room is to be insulted. Someone asks the band instructor, "Well, is the band sounding any better these days?" Or an American-history teacher may be greeted with "You know, you're the ugliest man I ever saw." What vanity a man may still possess after teaching a short time is quickly dissipated.

Frequently, though, the jibes, the off-color jokes, and the other tomfoolery give way to some surprisingly profound colloquy. Yet, even here, there is much opportunity for practice at deviling one another by assuming a pretended opposition. Far from being the setting for a cabal or Black Sabbath it may seem to be from the corridor, the room is perpetually filled with discussions which often point the way to what the jargon-lovers call "educational transfer," chances for a teacher to tie in his own subject area with other fields of learning. In this fashion, the give-and-take lounge talk can broaden a teacher's thinking, keep him on his toes where new or alien ideas are concerned, and strengthen his skill in leading his classroom discussions.

Apart from educational matters, the outstanding topic of the lounge is sex, but a close competitor is religion. On the subject of God as with any other, it is possible to find practically every theological position represented by the teachers. Sometimes I feel that I have been listening to a debate in a seminary after tuning in on or participating in such a discussion.

Some of my favorite arguments on the subject involved a young science teacher, Joe Walker, who had grown up only a block away from where I had been reared in Lima. Naturally, we had much in common, knew some of the same people, and often talked about that Northwestern Ohio citadel of conservatism. Generally, Joe was of existentialist persuasion, and he spent most of his spare time reading and talking philosophy. There was one issue upon which we differed strongly—religion. For a long time, he didn't realize this because of my apparent advocacy of doubt and opposition on the matter of religious faith.

One winter day, I dropped my role of pretense, however, and we had one of our most interesting talks. He was an atheist, he declared with conviction and not a little pride. God was man's invention—a damaging one, too, as he saw it. In actuality, Joe was one of the most religious people I had ever met, and I told him so.

"I don't see how you arrive at that conclusion about me," he exclaimed in surprise. "I don't believe in God."

"That's what I mean—you're a believer."

"A non-believer, you mean!"

"Same thing, in a way," I answered him. "How do you define *faith*?"

"Faith?" He puffed at his pipe several times and adjusted his glasses. "I'd call it belief in something where there's no physical proof."

"All right, so I would have to call you a person of strong faith." He laughed at my comment.

"How in hell do you figure that?"

"Don't you firmly believe in the non-existence of a god?"

"That's right. I said so."

"Do you have any physical evidence that God does not exist? Have you fully explored the universe and determined analytically that it is without a deity?"

"Now, wait a minute," he protested, "you're—"

"Okay. You believe absolutely in something without any physical evidence or lab analysis to back it up. That's your own definition of faith. You—"

"—you're asking me to come up with evidence, with proof where there isn't any."

"I'm not asking you to," I answered. "That's what you're already doing. Take a positive and a negative quantity—they're very real for a mathematician. That's the way with our religious views—I have a positive faith and you have a negative faith." He looked at me for a long time. I could have called him anything else but religious, and he wouldn't have been nearly so bothered.

"I can't see that," he said finally. "That's the kind of argument the Sophists would come up with—it's double talk."

"I think it satisfies the premise of your definition."

"You actually believe in God—I mean a deity that really cares about what happens to people?"

"I have to, damn it, Joe."

"Why?"

"Maybe for the same reason you feel you can't."

Joe leaned back in his chair, and there was a tinge of anger in his voice. "Now, let me tell you something. When my little baby sister died, there was a woman—a neighbor—came to our house and asked if the baby had been baptized. When my mother told her *no*, she shook her head and said, 'Oh, I'm sorry.' Then she went out of our house, still clucking her damned tongue. She figured my sister was doomed to Hell. Am I supposed to believe in a god that'd damn an innocent child because she didn't have water poured on her to the tune of some idiotic mumbo-jumbo?"

"I don't believe in a god like that, Joe. You're not talking about a deity—only the way some people represent Him."

"All right," he responded, "if there's a God, why does He let people represent Him that way. More people have been killed in the name of God than anything else. Look at the Crusades, the Inquisition—"

"I can't answer your question, except that every human being has two choices—selfishness and evil or sympathy and good—and every person finds it hard to choose the second way."

"You didn't always talk like this—something's changed you since I came here. You used to be a realist. Now you're an idealist."

"You're right, partly. I have had an experience or two here which have changed me. But I've been changing ever since I first saw the light of day and smelled the odor of the Solar refinery in Lima. You'll change, too. We all do."

"I never thought I'd see you become an idealist," he muttered, shaking his head sadly.

"You've got the thing turned around, Joe. I changed in exactly the other way, I think. Right now, you're the idealist, and I'm the realist."

"Boy," he groaned, "are you way out!"

"Maybe so, but look at it like this—in a way, aren't some of you existentialists saying that man doesn't need a god, that he makes himself completely what he is, without any influence of a deity?"

"I don't need a god. If a man has will and intelligence, he can stand on his own."

"Without any more qualification than that, I'd call your statement idealistic. That's Schopenhauer, though even he said that the individual will is part of the universal will. If you can look at the world and say that man doesn't need a god, that man can gradually build his own Utopian society, you're as optimistic and idealistic as they come."

"How can you say that you believe in an abstraction and still say you're a realist?"

"Because it isn't completely an abstraction—you can see it every day. Every man is a mixture of good and evil—soul and body, they're at war all the time. We're like that—well, you're the biology teacher—that Australian bulldog ant that old Schopenhauer talks about. The one that, when you cut it in two, the head and tail start fighting, the head biting the tail and the tail stinging the head right down to the death. With us, when a real crisis comes along and cuts us up, our soul and our flesh are at war. And, in my opinion, the flesh ordinarily wins. That's why man needs a god. Maybe he's partly master of his fate, but he sure as hell can't do much about his endocrines, his genes, or his impulse for genocide." In the closed-off corner carrell, the toilet flushed, and I grinned at Joe. "The animal is always with us, isn't he, friend?"

My answer came, quite by accident, from the other end of the room, where several men were discussing a related problem—one of the greatest hazards of the male teacher. "That *child,* as you call her," a voice boomed, "wants to go to bed with you, my friend. She may not even know it, herself, but you'll be wise to steer clear of dark corners in the hall when she's in the building."

"No, you're all wrong," a voice replied. "She sees me as a kind of father-in-school."

"Father-in-school, my ass!" snorted a third person. "*You* read the paper. Guy in my home town wasn't careful. Had this senior girl—all body and no brains—sign up for advanced biology. Talked him into a motel. Guess what cells he's teaching now."

"Lord, what a business this is. I've got one in my second-period class rubs her breasts against me till I've got a shine on the sleeve of my only suit."

"Yeah, but she's probably too damned naïve to know what she's doing."

"Like hell she is. You ought to see the silly smile on her face."

"You have to remember that they've got the brains of children even if some of them are built like women."

"She-it!" reverberated the first voice, blending his pronouns with great feeling, "they may have the brains of children, but some of them are playing the same game as that young babe that used t' teach here. Ahh, what's her name? You know the one I mean."

"The one that used to lay it all over the boys—tease hell out of them—because she knew it was safe? I think we've had several here who got their jollies that way."

"And some of these senior girls think the same way. Next year, they'll be operating the same way with college profs."

"At my age, their mothers look much better—if I were inclined to go astray, that is."

"Inclined, hell! Any guy could very easily get himself into the same sling as that biology teacher. That's one of the things that make teaching rough. Isn't that right?"

"Ask *him*. He's the guy that has all the girls in heat—not me!"

"I don't know where you jokers get that idea."

"Jeez, you oughta hear 'em talk. Look how they hang around his room! You can hear them panting halfway down the hall."

One of the speakers lapsed into a low-voiced anecdote, and I turned back to Joe, who still surveyed me in half-amusement.

"What would you say if your God were a big black man?" he asked. That was one of the favorite questions of an OSU philosophy professor under whose influence Joe had recently come. I resented the question because it is one ordinarily used to badger un-Christian-Christians and carries the inference that the person asked may be tainted with racist views.

"I wouldn't say anything at all except to be surprised that the God I believe in favored any particular color or form. I see Him as showing up anywhere and everywhere in the universal spectrum. What you're doing is supposing that I have some anthropomorphic deity in mind. You're thinking I must visualize and argue a long-bearded white man, or something."

"What about 'God created man in his own image'?" Joe quoted, with a bit of satire in his voice.

"If you accept God as spirit, then it's logical to suppose that the passage means man is endowed with part of that spirit. I don't know."

"What about your Christ?" pressed Joe. "Isn't he said to be God in a man's form? There's your anthropomorphism."

"If Christ was God in another person or form, it was temporary, wasn't it? It doesn't limit God to any given appearance."

"And that crap about a virgin birth?" he inquired, still looking at me as if I were taking my side of the argument out of the pure joy of shamming.

"Now we get into your field. You've heard of parthenogenesis in animals—that's a kind of virgin birth. Why couldn't it happen in a human being? And who is to say that such a phenomenon is not within a deity's power to supervise?"

"A deity's power to supervise!" he snorted. "I'd still like to hear you say why an all-powerful god would let evil exist in the world."

"All I've got is an idea, and it's not entirely mine. I don't know who began it, but William Blake—"

"Who's he?"

"Late eighteenth-, early nineteenth-century poet. Anyway, if I understand him, Blake believed that a knowledge of good grows mainly out of experience. It certainly stands to reason that if there weren't sin or evil Christ would have no function at all. Men wouldn't need forgiveness."

"All right, what about those that aren't sinful, that never do anything wrong?"

"Oh, my God, and you call *me* an idealist! I personally have my own answer. I don't think there is such a creature. Scratch the surface, and we're all of us beasts. Every one of us, flesh and spirit. Blake figured that people who do no wrong have actually failed to commit themselves to life. People like that would perhaps take such pride in their invulnerability to sin that they would turn their backs upon Christ. Blake saw the withdrawers-from-life as the greatest sinners and the most assuredly damned."

I still couldn't dismiss Joe's comment on God's being a big black man, and I had to touch upon race once more. "You were talking about a Negroid God a little bit ago. If God were a black man, it would put Albert Schweitzer into an awkward fix. Schweitzer, a great man, compassionate toward the sufferings of a backward, unfortunate people, spending his life among them—that was the man's spirit. Then the flesh, that noble organ we call the brain, rationalizing that the black man was not quite his brother. See what I mean? Even a Schweitzer can be guilty of benighted bigotry."

"But people can do good without God. Good morality is common sense, a matter of reason."

"How do you explain people who sacrifice themselves for others —not just saving lives, but giving up comfort, taking little or nothing in return?"

"I don't know—love, maybe, or pride or showing off or temporary insanity, or just good sense, a feeling that what they're doing is right," he answered.

144

"You mention love. You believe in love? I mean *love* in the sense of something besides a romp in the bedroom? You think there's something more than physical sense and orgasm in it?"

At this point, another voice in the lounge bleated painfully, "F'Chris' sake, how ya supposed to concentrate in here?"

"As long as you don't say it's spiritual. Science says a lot of love is strictly mental," replied Joe.

"And intangible?"

"Naturally."

"How do you know it isn't spiritual? How do you know the thing called a soul doesn't exist somewhere inside us and act as a catalyst in something called love?"

"How do you know it does?" he came back.

"Because love seems to me to contradict reason or common sense. Because I see the brain as being mainly the center of rational thinking. Because I believe that we feel beauty, love, and compassion with something else. I don't think that pure reason is capable of self-sacrifice—it's against the primal drive of self-preservation."

"Then if you're good you go to Heaven and if you're sinful you go to Hell?"

"That isn't what the true Christian believes. He argues that everyone is sinful."

"Not some I've heard," said Joe, relighting his pipe.

"I've heard that sort, too, but I don't call them Christians—or realists," I replied.

"Then you've got faith in something besides the human brain."

"I have to have. I've learned that wisdom is very different from knowledge. Wisdom comes from the soul, I think. I've found out, too, that whenever I've had the wisdom to feel compassion, it has paid off in big dividends. When you're concerned about someone else, you have less time to worry about yourself."

"I don't see how, according to your ideas, that you could belong to any church I've ever heard of."

"I can't honestly subscribe to everything that makes up the doctrines of any one of them, but you've hit the one big dishonesty in my religious practice. I do belong to a church, but mainly out of convenience and for my daughter's sake." He laughed at this as I knew he would.

"You let her be brainwashed? That's one thing I won't do. My little girl wanted to go to Sunday school with a friend of hers, and I told her absolutely *no*."

"I'm surprised at that, Joe, because, to begin with, I don't think you're an atheist at all. An atheist has closed the door—he no longer looks for a god. You? You spend most of your time arguing the issue with yourself and other people. When I said you have a negative faith, I didn't really mean it. You don't have any, but you're working like hell to find one. You wouldn't surprise me if you turned into an evangelist or came in here some day with a bundle of *Watch Tower* or *Upper Room* subscriptions. No, you're an agnostic, a questioner, and I'm glad to know this. The only educable mind is an open mind. But why do you close the door to your daughter's mind?"

"You think I want her conditioned by Sunday-school lessons? They get a grip on you once, and you can't see the other side," he explained. "Read Loyola."

It was my turn to laugh. "With her father to talk to, how could she fail to see the other side? No. I think you're doing exactly what you accuse the churches of doing."

Joe never really had a good comeback for that, though he may have developed one by now. He would leave Worthington a year later, still searching for a faith. He was an excellent teacher, always interested in subjecting the set ideas of society to dissection and debunking. Worthington High would sustain a great loss with his going. Subsequently, I hoped that he would some day read, among other things, H. G. Wells' *Outline of History*, particularly the chapter called "The Beginnings of Christianity." There he would be pleased to find an objective historical portrait of the man called Jesus, some eloquent attacks upon the early church-men's corruption of Jesus' teachings, and a clearer picture of the revolutionary which Christ really was. Possibly, when Joe really begins to understand the Galilean, he will see that such a man could not have been of this world alone, but of the Universal Spirit I worship.

I left Joe and another unfinished lounge dialogue that day to go back to 106 and a third-period English class. We were getting into the Victorian literature and it was necessary that my students understand how, even before the 1859 publication of the *Origin of Species*, Darwin and Wallace and the other evolutionists had caused consternation among some of the orthodox. I wanted my classes to understand how some who had accepted Archbishop Ussher's calculations for Old Testament chronology were angered and shaken by evolutionary theory. I tried to explain why people like Arnold, Tennyson, and Swineburne wrote poems in which they spoke, respectively, of a receding ocean of Faith, the difference between knowledge and faith, and of death's greatest virtue—eternal rest.

Then the tangle of definitions—agnosticism, atheism, theism, and the others had to be sorted out. The Fundamentalist point of view must, of course, be set forth with all its gradations. Finally, the story of the compromises between Scripture and scientific evidence that were made by many churchmen.

Before I asked the class to work with Thomas Henry Huxley and with Fitzgerald's translation of *The Rubaiyat,* I felt that they should be exposed to an effective expression of agnosticism in an American author whom some of them had grown to admire. I turned to the last chapter of Jack London's great autobiographical novel *Martin Eden* and read it to them aloud as dramatically as I could manage. I watched their faces as Eden reads that stanza from Swineburne's "Garden of Proserpine" in which London's hero discovers the solution for his satiation with and disgust for life:

> *From too much love of living,*
> *From hope and fear set free,*
> *We thank with brief thanksgiving*
> *Whatever gods may be*
> *That no life lives forever,*
> *That dead men rise up never,*
> *That even the weariest river*
> *Winds somewhere safe to sea.*

Then, looking up from the chapter with every sentence and gradually increasing the tempo and raising the pitch and volume, I tried to capture with my voice the cool calculation and desperate but deliberate measures that marked Martin Eden's suicide by drowning. When I had finished, the class sat hushed and horrified—even the loudest self-proclaimed agnostic among them. It wasn't enough. I had to pour it on, but good! I closed the book with a loud enough sound to jar several of the mesmerized faces in my front row.

"Oh, but that's not the whole story, not by a long shot," I said. One of the girls, looking half-relieved, spoke up then.

"He didn't die after all?"

"Martin was dead all right, but not the man he represented. It took Jack London almost seven years to the day, after the publication of this autobiographical novel, to get around to killing himself—as he had predicted. Seven years of 'To be or not to be,' of maybe worrying about that 'undiscovered country' that kept Hamlet from doing the same thing." Several of the students shuddered, all of them bug-eyed with incredulity. Finally, a young man spoke up.

"Did London drown himself?" he asked. I didn't want to tell him that the great author had put himself away with morphine sleeping tablets.

"That's the wonderful thing about literature, Tom. There's always something rather exciting to find out. You go to the library sometime today and see whether you can't let the class know tomorrow." I gave him several titles—two biographies and a good reference work—but I knew he'd have to get to the shelves quickly or every one of them would be in the hands of another student.

"Where can you get the whole poem by Swineburne?" inquired a girl. "I want to read that."

"Stop by the desk, and I'll give you my copy, providing you promise not to take a running dive into the Olentangy." The class laughed—they wanted something to laugh at.

"People don't really commit suicide after reading books, do they, Mr. Rousculp?" questioned another student.

"Are you kidding? I could give you quite a list. A former Japanese premier named Hideki Tojo was reading Oscar Wilde's *De Profundis* before attempting his own life. The first secretary of defense, James Forrestal was studying a play by Sophocles, *Ajax*, before he leaped about fourteen stories to his death. Another well-known person—" but the bell interrupted me at that point.

As the class filed out, one very serious-minded young fellow came to the desk. "Do you mind if I ask you a personal question?"

"Fire away," I told him. "If I can't answer it, I'll tell you so."

"You've never said what you believe—about religion, I mean," he said without adding the obvious interrogation.

"Is what I believe of any real importance to you? If it isn't, I'd be wasting my time talking about my beliefs, wouldn't I? If it is, then that's all the more reason why I shouldn't tell you. I might be taking advantage of my position and a captive audience in order to condition your thinking."

"The way you read that piece about Swineburne and Jack London sure makes me think you don't believe in God," he said, watching for some sign or clue on my face.

"Just remember, Bill, I'm trained to read and to act. Never forget that. You're going to hear a lot of people in your life who are a whole lot more convincing, even when they're taking you in. Only *you* can really determine what you can or can't believe—whether it's politics or religion or what have you. Even though *you* might be willing to disagree with me, there are some students in this class who would buy an idea or a whole credo simply because the teacher believed in it. If I started sounding off on my views, I'd probably violate the ethics of my profession."

I handed the girl who had come to the desk an anthology with Swineburne's poem in it, and the boy started to go. "Bill," I continued, "you have to remember that a teacher's job requires that he strike different poses, take different sides, to try to make his classes speculate and think. Of course, he's playing with fire. He'll regularly incur the wrath of the Americans for Democratic Action, the Daughters of the American Revolution, the churches, the veterans' organizations, the racists, the freedom marchers, the John Birch Society and every other group who'd like him to be their own propagandist. But inside his class, a teacher is responsible to the whole public and to his conscience at the same time. Outside the classroom, it's another matter. There, he should be active in any organizations whose aims he believes in, whether it involves electioneering, picketing, or praying."

Bill left for his next class, and I sat down at the desk to look over once more the quatrains of Omar Khayyam and to rehearse briefly the Satanic role I must assume, come tomorrow. Yet, though I play my part, I am, beneath it all, a fallen creature with a need for and a growing faith in God.

"Gene, I want you to tell me where that fifty cents came from," my mother declared firmly. "I don't intend to stop asking until you've told me." She addressed me always by my middle name as those closest to me do.

"But I don't know, Mother," I answered. And I didn't know. She kept after me, however, until she had reduced me to tears. I was past ten years old, and I had never seen my mother so upset, so ready to accuse me of doing something wrong.

While sorting out clothes, preparing to wash them on that Monday morning in July, she had found a half-dollar in some blue jeans I had worn nearly a week before. Even though a half-dollar would have had, in 1933, considerably greater value than it possesses today, it was not the amount that disturbed my mother. She was afraid, I suppose, that I had picked up the money around

The "Key" to a Better Understanding

the house, possibly had taken it from her purse, or perhaps had been given the money by persons unknown. When I began fighting back tears, she changed her tack. "All right," she said, "but just remember—eventually I'll find out where that money came from, young man. Sooner or later, you're going to tell me," she said ominously as she left the room.

I was crushed, helpless in the face of her accusation. The rest of the day I moped about the house. Now and again, I would see her turn from her work to cast severe or troubled glances at me. I must have fretted two or three days over the mystery of that half-dollar and the hurt over my mother's suspicions. Even my six-year-old brother would remind me of the charge weighing against me. "You bedda terl Mom, Zene!" he would warn in the dialect of which only he was master.

Finally, it was my little brother who made me recall the source of the money. He was standing on our front porch and staving off attacking hordes of Indians with his cap gun. As I sat there morosely watching him blink with each tiny explosion, I suddenly remembered.

Nearly two weeks had elapsed since he had got that cap gun and begun alienating everyone in the neighborhood, including the dog chained behind the corner grocery store. We had gone to my great-uncle's country store at Rousculp, Ohio, to buy our fireworks for the Fourth.

It was always fun to go to Uncle Claude's and Aunt Dawn's house, but the store was especially fascinating. It was the sort of country store that you can only read about nowadays. We could always expect candy or big slices of longhorn cheese when we went in there, and my brother was already wrecking his teeth on the jawbreakers. We always went to my uncle's before the Fourth because he would put marvelous elasticity into the little money we had to spend. He could convert twenty or thirty cents into an enormous sackful of caps, torpedoes, sidewalk snakes, ladyfingers, fountains, sparklers, one-and-a-half-inchers, the punk to light them with, and just about every other sort of fireworks excitement to widen a boy's eyes. He was, I think, the first man in rural Allen County to give fireworks displays, and farmers would bring their families from miles around to watch the night's activity.

This year I had had all of fifty cents to spend—a real bonanza—but my uncle, perhaps foreseeing the imminent breakup of my parents and knowing that money came hard for them, had refused to take any part of my half-dollar when he had handed me my bag of Fourth of July ecstasy. "You save that money, Jimmy," he had said, calling me as he did so often by my brother's name. I had carefully put the fifty cents back into the pocket of my jeans, and, with my mind on nothing but the hours of noise and fun I was carrying, I had forgotten his beneficence.

When I told my mother where the money had come from, she cried and felt terrible about her earlier doubts. Perhaps this event was one of the reasons why she was slow, in later years, to question me about matters in which I was entirely culpable. Certainly, I never forgot that episode in which I had felt so helpless in my innocence, and I am ordinarily careful to avoid judging my students before all the evidence is in.

The principal "felony" with which teachers find themselves confronted in their work is that product of laziness, fear, self-defense, and pure chicanery called cheating. Not so long ago I looked at a headline which blaringly announced: **OSU OFFICIALS BARE WORST CHEATING SCANDAL IN SCHOOL'S HISTORY.** Americans will recall with me the sensation caused by the dismissal of students caught cheating at the Air Force Academy several years ago. In the matter of cheating, I take exception with the optimist's view that it is the biggest news when people commit misdeeds. I disagree because academic cheating is not really news at all. It is mostly the product of normal human nature and dull-witted or unrealistic schoolmen.

I do not excuse dishonesty of any sort by anyone, but I do contend that discovered cheating is regularly a direct consequence of unrecognized and unapprehended cheating. In any school the carelessness or apathy of one teacher toward this problem can at least encourage similar dishonesty in other teachers' classes. I am inclined, also, to feel that, if the necessary care is not exercised, those schools with keener academic competition will harbor more widespread cheating, even though it is of a somewhat more discreet character.

I am too firmly set in my view of human nature to believe in any so-called honor system. Experience and observation require me to argue that, given sufficient motivation and opportunity, any student is capable of cheating, regardless of his past performance. Students with the greatest proclivity for classroom dishonesty seem to show up most often in the middle- and upper-achievement groups. Youngsters with the least academic promise are usually so numbed by the prospect of a test and so naïve about the shrewdness of some of their classmates that these poorer students rarely cheat unless they are sufficiently frightened over the possibility of not graduating or not being promoted. Ironically, the weaker student is most frequently discovered, generally because his technique lacks the refinement of practice.

So much has been said about students cheating because of pressure brought to bear upon them by their parents. That parents do sometimes build considerable anxiety in youngsters is without question. I have seen many unhappy effects of parental pressure. But for a school to blame parents entirely for scholastic deceit and theft is for teachers to abdicate their responsibility in establishing the correct classroom climate and proper preventive precautions. When students understand that complete impartiality reigns in a school, that discipline is not tailor-made according to the individual rule-breaker, that there are dire penalties for cheating, that their teachers are not blind to signs of dishonesty, that the rules have been formulated to protect the innocent, that tests or quizzes given during one period of the day will not be repeated in an identical form for subsequent classes, that the same tests will not be repeated year in and year out, and that monitors will regularly circulate and circumspectly check the work of the class during the administering of a test—then and only then will much of the cheating problem find a solution.

There are, however, additional steps that could be taken:

(1) Math tests might logically include more verbal problems and place more emphasis upon verbalized solutions rather than upon final answers expressed as numbers.

(2) Social-studies tests should frequently take essay form, requiring answers which would include the same basic factual content that objective tests require.

(3) English tests should always emphasize essay answers.

(4) Any course resorting to multiple-choice test forms could require students to mark their answers by blackening parallel lines on their answer sheets.

I will not pretend that these suggestions are new or that they comprise a panacea for the problem. Cheating is, I fear, a folly to which human beings will always be susceptible. If the other fellow does it, then it is wicked, but how often do we condone it in ourselves? We may be tempted to add questionable income-tax deductions, to ride the accelerator at five m.p.h. above the legal limit, to bring home an extra fish or pheasant, or to park illegally "for just a few minutes." We are fully aware of our misdeeds in such cases, but, worst of all, we often do them with our children as witnesses.

Cheating is not second nature—it is part of the primal fiber. We even cheat ourselves, if it's only the calories we sneak and don't count, the turned-down cards we peek at in playing solitaire, or the extra jigger of whisky in our "one cocktail before dinner." That it corrodes our willpower and stains our integrity we can easily forget for the nonce—it is sometimes merely the flavor of "the stolen fruit" which we savor.

Early in the school year, when my students are writhing in their writing as they take their first quiz from me, I customarily make a comment to this effect: "Now, people, we're sitting practically on top of one another in here, so I'm going to assume that, being human beings, some of you are going to be moved to check your answers with your neighbors. Therefore, I will ask each of you to help your neighbor out of his peril by putting your daintily perfumed hand or your hairy paw over your responses. If I find a paper that is not covered, I will penalize its owner. If your neighbor has the temerity to lean over and lift your hand from your answers, be sure that I will interview him in very short order."

If, during a quiz or test, I see a pair of eyes rolling about injudiciously, I try to avoid embarrassing the student who is yielding to his human foible. Instead, I immediately fire a question at him: "Did you have a question, Ralph?" or "Can *I* be of some assistance, Mark?" Generally, they shake their heads in the negative, and as they do so I give them a penetrating look with which I intend to communicate my full awareness of the misdemeanor I have forestalled.

But these methods and the others that I use are not original with me. Nor do such tactics guarantee that a classroom will be free of dishonesty. I dare say some cheating happens in every school, in every class. Like most teachers, I have caught the culprits, marked F's on their papers, and often talked with students on the subject. I have seen far less dishonesty in the past ten years because I have given essay tests, require most theme-writing to be done in class, and am not averse to telling anecdotes about the chronic cheaters (sidestepping identities, of course) whom I have known and to whom I have endeavored to administer the "cure," though I know there is no sure remedy.

One of the best illustrations that I can recall occurred eight or nine years ago. I cite this particular instance not merely because it reflects the slightly more camouflaged variety of cheating at Worthington. More significantly, the case demonstrates how much more readily cheating is implemented when the teacher is behaving in blissful idiocy. Though the miscreants were fully responsible for their acts, I must confess that my own sheer laziness —I called it "cutting corners"—provided the temptation, the opportunity. Finally, I should add that this was one of those occasions in which I had nothing but circumstantial evidence upon which to proceed.

Shortly after we had begun our language-review unit one year, I gave my classes their first test. After I had marked these papers, it seemed apparent to me that three students—Bob, Stu, and Cynthia—had shown an incredible degree of improvement. I had to recheck their papers in trying to satisfy my doubts.

On this evaluation, I had employed a commercially printed test. Many teachers employ such prepared tests, and, besides, it was much more convenient for me. It was so easy to rationalize that I was not sidestepping my appointed task. Now I could concentrate all my time on marking papers and add composition assignments, I reasoned. But I didn't understand the mistake I was making.

As I studied the test results, those three pupils' scores troubled me greatly. Something was wrong. Stu, capable of doing good work, had not been applying himself at all in the daily assignments and recitation. The grading scale, however, indicated a remarkable score for him—an A. Bob, I knew, had not yet made much progress; his daily work had averaged D or D–. Yet the test outcome for Bob was a B, a strong B. Though Cynthia had been doing generally good work in our language review, I was surprised to see that she had managed to draw the second highest grade in the entire senior class.

My first impulse was to say to myself "You're really teaching up a storm, old boy." Teachers keep a store of pleasant rationalizations on hand. Nevertheless, one disquieting fact began to romp about in my consciousness—the nagging awareness that Cynthia and Stu were "steadies" and that they frequently "doubled" with Bob and another Cynthia. "So they study together—so what?" asserted my optimistic and unsuspicious self. It was easy to suppose that the two Cynthias had conducted a highly successful review session for their boy friends. "Let's not be gullible about this thing," persisted my much stronger and much more cynical alterego—the side of me that judges others by my own rascality.

I began to compare their papers. They had missed a number of items uniformly, but this fact proved nothing. The items that all four had missed were among the most difficult problems on the test. Ah, but what had happened on Number 51—their answers were exactly alike in error. I went to the cabinet and looked for a while until I found the key for tests that the company sends to teachers using their materials. I never used this key because I have found that textbook makers or their printers sometimes unintentionally provide faulty answers. After some examination, I found what I was looking for. The incorrect answer which each of the four had supplied the fifty-first problem was the same incorrect response shown in the company's key.

Then I remembered that Stu's mother was a teacher in another school system and that the father of one of the Cynthias was a high-school principal who had offered me a job some time earlier. Either one of these parents could unwittingly—surely parents would never help their youngsters to cheat—have been the source for an advance copy of the test I had used. Still, I had to have more evidence. I could still hear a ten-year-old vainly protesting his guiltlessness over the strange presence of a four-bit piece in his trousers.

Everything that I did thereafter was motivated by my desire to make these four teenagers come to me and confess that they had known, before taking the test, what the questions and answers were. When I announced the test results the next day, I watched with sidelong glimpses for any reactions that might be mirrored in those four youthful faces. I loudly praised their individual progress, and I pointed them out as examples of what conscientious effort in study could do. Their aspects remained expressionless masks, and they seemed to accept my tribute with deep humility and modesty. "I'm a heel," I said to myself, "a fourteen-carat heel." I was mentally flagellating myself when I saw Bob half turn and smile covertly at Cynthia Number Two, whose pretty face appeared to glow momentarily with self-satisfaction and triumph.

After having announced that the subsequent test, about two weeks into the future, would follow the pattern of the first one, I waited till the end of the day, tore up all but one copy of the printed tests locked in my cabinet, and began to compose a test of my own. And I made that test as artful a document as I possibly could. Master Robert's smile and its reception had my spleen vibrating. I intended my test to be not only difficult, but informative. Among the questions on my work of detection, I included a dozen sentences that would lead anyone who was guilty to wonder whether I knew what was going on. For instance, two of the items ran like this: "If I were you, I'd get rid of the key" and immediately afterwards "When I know a student has cheated on one of my tests, I will not rest until I have the evidence, and neither will he." Still another statement reminded them that cheating on the tests would not help them in college composi- tions. I had a wonderful time, moreover, in throwing curves to sabotage especially anyone who had prepared to cope exclusively with the grammatical structures on the printed test I would have otherwise employed.

A dozen days later, I watched them take the test. This time my observation was much more fruitful. The facial expressions of each one of the four reflected shock over the change in tests, and three of them lost their poise completely as they encountered the messages inside the text. I pretended not to see the anxious looks they directed toward the desk. As they left 106 that morning, I saw Stu whispering frantically to Cynthia Number One. I knew that all I had to do was to wait, and I enjoyed every sadistic sec- ond. The following day, their faces were still as washed out as driftwood, and Stu stuttered over the recitation although he had obviously studied for the first time in days. Still I said nothing, gave no further hint whatsoever. I spoke to them pleasantly in the room and the hall and enjoyed the weekend knowing that they would not.

During the lunch period on Tuesday, I heard a tapping, light and reluctant, on the door of my empty classroom. Trying not to hurry, I covered the four yards from desk to door with a step or two and arranged my face for the expected callers. Two tearful young ladies, one of them almost hysterical, entered at my invi- tation.

"Here's the key," said the first Cynthia. She handed me a damp, folded copy of the answer sheet for all the printed tests. She looked like something the monster has just discarded in a horror movie, but her companion—the sobbing one—resembled a dying Camille.

"Bob and S-Stu will be here to see you a-after school t-today," said the second Cynthia, trying to pull herself out of her death- bed. Standing there without their usual veneer of "senior-itis," they waited expectantly for me to rage.

"We're ready to take any punishment you give us," they cho- rused. "We feel awful." They made me feel that my work was well done—their penitence was important. I had to fight to keep from laughing at them.

"Of course," I told them, "you'll have to take an F on that first test. And you probably had trouble with yesterday's test, too."

They nodded in unison, still nervously waiting for me to add some dire disciplinary action, terrible to their minds because of its unknown nature. "I rather think," I concluded, "that you've punished yourselves far more thoroughly than I ever could. At the same time, I should warn you that, if I find you out of line again, it'll cost you a great deal more."

The boys did come in after school, and I said similar things to them, though in a somewhat tougher diction. It all turned out well. I think they became better students for the experience, and I know I became a wiser teacher thereafter. When I went home that night, I was whistling as happily as the boy who found out suddenly he had not only fifty cents to spend again but an additional fifty cents from his mother for honesty.

"Do seniors change much from year to year?" The student hall-monitor in the west wing had seen me pause in the corridor to look up at one of the composite class pictures.

"Oh, I think they do, but some of the other teachers might differ with me," I answered.

"I've seen you looking at that one every now and then. That must have been one of your favorite classes." He walked to where I was standing and looked up.

"I've liked my classes every year, Paul, but—well, this was the only year I had every senior in 106."

"Gee, they had only about a third as many kids as we do. Their football team any good?"

"They got clobbered seven out of nine games." I laughed. "They had it worse than your team, even."

The Rebel Stranger

"That's pretty bad," he chuckled. "Hey, there's a pretty smile." He pointed to one of the portraits.

"You mean *her*? That picture isn't a good one, really. Her smile wasn't just pretty—it was devastating. Oh, she was a holy terror, a rebel first-class, a beautiful fire that nobody will ever put out."

"A rebel doesn't change things at Worthington very much," he said with some scorn.

"Well, this one changed one thing."

"How's that?"

"Well, Paul, she was the first student that ever made this English teacher turn out some writing of his own." I didn't tell him much more than that about the girl. Yet, had it not been for her, my *Chalk Dust* might never have taken form.

She came to Worthington at the end of her sophomore year and created a not-so-mild sensation the minute she set foot in the hall. Talented, intelligent, and strikingly pretty, she was immediately "rushed" by that elusive, exclusive, abstract entity called The Clique and had little difficulty in gaining acceptance by her class-mates. She never lacked dates and invitations—at least, not at first. Standing about 5'2" or 3" tall and wearing her black hair in a variety of styles, she used her dark, Eurasian eyes to such full advantage that, wherever she moved, she did a beautiful job of separating "steadies" in the school. The Clique soon began to re-gard her as the Menace to the social status quo. Whenever girls saw her approaching in the corridor, they automatically ushered their boyfriends to another, safer quarter of the building. She was by nature coquettish but derived, I suspect, little satisfaction in such a role. It was just that she loved to rock the boat of social stability and complacency.

Of all her traits, that spritely unwillingness to conform, to sacri-fice any degree of her independence, was both her greatest strength and her own worst enemy. By the middle of her junior year, she was at war with The Clique, though the rest of her class-mates, seeing her as a genuine nonconformist, continued to seek her friendship and company. As a student, she never really liked Worthington, and she saw the school as a mirror of what she felt were the town's narrow, provincial attitudes. Having spent her sixteen years in two other states, she had seen other ways of life. Thus she did not hold Worthington High in the almost holy awe with which part of Central Ohio regards the school. Still, she joined numerous activities and was an important voice in the music presentations. She was a leader, too, in the senior-class activities.

Her Kuder Preference Test results indicated that she was prin-cipally interested in music, but the profile also pointed to her strong liking for the "Artistic" and "Literary." Her intelligence quo-tient stood officially at slightly under 120, though I am convinced that it lied in its paper teeth, that she was one of our brightest stu-dents. She detested math and science, geometry and biology hav-ing brought her worst grades, according to her transcript.

At home she rarely found opportunity to talk with her father, but apparently she was very close to one of her three sisters. The strongest influence in the household was her mother—a rather austere, outspoken woman whose ambitions were centered in her

162

family and whose identification with her children's successes was quite apparent. I met the woman only two or three times during the two years in which I was her daughter's teacher. The first time, the mother looked at me closely and said in an unemotional and cryptic fashion, "My daughter speaks of you frequently." Just that! So I couldn't really determine whether her daughter's references to me distressed or pleased the woman.

The girl first came to 106 for junior English, and it was immediately evident that she enjoyed the class. I very much liked having her stop by the room at odd times of the day to tell me about her thoughts and the insignificant and amusing events in her school day, or the latest gossip that her elfin behavior had stirred. I gradually got the feeling that I was serving her as a sort of father pro tem, but I frankly drew much pleasure from her patter and wit and her remarkably shrewd and mature understanding of people. She was one of those personalities whose sparkle can relieve one's darker moods, and she always seemed to know when I needed brightening.

We had been reading *John Brown's Body* for several weeks, and one day I brought in the recording of the platform drama. That morning we listened to Tyrone Power's inspired reading of Jack Ellyat at Gettysburg. I still marvel that Benét, who had never seen battle, could have reproduced so accurately the emotions of a man in combat. When the bell had rung, the Rebel stopped by the desk, her customary smile gone from the parted lips, her eyes bright with empathy and wonder and—and her voice different with a strange, soft music.

"I watched your face when we listened to the record—that part about Gettysburg. You almost made me cry."

I must have flushed—most often I prefer that my students not know my deepest feelings. It's my only inhibition in the classroom. It may weaken my teaching, but I can't help it. There are parts of me, aspects of my nature, that I have ostracized from Room 106, or tried to. Her comment disturbed me. That part of the recording never fails to tear at me, though it also holds a grisly fascination for me. I was on the defensive when I answered her, but I tried to brush her statement off as a joke. "What do you mean?"

"You must have known something—seen something like it. It was in your eyes. I could feel it all over the room. And when you—" Perhaps she was sensing "it" once more, for she left the words hanging. Then, too, students were coming in already for the second-period class—seniors with the usual absence slips to be signed and passages in *Macbeth* to be explained. "I'd better run or I'll be late. American history, you know." She made a child's mouthful-of-medicine face and hastened out the door.

I thought about what she had said. Apparently, the mask I strove to hide behind was not so impenetrable, after all. *How many others in that class had sensed my feelings?* I had to know.

At noon that day I stood in the lunchline (as Worthington teachers did before they were given a lunchroom of their own) behind another student from my first-period class. Usually he was a very perceptive person, and if I had displayed any agitation in class he certainly would have seen it. "Say, Don, what did you think of the recording we heard?"

"Hey, that's cool!" he responded.

"The first time I heard it, I thought it was tremendous, but after hearing it a couple dozen times I don't get quite the same charge out of it," I lied glibly.

"I bet you do get bored with it," he said, picking up a tray and looking across the counter to where a woman was ladling soup. Apparently he had not discerned any untoward show of feelings in his teacher that morning. What had the Rebel seen that Don had not?

That evening she stopped by the room. I was recording quiz marks, and I thought at first, probably because I had just noted a C beside her name, that she wanted to inquire about her grades. My quizzes frequently gave her fits. A second look at her, however, assured me that she had something very different on her mind. "I just wanted to say I'm sorry—about what I said." She wasn't very convincing.

"No, you're not really," I said. She blushed at that, then admitted it.

"Not really, no," she shuffled my words. "But it wasn't any of my business, and—"

"Why should you be sorry? You were right. That part of the record does get to where I live. I'm the one that should be apologizing—to the class. When I was in high school, I thought there was nothing more revolting than seeing a teacher get all choked up over poetry or anything else."

"But I don't think anyone else knew how that battle scene bothered you—nobody said anything, anyway."

"You knew it."

She looked at me a moment, then said quietly, "I know. I think I always know what you're thinking—how you feel about things."

I had to ponder that remark. If she was being truthful, she hadn't merely stolen a peek behind the pedagogical mask—she could see right through me daily. I liked to think I was somewhat inscrutable as a person and fairly unpredictable in the classroom. I had always prided myself on living outside the scheduled or well-grooved patterns and routines. I had tried to play a repertoire of roles in Room 106. I wanted to believe that my students seldom had assurance of what tack I would take in dealing with a subject. Now here was the Rebel candidly suggesting that she hadn't been taken in at all by the act. She had to be kidding!

"You *always* know what I'm thinking?" I leaned back in my chair. "Well, you might just be shocked sometime over my thoughts." I said it facetiously, but there was more than a grain of truth in the idea. "You're dangerous. You know that?"

"Maybe." She smiled, but wistfully. "How old were you when World War II started?"

"Just out of high school—Class of '41. Why do you ask? It's not nice, you know." I knew she was still thinking about that morning.

"I was wondering what you were like then."

"Not very good, I'm afraid. I thought I was a real tiger when I was only a bad-mannered tomcat. Like that expression I hear some of you using, I was a crazy-mixed-up kid, I guess." I didn't care for the direction the conversation had taken, so I swung back to the thing I really wanted to know. "Look, I'm curious. What made you think I was upset this morning? I must have done something."

"Not exactly." She looked off to one side as if trying to bring a picture into focus. "Your mouth looked different, maybe, and—well, you were looking out the window. Oh, and your eyes, they—they didn't look like your eyes."

I'm not used to having students discuss my facial expressions, and I had to make a joke of that. "Like I might have had a rough night last night?"

She laughed, chidingly. "Oh, you! No, you were just different." She looked serious again. "I guess that record *did* remind you of something."

"I think so. Something, maybe, that's a long way off, that I've tried to forget, even." When I looked up, I saw that she was hanging onto my words with an expression of compassion. For a second I had the odd sensation that she was the teacher and I, the student.

Several voices passed in the hall outside, moving in the direction of the music wing.

"Oh," she exclaimed, "I've got to get to ensemble. Bye." As usual, she flashed out of the room as quickly as she had appeared.

The Rebel had caught a glimpse of my past—some splintered moment out of the dark events which had brought me to this classroom and which even now were undoubtedly influencing my teaching. Perhaps I did not know myself as well as I thought I did. For years I had been requiring young people to dissect their own lives, but failing meanwhile to follow my own instruction. *I should begin to examine myself*—to rid myself, if possible, of the counterfeit man whose minting was already suspect in one pair of eyes.

I began to force myself to think about some moments in my life that I had banned from my consciousness. I turned to old papers that I had long since abandoned. Both before and after the war I had made some notes, and though some of them had been scribbled in an indescribable mixture of alcohol and agony they brought back now many vignettes of my childhood, adolescence, and career in homicide. It was very hard to relive certain of these events. But it was only too easy to dream of such things.

There is no complimentary ticket into the cyclorama of one's own soul. Though not exorbitant, the price is dear. During the ensuing spring and summer, I tossed at night through a succession of terrible dreams. I say dreams because they contained variations, but most of them ended in precisely the same way. Each time I would awaken trembling from a grotesque scene in which I leaned over a dead boy, and in every dream it was my own face that I saw. Those dreams even followed me into the classroom. One day while I was writing on the board, the chalk dust on my hands became all at once another kind of dust, the dust of lava rock— and then, for one horrifying instant, I saw blood pour over my fingers. By now I knew whose blood it was.

His name was Strain—Corporal Strain. I never knew much more than that, except that he bore a remarkable and unfortunate likeness to me. The men in the second battalion used to mistake him for me whenever they saw him shaving or emerging from the showers or performing in any situation where it was not immediately possible to determine his rank. Someone said that he was from somewhere in the East and that he was a quiet fellow. Someone said he wore his ragged moustache because he thought his look-alike looked good with one. A PFC who knew him told me that Strain had wanted combat duty and had requested a transfer from a soft Stateside, peace-side assignment, much the same way I had written the Commandant a year or so earlier. Perhaps he was another glory-hunter, come to the islands in search of himself and Life, come to the edge of Hell for Vergil's wisdom. I never knew.

I had seen Strain at the Maui base on various occasions—on liberty in Wailuku and Kahului; at the Division's Red Cross recreation center, where everybody went at times to reassure himself that there were still women; and in the battalion "slop chute," where Strain drank Cokes and sat watching the phenomenal capacity for beer that some of his acquaintances demonstrated. I saw him there one night, grinning at a bunch of thoroughly beered young Marines. They, in turn, were enjoying the antics of the battalion mascot—an English bulldog clad in his little jacket of Marine Corps scarlet and gold and lapping enthusiastically at the puddle someone had poured from a bottle. I don't recall ever having talked with Strain.

The last time I saw him was on Iwo Jima on March 13, 1945, two days before the island was secured and only one day before my own bloody exit. Easy Company and his outfit, too, were by that time shredded into remnants. The chaos and carnage of that March day had found our two units sharing a common piece of ground, most of our officers dead or wounded, and only a few NCO's alive and unhurt. We were located at the intersection of two draws, the smaller of which looked more like a ditch. The larger one, along which we had been moving toward the last "pocket" of Japanese resistance in our sector, led presumably to the Pacific and the northeastern shore of Iwo. At the moment, however, that Easy Company had reached the intersecting ditch, that pocket seemed suddenly to become the whole two-pants suit of Japanese courage and tenacity. Great caves, some of which were later discovered to run a half mile or more, had become funnels through which poured a surprising number of surviving Japanese dedicated to the proposition that we should either go home or stay permanently.

I've tried several times to write of that day, but each time I've torn the paper to confetti. Maybe I'm not ready yet. Maybe down deep I feel that the boys I saw die in that draw deserve greater privacy in their final moments. Maybe I can't look at the greed and self-aggrandizement in the world today after contemplating the screams and dying sounds of the past and still write in language that is coherent and fit for reading.

I will say simply that the rate of casualties among us was, for a short time, nearly proportionate to what it had been on the beach. Eventually I found myself behind a pile of lava rock, firing rapidly at scurrying figures. At first they had looked like our own men, but it soon became evident that they had donned the camouflaged helmets and dungarees of our dead and were gambling in an all-out bid to penetrate our lines. They were successful enough, as a matter of fact, to drive a wedge into our left flank. We were soon aware that one of their automatic weapons had begun a cross fire down the smaller draw, from which we were firing.

There is a noble tradition, probably invented in an inspired office atmosphere, that Marines never retreat, that they merely participate at times in what are called "orderly withdrawals." Frankly, I was about to suggest to the others in what was left of the platoon that we "beat it the hell out of here," especially when Japanese bullets began to chip the rock inches above my head. I had just pulled back from a slit in the rock and had just motioned to the man on my left to move back when someone from my right ran up to the position which I had vacated and eased his rifle into that notch of rock. I moved forward to warn him away. As I did, I heard something that sounded as if someone had kicked a broken, waterlogged rubber ball, and I saw a sprinkle of dust.

I caught him as he fell, but not on purpose. He simply fell back toward me, and I grabbed and held him, largely out of a reflex action. His mouth moved once—he was already dead, having caught a Nambu .31 squarely in his forehead. The back of his head was—my God, some of him was on me. I let go of him and half kneeled in horrible fascination. Now, in those staring, unseeing eyes, I saw my own. The face was like mine, too, except younger, less weathered, possibly fairer complexioned. It was like looking at myself in death, and I pulled away from him in dread. When my stomach stopped jumping, I saw his name on the cover of the helmet which had been knocked to the ground. The stenciled letters read: **STRAIN, S.C.**

There was another rattle from the Japanese automatic on the left, and I turned to see that the others were clearing out. The next ten minutes found us in bent-over, headlong flight back to the shelter of higher ground. But even after I had joined the others in safety, I felt that I could never in my life run far enough, that there would never really be another place of certain refuge for me in my existence.

Someone passed Strain's body after I had left it, and the word was out in another unit that I had been killed. A final touch of irony came on the following day, when I was hit by the same kind of bullet only a few yards northeast of where Strain had died. It was almost as if Destiny had erred and then tried to compensate.

When I came back from the islands, I intended to find out more about Strain. I never got around to it; I sought instead to lock him away in my mind. Perhaps I feared that I should have been his stand-in, that there was more to warrant his having survived instead. His was one of the ghosts that followed me, that relentlessly pursued me as I sought to lose myself in the animal comforts available to a Fourth Division Marine in our "sponsor city," Los Angeles. But somewhere in that blur of lights and bottles and inviting eyes that followed, I had eluded him. I had put his name upon a bundle of papers and had hidden them from sight. Then a classroom and a record and a girl had brought his spirit back, not to torment me but to release me from that volcanic rubble. To free me from that place where his soul found peace and where my own spirit began to comprehend its shallowness and purposelessness. Today I can even think that Strain would approve of what I try to do in 106.

My return to my classroom in the September that followed was not without some reluctance, however. The dreams that had shattered the summer nights had ceased, but they had left me considerably altered in appearance. I had lost weight, and I was also afflicted by what the dermatologist calls *alopecia areata*. I had grown accustomed to the male-pattern baldness that was moving my forehead boundary, but this new variety of hair loss followed no pattern whatsoever. When school opened, I looked like something a large cat might have dragged home from Hiroshima. I don't think my concern over my appearance grew out of vanity. But I hated seeing the expressions of shock on so many faces.

In other respects the purgation that had racked my whole self during the preceding months left me in a better physical and spiritual state than I had possessed since the war. I plunged into my work, determined that I would be a better teacher even if I did look like a mutant. The routine tasks at the school before the students arrived that fall seemed easier and more enjoyable.

That senior class was probably my favorite of the many I've seen pass through. Some of their junior-class teachers had complained about them, and at least two of their senior-year instructors picked up the refrain. The major grievances were characteristics that I enjoy in students, though. These seniors wanted to know the *why* of things, and they were perfectly willing to challenge a teacher when they thought he was wrong. I reveled in every minute of that year. Even on the first day, I decided that I was going to like them.

Throughout the morning hours I looked in vain for one face among them—the Rebel's. I felt a bit of discomfort in the prospect of seeing her—I guess I didn't want to watch that "Oh, what happened to you?" expression come into her eyes. It was a foolish idea, without a particle of logic, to be concerned about one student's reaction, but I liked and respected her and I especially didn't want her to look at me as if I had leprosy.

She came in at high noon—my fourth-period class—with that bouncy little slippered march of hers, the sable of her hair slightly auburned by the sun, her eyes asparkle, her nose crinkling with her smile. "Hi," she sang warmly. "It's good to see you." She lit the whole room with her pert loveliness. I should have known how she would greet me. Had I been Quasimodo, Martian, and Phantom of the Opera rolled into one, she would have been oblivious to my appearance. Perhaps Strain would have liked her as I did. I grinned back at her and reached for my seating chart. My Rebel was back in 106, and everything seemed right with the world.

We shared the same sort of warped sense of humor, she and I. Early in the year she was dating a member of the football team, and one day when I passed them standing together I said to him, "Good night, Bob! I see you with a different girl every time I turn around." He writhed, of course, but she enjoyed that. Many times in class, the Rebel would grin at subtleties which the others missed completely.

I believe that somehow she understood me as well as anyone ever has. Even more remarkably, I could frequently read her feelings. It was downright eerie at times. If I had a half-dozen possible composition topics on the board, I knew invariably which one she would select. In another instance, the odds against my knowing her writing topic were much higher. On a February afternoon, I asked the class to write descriptive essays on "someone in your English class." I looked back at her during the classroom writing and knew immediately her subject.

The portrait of me that she handed in was such a glowingly idealistic view of me that I will refrain here from reproducing the copy that I keep in my files. She titled her paper "Chevalier Sans Peur" and the sentences that followed treated her subject in a very heroic light. That she should see me in such a way meant so much to me that I began to worry about my exact feelings toward her. I had to admit now something that I had been trying to ignore. Unquestionably, I had a favorite among my students—for the first time, I was guilty of what I considered to be a clear breach of ethics. She must have known this—she knew me as well as the lines in any of the plays and musicals in which she performed.

With exactly what feelings she had written the paper, I could not know. That I held some special significance in her life, there was no doubt. Whether I represented a father-image or an abstract maleness or something more complex, I could not let her go on thinking I was any kind of hero. I thought then—rightly so?— that a hero should not be a balding, thirty-five-year-old husband and father whose wartime memories could still give him bad dreams. She had furnished the impulse that had led me to go back and to face past terrors, and now at last I could tell her—and anyone else who was willing to listen—the truth about myself.

The night I read her essay I began to write *Chalk Dust*. Within the next several weeks I wrote several other short narratives, and I used all of this material as the framework for language proofreading tests in my classes so that she could read this material and see the unheroic stuff of which I am made.

Knowing her, I have sometimes wondered whether the Rebel planned it that way. Nevertheless, she made me write. She left me with a new type of testing, a better feeling about myself, and the beginnings of a book. She was the greatest argument for ESP or clairvoyance that I have ever met. Perhaps she had known someone very much like me. Maybe in some peculiar mode our minds operated on the same wavelength. She knew, no doubt, that I did not want to say goodbye to her at graduation, and she refrained from coming to the room.

"That girl you were talking about—" broke in the hall monitor, "was she ever a queen?" I started to tell him that a girl like the Rebel is rarely voted a high-school queen, but that wouldn't have made sense because I'd never met another one quite like her. Besides, I had a better answer:

"She was in Room 106."

Toward the end of October, 1964, my brother and I had one of our two-or-three-times-a-year conversations. We've always been somewhat like Dumas' Corsican brothers—i.e., we've always had the capacity to know how things are with each other by a mere glance or word. And we've always been given to plain talk, never skirting issues.

"Okay, who *is* she?" he asked finally as the two of us sampled some of his Scotch in the otherwise deserted kitchen of his new home.

"Who's who?" I returned, sounding like a volume of self-advertisement.

"Who's the woman on your mind?"

"What woman? Whaddaya mean, Jim? You know I'm a happily married man, and I'm too—"

Cecil B. and I

"Hey, this is your brother talking. And I know that absent-minded look on your face."

"Honestly, Jim, what would I want with another woman?"

With a show of mock nobility, he ignored the question. "Well, maybe I'm wrong, but when you sit around like you're somewhere else and stare and smile at a sirloin the way you did today, I'd swear there's something female behind it."

I loaded my voice with hushed, confidential accents and leaned toward him slightly. "Well, I might as well level with you. You're right. I admit it." The grin dissolved from his face, and he looked quickly and surreptitiously toward the door and the sound of voices in the next room. When he turned again to me, he was all seriousness.

"Just remember, Gene—the family curse!" he cautioned, reminding me of the rather embarrassing proclivity among our progenitors for polygamous pursuits. Then, in still lower tones, he asked, "Who is she? What's her name?"

"Ruth," I said, thoroughly enjoying his discomfiture. "And I want you to meet her, Jim. She's a raving beauty." He had a mouthful of Scotch and soda, and he nearly choked.

"Meet her!" Shocked by the suggestion, my little brother momentarily lost all discretion, and his voice rose about ninety decibels. Then he caught himself and cast another troubled glance toward the living room, where our wives were still talking mother talk. "Are you out of your mind?"

"Jim, when you see her and listen to her, you'll know why I just want to take her and travel."

At that moment he was exasperation in technicolor with stereophonic sound. "Yeah. A guy I know took one, and his wife's had him traveling for months."

"Tell you what, Jim. Why don't you plan to bring Pat to Columbus on Friday the thirteenth, and we'll take our wives and go see her together."

"Take our wives!" This time he really did choke. When he eventually decided whether the Scotch should take the high road or the low road and when the strangling sounds had ceased, his handsome features were a shade redder. "Friday, the thirteenth! Brother, you are something else. You're not safe running loose on the streets."

"Look, the way I've got it set up, no one will be the wiser. We'll just be seeing her and hearing her—we won't actually be talking to her."

After a while, he reluctantly agreed to come to Columbus on the appointed weekend, and I couldn't resist giving him another jolt before departing. As I slipped behind the wheel and prepared to back out of his drive, I called through the window, "You're really going to dig her lines, Jim." He was shaking his head as I drove off.

As I recall, he was still shaking his head when he arrived two weeks later. It wasn't until he had opened his printed program in the undersized Worthington auditorium and had seen the title of the play I had been rehearsing for more than a month that the climax occurred. I saw him stare at the words **DEAR RUTH,** behind which the sun gradually rose in a glorious dawn. Then he gazed at me and saw my grin. A murderous light appeared in his eye briefly, and then we both began to laugh. I laughed so hard that several acquaintances sitting close by were convinced, I'm sure, that I was suffering pre-performance director-itis, that the work on the play had brought me to the snapping point.

So much for my bad joke. Later, I told Jim that he hadn't been totally in error. "You were really right, Jim. I am in love with *Dear Ruth,* with that whole sweet bunch of kids. It goes deeper than I can tell you."

"I dunno," he muttered. "You still sound as if you had a woman on your mind."

I didn't tell him what I was thinking. There was a half-formed sonnet in my consciousness as I considered how much I would hate bringing my work with those kids to a close. There was something else, too. It had been a bright seed planted some half-dozen years earlier and lying dormant in my mind. But it began to grow that night. I knew all at once, and for the first time, that Love, though it be manifest in an infinite variety of relationships, is nevertheless a single emotion born of a single Force. Love is the irrepressible, overwhelming desire to *give.* Love never takes. If it receives, then it merely accepts those gifts which, in the heart of the loved one, demand return. For Love receives in giving, and it finds its only true consummation in the tenderness of sacrifice.

Then I heard my brother's voice, which is nearly identical with my own, mingling with the words in my mind. "That play—you really go for that stuff, don't you?"

"Yeah, I really go for that stuff," I answered. "I really do."

Anyone familiar with *Dear Ruth* knows that Norman Krasna's situation comedy is a great audience pleaser, and my high-school artists had the most responsive audiences I've ever seen at amateur performances. Later in the year, the cast was invited to another high school planning to do the same play. After one rehearsal, our troupe (with only one replacement) gave an admirable demonstration performance for our hosts. That cast was as nearly perfect as any I have ever worked with—the father, the teenager, and my Ruth made the principals in the MGM film look sick. I would have liked nothing better than loading those performers on buses and showing them off from one end of the country to the other.

That was the first conventional play that I had directed in a dozen years. Quite honestly, I am inclined to oppose the very widespread practice of regularly assigning English teachers to direct plays. In the first place, few English teachers are adequately trained for producing plays. Drama has a legitimate and important place in any school's curricular and co-curricular program, but theatrical arts are best handled by a speech-and-drama teacher. If an English program is to be what it should be in a high school, the busy English teacher must not be annually saddled with such time-consuming undertakings in addition to his regular chores. There are those, I'm sure, who will disagree with this contention, but the National Council of Teachers of English and the National Association of Secondary School Principals will generally support my view.

On the other hand, a once-in-a-while go at play-directing might profitably be offered a teacher of English. In this spirit, Bill Lane had asked me in 1964 whether I'd like to do a play again. I think he knew that I had missed working with commencement productions and senior-day skits and probably thought it might do me some good. It did.

I am not thoroughly trained for such work. Though I had had some acting experience before coming to Worthington, I possessed no working knowledge in set design, lighting, sound, makeup, and various other facets of theatrical production. My first teaching contract, however, called for me to direct a junior-class play. The only strengths that I could bring to such a task were a fairly good ear for the proper inflection of lines, some awareness of how to block stage positions and movements, and a very great interest in theater. Otherwise, my approach to directing a play was virginally naïve, utterly pristine in its ignorance.

It seemed to me that I couldn't go wrong with a good mystery melodrama, so I tried to get the rights to John Willard's *The Cat and the Canary*. That play being tied up, I settled for Bayard Veiller's *The Thirteenth Chair*, another who*did*it. The real murderer in our production of the play was the director, but I didn't know how bad a job I was doing. Of course, I had accomplices. What should have been two of the scariest portions of the play were uproariously funny. After being stabbed to death, our first corpse bumped his head and said "Ow!" A knife, which was supposed to frighten the characters by falling suddenly from ceiling to table, missed its cue, and two of our performers just had to look up and wait for it.

I learned a big lesson about permitting dialogue with profanity in plays intended for young audiences. If the audience is too young, profanity may lose whatever effectiveness it was intended to have. The superintendent tried to tell me this, but I had to learn the hard way. We gave a matinée performance for some of Worthington's elementary students, and that's where I discovered the truth for myself. In the middle of some important first-act exposition, one of the actors declared, "I don't give a damn what he was—he was my friend." Immediately, a little boy up front shouted to an acquaintance three rows away, "Did you hear that? That was your brother said that. He said *damn!*" The audience lost a dozen or so important lines that followed.

As seniors, the Class of 1951 decided that they wanted to do another melodrama. Although they did a very creditable job with James Reach's *The Old Man's Money*, one of our performers gave me much more heightened suspense than the playwright had planned to provide. In the climactic scene, the girl who played the nurse was supposed to discover that some medicine had disappeared from a container. On the night of the dress rehearsal, my actress picked up the small box very dramatically, opened it, and then exclaimed in a beautifully pitched voice: "There are *five* mills pissing from this box, not one." I needn't say that on our opening night I waited tremulously until that line had been properly rendered. With a little more experience or good sense, I would have altered Reach's "missing" to "gone." The young lady who put me through that ordeal is now a teacher, and I wonder whether she still blushes at the recollection of that so-easy transposition of sounds.

Sometimes, I found it desirable to make minor changes in a set, too. In one play we had the custodian build an oversized TV console, and instead of using a radio broadcast, we put the smallest boy in the class inside and equipped it with lighting. We had the first color TV with instant tuning in the country. The boy who was our newscaster has grown considerably, I might add. The last I heard from him, he was one of the Secret Servicemen assigned to Jackie Kennedy, Caroline, and John-John for a year or more before the President's assassination.

The Worthington Class of 1953 found me a somewhat wiser, more polished director. While their junior- and senior-class plays reflected my improvement, the class nevertheless experienced certain misfortunes. When one of my actors was to hit his antagonist over the head with a pistol butt (or seem to do so), the blow was miscalculated, and the fellow on the receiving end was all but knocked out. Happily, this *faux pas* occurred during a rehearsal,

177

not a performance, of the junior play called *Who's Batty Now?*

The victims of such thespian overeagerness were always forgiving, but in every high-school cast there is one performer whom the others enjoy teasing past all patience. The young man whom this group especially enjoyed bedeviling was a very intelligent, scholarly boy, who is presently teaching college English. Backstage and out of my sight, they would hide his hand props, hold him, or otherwise delay his entrance cues. Once he nearly ran through a flat trying to get onstage in time for me. Twice during our rehearsals they fixed his car so that it wouldn't start. I finally had to call about five boys to one side and set up some prohibitions on this game.

Even in working with *Dear Ruth* years later, I found that the play's Albert was being pestered by some of the stage crew. On one occasion—it was our opening night—when he was to look out the window and say, "There's someone out there," my technical director, unseen by the audience, held up a *Playboy* nude for Albert to see. Because he took his acting seriously and very nearly "broke up" on stage, he was furious when he complained to me about the incident.

Some of the same accident-prone youngsters worked with me when the Class of '53 presented Frank Vreeland's adaptation of Lloyd Douglas' *Magnificent Obsession*, for their senior-class play. Once, when I had instructed the young protagonist on how to disarm a knife-armed assailant, I found that I had taught too well. My "heavy" was very nearly laid up with a broken arm.

I was extremely proud of our *Magnificent Obsession*, though. There was only one noticeable flaw—the sound-effects man produced the brake-squealing, glass-shattering clamor of an automobile collision several lines before one of the characters inside the house was prepared to say "Sounds like a car—"

The worst accidents in any of these plays, though, were suffered by one of my student directors. She was a tall, intelligent, very helpful girl who was going through "that awkward phase," apparently. In the course of helping me, she fell onstage, backstage, into the orchestra pit, down the stairs leading from the proscenium arch, and over seats in the auditorium—all at different times, fortunately for her. Just when we had a somewhat effective scene being played, I would hear a loud crash and turn to see the student director stretched out like Caesar in the Senate. She always took her worst spills when she was being careful. I saw her a few years ago and couldn't get over the change—her semicircular canals were functioning very nicely and, as far as I could tell, there wasn't a bruise on her.

When Harriet Somers brought her training and experience to the high-school staff, it seemed logical that I bow out of my work as a class-play director. The commencement productions would take a great deal of my time and would let me go on at least one binge of creativity per annum. Besides, I wanted to begin writing stories and even plays.

My first and only full-length play was a fantastic melodrama called *The Mantis House.* I wrote the first two acts during the summer and fall of 1954, and when the juniors wanted to do it for their class play, I threw together a third act and turned it over to the young drama-and-speech teacher who had been hired to replace Mrs. Somers. Meanwhile, I tried to sell it to several TV producers, including the old Studio One and NBC's TV Playhouse. I was aware that there were weaknesses in the play, but I was hopeful that someone's adaptation might alleviate these problems. My failure to market the play was softened by the very fine high-school production that the students gave. Later, Row Peterson's drama editor suggested revisions, but by that time my bookstore moonlighting was taking up most of my spare time. *The Mantis House* gradually became a cold cocoon in my file.

With only a scaffold stage and a shortage of rehearsal time, my work with commencements and senior-day skits was always hampered with miseries. My Father Time very nearly lost his sheet in the 1956 commencement. In our take-off on the *Wizard of Oz* in 1959, the lion lost his tail. In 1960, a boy miraculously escaped serious injury when he fell off the stage and landed headfirst on the gymnasium floor. Two years later, during the senior-day performance of *Gremlin in the Kremlin,* our cardboard-and-wood Russian tank fell apart. By 1963 I was sure that I had better stick to farce-comedy, that laughter was my forte.

After *Dear Ruth,* I directed one last play—Samuel Taylor's romantic comedy *Sabrina Fair.* With the help of Worthington's new art teacher Todd Kuyper and several of his students, we had a prize-winning stage set, and the performers were equally strong in their work. But with the sadness of that November—Dow Nelson's death—naturally the play did not draw heavy audiences at any performance. It was not a time for romantic comedy, though the production was one of the two best plays I had ever directed.

Afterwards, I told Bill Lane that I thought I'd better quit while I was still looking good at the job. We had three first-rate teachers of drama on the staff in as many years, and I was beginning to devote increasing time to my *Chalk Dust*.

Obviously, there are no Cecil B. DeMilles in high schools just as there are no Knute Rocknes—and there shouldn't be. In public education the emphasis should be upon teaching, not upon professional entertainment. Not long ago I heard of a drama teacher in another high school who consistently brings in professional choreographers and stage technicians, all in order that her plays may have the professional touch. I am inclined to doubt that dramatics in that school have very much relationship with teaching.

Indeed, one of the great sicknesses in American high schools today is that teachers can grow too much concerned with winning and lose sight of a greater responsibility. On too many high-school basketball floors, gridirons, or stages, young people are no longer permitted to experience the sheer joy of playing the game or the scene. Thus too many teenagers become little robots, watch movies and hear reports from scouts on next Friday's opponent, spend more and more time practicing, attend special training camps (some of them on the fringe of league rules), or are told that their failure to participate in a spring sport will remove them from consideration for a fall or winter sport.

The problem may be related to the illness of mothers who put padded brassieres on ten-year-old girls and send them to school to compete for boy friends, but there is no excuse for one who calls himself a teacher to rob youth so completely of educational breadth and joy in learning. The coach—of drama or sports—who indulges in the fantasy that he is running a Broadway show or a big-league team is hopelessly lost in immaturity, ruthless and selfish ambition, and an unwillingness to accept his responsibility to teach and to try to help the losers, too.

"But shouldn't we strive to win, as in life?" comes my critic's question. "Of course," I reply, "but your version of the play or the game has only one real analogy in life—war and the exploitation of individuals, which I do not teach." Generally, we operate as individuals in life, and we have to make our way as best we can through setbacks and losses. We can't recruit the twenty-one best strategists to help us out in achieving our goals or defending our gains. Life is *not* a game, in spite of all the locker-room clichés— only a first-class dolt would make that comparison. Sports are an important training ground for the individual just as drama, debate, and service organizations are practice for living. Dow Nelson's success as a football coach grew out of the same source as his teaching success, for he always saw the individual player or student as being more important than the score or the class median on a test.

When one of my students fails a test, I don't tell him that he can't take the next one. Sometimes I work with young people who will never stand up well in academic competition. Often among the people who try out for a play cast are those who will have great difficulty in establishing the illusion I want to create in the production. But I don't automatically send them away and recruit someone else. I have never told a student that he must give up band or track in order to be in my play—for it's not *my* play. As a play director, I have tried very hard never to let myself be carried away with the notion that I am working with *my* plays, though I have always referred to the actors as being "mine," out of my affection for them. In reality, the plays belong to the young people with whom I work.

So far as I know, students have never been required to join the Thespians in order to participate in class plays. Nor will I pout and rant and threaten the members of my cast or crew because of their errors, nor call attention to their failures in school assemblies or after final curtains. I do try to correct the young, I show them what I want, and I urge them to do their best. I have never had reason to suppose that they did any less than that.

I have never apologized for play casts, either. Sometimes, we teachers are tempted to hide behind our papers and behind our students. When things go well, we like the credit, but "fall guys" are convenient when the results are not quite as we would have preferred. Nobody ever looked better than the man they called "the little Napoleon" of the Civil War—General George McClellan—and nobody ever had more excuses for his personal failures. Most often, his scapegoats were his subordinates. Maybe that was the real reason for Lincoln's calling the Army of the Potomac "General McClellan's bodyguard."

My best casts were never without their shortcomings, but they overcame these in large part. They did so in spite of the director's faults, and they succeeded in their spirit. Spirit is the big winner every time—it will make pure brawn or brain look very bad very often.

But I hear the other side answer, "He's only a play director—an English teacher!" And I must reply, "Thanks, but not really. Nevertheless, I have been trying." Yet it's a poor answer to those who do not comprehend that in trying lies the greatest, sweetest victory.

I do not like to strike a set—in a way, it suggests death. There is a feeling of loss and finality about it that I cannot make myself accept. The Saturday that saw our last scheduled performance of *Dear Ruth*, I had to let my young cast and production staff know that I shared their sadness in bringing our work to its conclusion. My sonnet-thoughts had found words, and I enclosed a copy with the brief note I had written to each of the students who had contributed to the play's success.

About fifteen minutes after the performance had ended, I headed backstage to be certain that everything was secured and the lights were all off. On my way I encountered one of the girls in the cast. She had been looking at the darkened stage, and the tears were streaming down her face, making fantastic patterns in the makeup she still wore. The play had been important to her in establishing friendships and providing happiness. Her father, who had been fighting a long bout with alcoholism, had come that night to see her perform—one of the rare occasions, apparently, when she had beaten out a bottle for his time. She didn't want the play to end, she sobbed. I assured her that, for me, it never would.

As the small figure was swallowed by the shadows of the play-bill-littered aisle, I leaned to pick up an envelope she had dropped in her distraction. I knew what was inside—

SOUNDS FROM A DARKENED STAGE

AND NOW OUR LITTLE HOUSE OF CANVASSED PINE
MUST STAND IN DARKNESS—SOON THE WALLS WILL LEAN
TO HAMMERS AND TO HANDS THAT WILL CONSIGN
EACH FLAT AND PROP THAT MARKED OUR FLEETING SCENE.
WE CLOSE AT LAST THE PENCILED, DOG-EARED SCRIPT
AND PUT ASIDE THE PAPER LIVES WE LED,
SUPPOSING THAT, BECAUSE THEIR STAGE IS STRIPPED,
THEY LIE IN BLUE-BOUND SEPULCHERS AS DEAD.
BUT THEY WILL WALK THE YEARS UPON THESE BOARDS
AND SHAKE A GHOSTLY AUDIENCE TO MIRTH
BECAUSE THE HEART IN EACH OF US RECORDS
THE LABOR AND THE LOVE THAT BROUGHT THEM BIRTH:
THEIR PLASTIC LILACS WILL FOREVER BLOOM
AND BRING A PHANTOM FRAGRANCE TO THIS GLOOM.

There is a strange, unhappy philosophy afoot whose adherents insist that education must never be fun—that laughter and learning are incompatible. I feel assured that these prophets of gloom have always been on the scene, though. No doubt the sound of laughter emanating from Plato's Academy raised many a Greek eyebrow. The devotees of deadly seriousness are especially articulate in times of Sputniks and Rickovers, and they occasionally infiltrate my profession, where they must ultimately be miserable in their work. Shakespeare recognized the need for comic relief, even in the presence of death, but the Pallbearer School of Pedagogues steadfastly decline to accept the truth about people—that, where there is no joy, there is no real life or growth.

At rare times youngsters come to Room 106 who have plainly been conditioned by cheerless homes or somber classrooms. Such

TG9F: Thank God 9t's Fun

students regularly show shock and discomfort over the laughter in a school. Even after adjusting to such an atmosphere, they continue for a time to check other faces to determine whether and when it is appropriate to smile or chuckle.

I don't wish anyone to suppose that the main business of my classroom is to entertain. Like most English teachers, I take my work quite seriously. At the same time, I will sacrifice any of the perennial totems or fetishes of false dignity and pseudo-propriety propounded by the Pallbearer's ethic. Some few in my profession would question my reading portions of Richard Armour's *Twisted Tales from Shakespeare*, lampooning Shelley's "Indian Serenade," comparing Elizabethan lyrics with modern "pop" songs, referring to the sad-eyed Petrarchan lovers in the school corridors, showing the implications for high-school romances in Hume's essay "Of the Tragic," or doing a number of other things in my classroom which provoke laughter. Still other observers would be thoroughly troubled by the original character monologues which my students write and enact in Room 106, for at times my classroom family show not only surprising insight into human frailties, but also some propensity for racy humor. In this respect, I must add, they are always less ribald than Shakespeare's Mercutio and much more tasteful than many of our late-show television performers.

It is curious that, though the logician's thinking process requires us to set aside our emotions, it is these same emotions which most often trigger creative thinking and humanism. Thus I find that students remember longest those authors and experiences which have stimulated a sense of humor, horror, hurt, harmony, hostility, heterodoxy, and *hybris*. When young people laugh at Thurber's Walter Mitty, shudder beneath the dread arc of Poe's pendulum, share the pain and futility of Wilfred Owen's totally disabled soldier, move through the wonderful warmth and merriment of Saroyan's *My Name Is Aram*, understand the prejudice and hatred for nonconformity in H. G. Wells's "The Country of the Blind," find William Blake's views at odds with their own concept of God, and thrill with pride as Stephen Vincent Benét pays reverence to the American Muse and our national heritage—when students feel such emotions, they are much less likely to forget.

Of these emotions, laughter is among the most important, especially for one who believes, as I do, that the man who does not laugh can not love. As the often gloomy Thomas Carlyle once put it, "The man who cannot laugh is not only fit for treasons, stratagems, and spoils, but his whole life is already a treason and stratagem." In emphasizing the value of laughter, I am talking about men's capacity to laugh not merely at others but at themselves as well. When we smile at Walter Mitty, we are in effect learning humility since we must inevitably come to see him as no more than an exaggerated version of ourselves. When we are led through literature to see our own foibles, we become more tolerant of others, more cognizant of our human ties or, as Maugham phrased it, bondage. Though it be trite, it is nonetheless true that most of the misery on our planet has been nurtured by our inability or unwillingness to understand (and thereby to love) one another. Sometimes it is hard to hear that Voice of two thousand years ago above the din of the sonic booms and the bomb tests. But we can hear that living sermon above, in, and through innocuous laughter and good cheer. And so we laugh in Room 106.

I suspect that teachers who discourage good humor suffer from not merely a slowness or opacity of wit but also a deep-seated sense of insecurity—fear that they themselves might be the objects of laughter. To such people I can only recommend that there are other vocations. Teaching is too great a task for one who is thin skinned or for one who holds his own image in awe as something inviolable. Most young people have an uncanny capacity for recognizing the stuffed shirt and an unusual sagacity in searching out the Achilles' heel. The person who cannot bear publicly making a mistake or otherwise revealing his imperfections had best get away from other human beings, especially young ones.

On those days when I begin to take myself somewhat too seriously, I am often grateful for the medicinal effects of student laughter. One day when one of my classes and I were struggling fitfully over Addison and Steele, there was a rap at the door. I usually teach with a closed door to shut out corridor sounds and unsolicited ravens, but on this occasion the door was open. Outside stood an attractive young woman whom I recognized as the maturer version of a former student, one who had graduated three and a half years earlier. Feeling that the class had reached a temporary saturation with me and with eighteenth-century satire and social criticism, I gave the students the remainder of the period for study.

"Excuse me, people," I said, motioning to the door. "A former student of mine." (I always call my classes "people" because I prefer never to forget that they are.) I smiled at the visitor and walked to the door, the students in the first several rows eying the entrance with much interest. "How are you, Jacquie?" I said, taking the young woman's hand.

"I wanted to show you something," she replied. She reeled in a leather leash at the end of which tottered a small, disoriented tot. She held the child up, and he finally found my face and grinned broadly, vacantly, and bitelessly. I thought he was cute and said so. I always feel awkward with an infant, but Jacquie handed him to me. He gurgled two or three times, threatening to decorate my vest with pabulum, and then emitted two syllables that turned my eavesdropping class into volcanoes of mirth. "DAH-DEE!" he shouted, then smirked at me.

My first laughter wasn't very genuine—I think I was troubled over my teacher-image—but after a moment I thought it was very funny, too. Before I handed the child back to his embarrassed mother, I muttered to him in an ugly tone, "Wise guy!" Somehow

Addison and Steele were less formidable for that class the next day, probably because, together, we had laughed at me.

Sometimes the incidents that amuse me do so only in retrospect, and many times I alone can fully appreciate the humor. Once, in a junior-English section, I noted that Eddie, my biggest single challenge that year, was indulging in one of his favorite diversions—looking out the window. This time, though, his usual blank gaze had been supplanted by a wide-eyed, indignant expression. Eddie showed interest or verve only rarely, regardless of whether it was inside or outside the room, and I hastened back to see what had so moved him. Just to see that intentness on his face was exciting. We were working with poetry, which Eddie had given up for Lent, and I had possibly become callous to his daily expressionlessness.

He was so engrossed that he didn't even worry about my reaction to his inattention. Instead, he pointed toward a truck that had parked close to the back entrance of the cafeteria. "Look, sir," he said in a stentorian whisper. By this time most of the class were half-risen from their seats and straining to see the source of Eddie's concern. As the driver of the truck came back up the steps from the cafeteria and pulled two large, brown paper bags from inside the vehicle, Eddie gasped lengthily and I saw what was the matter. The bags were marked in large bright-red letters **DOG FOOD.**

"Did you see *that,* sir?" Few of my students "sir" me, but Eddie had been in quicklime with me so often that he had adopted this verbal tactic, which never failed to catch me off balance.

"Yes, I can see, Eddie." I realized that he was not alone in his dismay, that others were now reacting as Eddie was. Clearly, the class's work with Edwin Arlington Robinson could not proceed for the moment. I had the greatest faith in and affection for our cooks, who were disgracefully underpaid, and I felt that I had to dispel any suspicions the class might have about cafeteria economy and the daily "blue-plate special."

"Now, there is a very logical explanation for those bags, Eddie. I don't know what it is, but I'll go right down and find out. While I'm gone, people, turn to page—" I gave them something to do while I slipped downstairs and cornered a cook. "Mrs. Marks," I began, trying to be casual, "some of my—ah—students were—well—wondering what is in those bags they just brought in. Ah—you know. The ones with the—ah—big red letters on the side?" She laughed, as I had hoped she would, and motioned me to the storeroom, where she opened one of the sacks.

"See? Green lima beans."

"Oh, well, I knew it must be something like that—and I thought I'd better let the kids know. By the way, why *these* sacks?"

"Our government-surplus supplies come with all kinds of markings," she explained.

I was not able to satisfy the class until I had spent another five minutes clarifying the government's lunchroom subsidy program. I could see that Eddie still retained some doubts about the matter. When we had talked about Robinson's "Richard Cory," in which the poet tells of a man who presumably has a perfect life but who commits suicide, I put in another pitch about our not always being able to see from the outside what's really on the inside. After we had equated Richard Cory with a bag of beans, Eddie seemed temporarily content.

Three weeks later, his calm was sundered once more, and this time there was no restoring his equanimity. In the midst of a discussion on Eugene O'Neill's contribution to American drama, Eddie's eyes once more swung window-ward, and, if he had looked indignant before, it was with sheer horror that he cried out now. More supplies were being unloaded, but this time the bags were stamped, in large black letters: **MANURE.**

Quite unwittingly I did do some damage to the cafeteria budget that year. I had been working in several classes with Stephen Vincent Benét's *John Brown's Body.* At one point the poet's treatment of Civil War prison camps seemed to deserve some additional detail, so I brought into the room some material from an old military history. So that the class could more fully grasp the terrible circumstances of POW's in that day, I read some passages describing the horrible lack of sanitation and the advanced stages of scurvy in which, for instance, men's teeth fell out and their gums broke off in chunks. I would have supposed that, if anything would, this might provide an object lesson on the human need for fruit and vegetables. At lunch, however, student after student went through the line without ordering. The cooks had prepared a delicious soup with large pieces of meat floating in it. I learned, later, from the cooks just how effective my teaching had been that day.

I get many free lessons in semantics via my students, usually without warning. They are always alert to the *double entendre,* to the unintended pun. I don't feel that their absorption with the risqué marks them as having fouler minds than the rest of the species, but they are a rather sophisticated, alert breed. Because

I can become thoroughly involved in my subject matter, I am sometimes caught off guard.

Not long after I had begun teaching, I began to feel the weight of the bookkeeping tasks required in a school. Especially did I writhe under all the procedures for handling student absences. It seemed to me that I could easily devote at least five minutes at the beginning of every period to signing re-admission slips, assigning makeup work, and discussing pre-excused absences. This time loss was very irksome because I learned early the value of getting a class started as soon as possible after the bell. Still working very hard to establish the kind of classroom atmosphere in which I could teach with any degree of success, I was from time to time delinquent in my other responsibilities. Occasionally, I would forget until the class was underway, and then I would have to stop and take care of a sometime absentee. One day in a world-history class I had to leave Napoleon's cuirassiers poised in mid-charge on the crest of the sunken road of Ohain. If I hadn't delayed the French debacle, a student would have left my room without having an absentee's excuse-slip initialed.

"Do you have a pink slip?" I abruptly asked the sweet little girl in the front row. She dropped her jaw and stared at me, and her face began to approximate the color of the form requested. "You'll need a pink slip," I said and smiled, thinking that I had startled her. Now her face was red.

When the class began to laugh, I remembered that the girl was rather new to the school and might not understand. In rephrasing, I committed my second faux pas. I still had not grasped the reason for her blushing and the cause of the class's amusement. "You surely have a pink form."

I tried to say it gently because I didn't want to frighten a new student, but the laughter of the others grew in pitch and fever. Thinking that they were being rude to the newcomer, I stopped and really read them the insurrection bill. After they had assumed a smiling silence, I turned to the girl once more. "I realize you're still getting used to us here. When you came in today, didn't anyone make a pass?" The class howled at my third strike, and the girl began laughing, too, with relief as she finally comprehended what I was trying to say. Napoleon didn't lose the Battle of Waterloo that day. I did.

One of the cardinal rules of teaching, I think, is to watch the students' faces. Generally they will tell you when you are getting through to them or when you are badly botching the job. Expressions on faces will warn you of errors, of the need to rephrase, or of the desirability of some new approach to the material. Nowadays I focus principally upon students' eyes, but Before Myrna I was confident that other facial expressions were dependable.

Myrna was a beautiful girl, but singularly unintellectual. Long dark hair, soft brown eyes, and almost total apathy toward history were her most striking features. I believed that she enjoyed the class, though. Rarely absent, she would sit, smiling prettily from bell to bell and looking about at objects in the room. I did not call on her frequently to recite because it was always an embarrassing, discouraging, and academically sterile experience. Her world was a twilight zone, brand new every day—and so was world history. What we had talked about extensively on Wednesday was still new and mysterious to Myrna on Thursday.

Once, however, I felt that I was communicating to her. I was using (without properly crediting) some of Warner F. Woodring's vivid description of the Spanish Armada and its helplessness before the English seahawks. As I paused in my presentation, I glanced at Myrna. There was a look of fascination, of a new horizon transforming her features. Her eyes shone floorward, where she was, it seemed, witnessing the destruction of King Philip's fleet.

With what appeared to be a major educational breakthrough to my credit, I felt inspired. It is possible that we sank more galleons that afternoon than had ever sailed out of Cadiz harbor. Moreover, until the final bell Myrna's eyes never shifted. I had already dismissed the class and most of them had gone before she rose and came to where I was standing no less triumphant than Drake and Frobisher. They had won only a sea battle, but I had won Myrna.

"Mr. Rousculp," she sighed quaveringly, "your shoes look just like great big chocolate bars."

Though some student aspects are misleading, there was never any mistaking Joel's feelings about my classroom. His manner in 106 was one of utter tranquility. Daily, he made me feel like a wicked warlock whose spell put Beauty to sleep. He wasn't malignant about it or purposefully rude—it was just that my voice held for him the properties of Sodium Pentothal. He was a happy boy. Even when I would awaken him, he would smile agreeably. For about five minutes Joel would sit there looking very much like a cocker spaniel in heat, and then he would lapse into his customary catalepsy.

I grew convinced over several weeks of Joel that he possessed a constitutional contentment, that this was his greatest foe. Of course, I could not let him sleep away his diploma, and I tried a number of approaches—I dropped books beside his desk, hung **DO NOT DISTURB** signs from his right ear, had my students do unplanned choral reading, spoke to his parents, spoke to Joel, stopped speaking to Joel, moved him into the hall when he became asthmatic, and set up a schedule of sadistic harassment.

Finally, after sounding reveille one day, I sent him to the health office with the standard referral card, on which I wrote: "This child is in serious need of assistance. He has been bitten by a tsetse fly." I never knew what took place in the nurse's office, but when Wyncken, Blyncken, and Joel returned he was wide awake. Thereafter, whenever he did drift off it was only for brief intervals, and, always upon awakening, he would search the air above him as if looking for some winged predator. I felt rather guilty about Joel—when he left Room 106, he was beginning to develop a small line across his forehead.

Nobody furnishes me greater amusement than the young hypochondriacs I find so frequently in Worthington High. Why we have such a large number of them, I cannot be sure. That many doctors have made their homes in the community may have had the effect of drawing families prone to pseudo-illnesses. Possibly hypochondria thrives here because suburban mothers find more time to worry about their family's health. Surely the presence of a well-known sanitarium is more closely related to effect than to cause. At any rate, the school nurse is daily afflicted by a number of young people with imagined ailments.

From my point of view, few sights are so incongruous as that of the very robust person who is incessantly fretting over the microbes that menace him. One of the most capable young men who ever sat in 106 was beset by exaggerated health anxieties. Shortly after the class had begun one day, I saw Barton staring at his thumb. All 6′ 2″ and 195 pounds of him was intent upon that prehensile sausage. I couldn't help noticing his turning it all about and rubbing it gingerly, because usually he was hard at work. Except that it was larger than most, the thumb revealed no special features. Having no background in pediatrics, I began to speculate whether thumb-suckers, once cured, sublimated their drive by thumb-watching.

When I couldn't stand the spectacle any longer, I stepped to the corner of the room where Barton sat and asked him what was wrong. Grateful for my concern, he showed me a tiny black wound in the thumb. He had jabbed himself with a freshly sharpened pencil and was wondering how long it would take for the infection to set in. I explained that amputation was rare in such cases and that since he had washed the pollex with soap and water he should relax and let his white corpuscles take over. It was hard for me to imagine the big tackle's being so upset over such a minor scratch.

My reassurances were to no avail, however. Before the end of the period, Barton asked for a pass to see the nurse. I gave him the necessary yellow slip, but he returned soon. The nurse sent him back to me with a note which said, in effect, that this same boy had been in her office three times earlier that same day with the same complaint and that he was about to drive her "out of her gourd," because he had been adequately cared for and advised.

There are some things that nobody expects ever to happen in a high-school classroom—at least, not until they have come about. Early one year I was working with a group who had been reading George Orwell's *Animal Farm* and enjoying it very much. Naturally, I wanted them to appreciate such literary matters as the author's parody on Shelley's "Song to the Men of England" and, of course, the parallels between the fantasy and the communist and fascist dictatorships.

Because I wanted them to draw their own conclusions inductively, I set up a program of oral reports and assigned topics to individual pupils: Lenin, Trotsky, the MVD (Secret Police), the Five-Year Plan, etc. I printed each of these topics on the board and put a student's name beside each of them. As I got to the last name on the list, I wanted to check its spelling one last time. "Marty, I've noticed that the office spells your name differently sometimes. Have I written it correctly here?"

Marty leaned forward and studied the green chalkboard carefully. After what seemed to be two or three minutes, I wasn't sure whether time was passing or standing still. There was no sound in the room, from Marty or anyone else. I began to feel awkward. "Well? what do you think, Marty?" I tried to be patient—after all, it was a twelve-letter name.

"We-e-e-ll—" he began, then leaned back and pondered the board once more. Breaking the silence helped, anyway. Feet were beginning to shuffle, someone coughed, and a girl in the back row giggled in a low key. I was wondering how I could possibly reword my question. By now Marty had written his name on a piece of paper and was carefully comparing it with my version. I kept thinking, *My God, this isn't really happening.*

Just as I was seriously considering going to the health office myself, Marty came to life. "I think," he said with great deliberation, "that your second E should be an A." "Thanks," I replied with much sincerity. I hastily corrected my spelling and went on discussing the assignment.

The punch line didn't sound until after my last class that day. I was coming out of the teachers' lounge when Marty dashed up to me excitedly. "Mr. Rousculp, I told you wrong. I called my dad up at noon, and between the two of us we figured out that you were right all the time."

It was the end of the day, so I went back into the teachers' lounge and hid. I had to take another time-out before I went back to my room to correct the spelling of Marty's name on all my records for the second time that day. I lit a cigarette and stood looking out at the parking lot, where buses were arriving and ingesting the lines of waiting youngsters. Then I began to laugh, not at the boy who couldn't spell his name, but at myself and at the foolish assumptions that people in my profession sometimes make.

Too often we conclude that, because a young man appears physically mature and healthy, he must have nothing of the child left in his nature and that, because we are using simply phrased language, our meanings must be unmistakable. We convince ourselves too readily that a boy who falls asleep in a classroom must be physically or mentally abnormal when, perhaps out of necessity, he is spending long after-school hours at a man's job. We forget that young people, like their parents, are habitually disposed to accept, as truth, that which they read, whether it happens to be a newspaper editorial or a stenciled **MANURE.** We sometimes spend hours preparing spelling assignments, never doubting for a moment that, as a boy is sixteen, he can spell his own name.

Such mistakes in a teacher are often as absurd and usually less excusable than his students' shortcomings. With a little thought, I find it difficult to laugh at one of my students without laughing at myself. To laugh at one's self is to learn humility, and humility is essential to an educable mind. Far from being incompatible with learning, laughter is one of the great vehicles for intellectual growth. The outstanding professional comedians, including some of our keenest satirists, have always known this—even in their most slapstick sequences, there are glimpses of universal truth. Charlie Chaplin, Harpo Marx, Jimmy Savo, Emmett Kelly—all the great clowns have understood that between laughter and tears there is only a gossamer of distinction.

I recall having once read a comment damning Red Skelton for his "cruel characterizations" of an alcoholic and a punch-drunk prizefighter. It was clear to me that Skelton was demonstrating far deeper human feeling and perception than the entertainer's critic. What had seemed cruel to the latter was evidence itself of the implicit sympathy in Skelton's treatment.

Genuine laughter conveys only warmth and delight, and it is good for both students and teachers. It is possibly the greatest blessing of the chalk dust. Actually, the sort of laughter that creates hurt is not true laughter—it is the sound of anguish and hate, and this is the only variety of amusement that I discourage in Room 106.

Some years ago a young lady in one of my junior-English classes was struggling with a severe speech impediment. Once, when she was stammering in her recitation, two of the other students began to snicker. I gave them a scalding look and called them in later that day.

"There are several steps we might take," I told them. "Obviously we owe her either an apology or a chance to get back at us. I suppose we could set up a schedule in which we pick out some little thing about everyone in the class and take several minutes a day to laugh at whoever is to be the day's joke. Each of us has something that he doesn't like others poking fun at. Some of us bite our nails, some of us are shorter than others, and some of us are so insecure that we feel better when we can find someone else's sensitive spot."

Before they had left my desk, the boy who stood about an inch over five feet and the girl who was a chronic nail-biter agreed that their classmate's stammering was not really good for a laugh. Not that I had solved everything—about a week later, I overheard my stutterer say to the boy, "W-well, if it isn't T-tiny T-tim!"

"Glory be to God for dappled things," wrote Gerard Manley Hopkins. With something of the same feeling, John Ruskin wrote, "Shadows are in reality, when the sun is shining, the most conspicuous thing in a landscape, next to the highest lights." My world of teaching is of a pied beauty, a mixture of light and shadow, of laughter and sorrow. If the chalk dust has been the medicine of my life, it nevertheless burns the throat and stings the eyes.

I am too close to my story, too much moved by its impact upon me, to tell it well. The two boys of whom I write deserve to have their stories told, however, and as simply as it is possible to do so. So far as I know, they were not acquainted with each other. Certainly, they were very different from each other in many ways. Offhand, I can think of only three or four things they had in

Chalk Dust Gets in Your Eyes

common: each was a senior in Room 106, each is a subject in the newspaper clippings lying here on my desk, each affected my life very significantly. A single conversation brought them together, and so they must remain in my story of John and David.

In the fall of 1961, when I made the monologue assignment, I was worried about John. True, his writing was weak, his grammar quite bad at times, and his reading extremely slow. Still, he was showing improvement in these areas. The monologue would be another matter, I feared, for John was very likely the quietest boy who ever sat in my classroom.

Nor did I prove helpful in selecting his seat. I had not yet realized that my farsightedness sometimes causes me to overlook the front row and to overwork the back row in conducting recitations. By seating John in the front of the room, I inadvertently aided and abetted him in his natural reticence to speak up. By the time I had begun to compensate—to stand farther back and to collect additional chalk dust by rubbing against the board—John had already cultivated a chronic silence, unbroken except when I called upon him specifically.

His responses to my questions were usually distinguished by brevity and a look of embarrassment. In this respect, he made me think of his sister Evelyn, whom I had taught two years earlier. I know now that I should have visited their home and met their parents. In failing to do so, I missed the chance to be more helpful to them. Someone told me later that the parents had migrated from a country in south-central Europe and that English was a second language in the home. But this was another teacher's impression. I didn't know. If I had possessed more understanding of John's background, however, I might have been able to do more for him.

The boy was extremely conscientious and cooperative in everything the class did. When I began to talk about the monologue requirement, however, his face showed considerable alarm. I make it very hard for a student to back away from this assignment—harder, I think, than actually giving the monologue. "I'm pleased to say that, over the years, only a few students have been cream puffs—so shy and milquetoastish that they just couldn't bear to give one," I tell them. Properly inflected, this statement is an excruciating thorn for those in a classroom who are thinking that they can't possibly do what the teacher is asking. Perhaps I am wrong to wield such a weapon—I've worried about it often—but it contributes, no doubt, to my .995 average in monologue results.

It seemed inevitable that John would stop at the desk to ask whether there were some alternative to giving a monologue. I expected him to broach the issue at the end of the period. He wanted to, I could tell, as he walked slowly from the room. He didn't say anything till the next day, though—when he could no longer put off seeing me. I had my briefcase in hand and was just about to go to a staff meeting when he appeared at my desk.

"Mr. Rousculp, I think I'm going to be a cream puff." He said it in such a manner that I knew he must have braced himself for that speech. I set my briefcase down and tried to affect surprise.

"John! You? Ah, you're kidding me!"

"No," he said simply, his cheeks flushed and his eyes fixed on my Grecian-urn bookend. "I just can't give one of those monologues."

"John, did you ever see a cream puff in a bakery?"

"I've seen them sometimes at the store where I work." He edged a foot toward the door as if he wanted to terminate this discussion as quickly as he could.

"They—well, you know what they are—thin-crusted, soft inside, just lying around for someone to take a bite out of them. You're not like that, John. If anyone takes a bite out of you, you'll bite him back."

"I—I don't know. I—" The color on his cheeks grew redder.

"Well, I *know* you can do as simple a job as a monologue," I told him confidently.

"Even if I could," he conceded, "I wouldn't know what kind of a character to be."

I glanced at my watch. The meeting would have already started, and I had to get to this one. I don't like most meetings. Worthington's chemistry teacher, Dan Wingett, defines *Hell* as "a long meeting at which people keep talking and talking and nothing ever gets done and, meanwhile, you keep looking at the clock because as soon as this meeting is over you've got to go to another one." Nevertheless, I had to leave John to get to the meeting.

"Look," I told him, "you keep thinking about it and, above all, don't brainwash yourself with I-can't-do-it's. If you don't come up with an idea, I'll be here tomorrow night, meeting or no meeting."

Twenty-four hours later he was there, waiting for me, when I returned from the duplicating room with a sheaf of the forms I use for evaluating monologues. "Any ideas, John?" I inquired, trying to pick up my optimistic tone of the evening before.

"No," he said. "I can't think of anything at all." He was the portrait of gloom. I could tell that he was prepared to say "It's no use."

"Sit down, John. We'll talk a bit and see if we can't think of something together." He slouched into a desk-arm chair, and I angled myself into one beside it. "What about your neighborhood?" I probed. "Aren't there any peculiar character types that live around you? There's always one oddball, anyway, on every street."

"I don't know the people around there very well—I work in the evenings, and—"

"Hey, wait a minute. Where did you tell me you work?"

"A grocery store, down in Beechwold," he said spiritlessly.

"What kind of work do you do there, John?"

"Carry-out boy," he answered, "but I do other things, too— stamp prices and sweep out the—"

"A carry-out boy! Why, you're all set," I said, still plugging for an Academy Award with my show of enthusiasm. "Nobody in the world, John, runs across a bigger assortment of personalities than a grocery's carry-out boy. I bet you've met people you couldn't please if you drove them home and cooked their meals and then offered to do the dishes."

He came to life a little bit. "You mean if I took a character like someone in the store, it would still be original?" He was looking off toward the bust of Goethe on the file cabinet. There was a half-smile on his mouth, and I could tell he had someone in mind.

"It would be original if you added some little touches and invented some things for the character to say, or maybe exaggerated the person somewhat." I didn't want the job to sound as hard as it is—I played the line and let him run with the plug at this point.

"Could it be anyone in the store?"

"Anyone but you."

"My boss," he said musingly. Then his eyes lit up. "What about my boss?"

"Sure, you can do your boss. What's he like?"

"Well, the funniest thing about him is the way he doesn't want anyone to smoke in the store—he says it's messy and a fire hazard."

I didn't see anything very funny about his boss's prohibition on smoking, but I didn't want to throw a soggy mattress onto his idea, either. "Yes," I said, "that sounds like something you could work with." My own enthusiasm flagged a bit.

"That's not the funny part," John went on. "What kills me is the way he sneaks down into the basement every so often to puff on cigarettes, himself."

"Now, that's good, John. All you have to do is to make him very pompous when he's laying the law down to the others and then have him creep downstairs and back as if he's scared to death someone will catch him. And then you could—"

"I just don't know. I don't think I could do it here—in front of the class."

"Everybody and his brother is thinking the same thing, John. Everyone's scared of the idea, but some of them don't let on. What you have to do is to make up your mind that if they can do it you can, too."

John breathed deeply and somewhat tremulously, but he looked as if he might, like Macbeth, be ready to "bend up each corporal agent to this terrible feat." At the door he had one afterthought, though. "Mr. Rousculp, there's no way my boss could find out about this, is there?"

"Not a chance," I assured him. "But don't let your model catch you watching him."

Though I can readily project myself into the characters and situations my students present, my obligation to evaluate their work requires that I see them as members of my classes. Therefore, I identify with them as well as their characters as they struggle with this challenging task. I realize that for young people like John a monologue is an Herculean labor.

Knowing this, I experience a personal tension comparable, I suspect, to what the nervous monologist feels. As John's turn came gradually closer on the calendar, I began to have second thoughts: *What if he flops? What if he folds and fails to give one? If he withdraws, then, into a permanent vegetable silence, to what extent will the fault be mine?* I am sure that such anxieties will seem trivia to people outside the profession, but they will always follow me in my work.

The day came, and John sat rigidly waiting for his name to be called. I scheduled him early in the period so as to relieve him of that intolerable marking of time. I was probably making it easier on myself, too. When I called him and he stood up to explain the physical setting for his monologue, I leaned in suspense and tried to make a mask of my face. I could see some of his classmates staring in amazement that he should undertake to give such a performance. Not John, they were thinking, not the boy who blushed when he recited and who never spoke more than a few quiet words. What had happened to the boy who almost always had taken F's rather than get up for oral book reports?

I've forgotten portions of John's monologue because I was too much involved with what was happening to him. I remember, though, that he used the side of the classroom as the "stairs leading down to the grocery basement." He did a good job of depicting the boss who was breaking his own rule, and the class enjoyed the character and situation. He was doing very well when, all at once, he forgot his lines.

Then he did the most difficult thing of all. He stopped, looked back at me, and said, "Mr. Rousculp, I'd like to start over." I knew what he was going through, and I could only nod my approval to John. This time, he made it through the four or five minutes of lines and pantomimes and returned to his seat with the applause of the class. I was glad that this was the last class of the day. I wouldn't have been good for much else.

John sat beside Nick, Worthington's first-string varsity fullback. Though Nick had big problems of his own, he was quite an extrovert, jovial and generally well liked by his fellow seniors. If there was anything that Nick respected, it was raw courage. When the period ended and the class rose to leave, I saw Nick reach out and clap John on the shoulder. "Really a good job, John!" said the fullback. As they moved through the doorway together, it seemed to me that I could almost see John growing in stature and young manhood. That day had marked a personal victory for him. He had defeated the greatest antagonist in life—himself and the nameless fear that governs so many people.

Early in 1962, and less than two months after John's monologue, I bought a house in the Beechwold section. Some might question why I don't make my home in the Worthington School District. In addition to finding less expensive but equally desirable housing three miles away, I enjoy much greater privacy in my after-school hours and I believe that I can deal with my students more justly and impartially than I could with my neighbors' offspring. Of course, my definition of *home* demands some hairsplitting—a person cannot teach for two decades in a community and not "live" there, in a sense.

The store in which John worked was only five blocks west of my new house. I had forgotten, as a matter of fact, that he worked there until he hailed me from across the parking lot outside the store. Afterwards, I made it a point to stop at the store occasionally, even though their prices were a trifle higher on some items.

The people in the grocery thought highly of the boy. The owner talked about what a fine worker he was. The store manager, whom I took to be the "boss" of the monologue, obviously liked John. The young fellow continued working in the store long after his graduation.

John always wanted to know how my new crop of seniors was doing. During monologue week, I invited him to come up and sit in the classroom. Though he couldn't leave his work, he began talking excitedly about that day when he had performed. He'd never forget it, he said. I told him that I wouldn't either and that, without using his name, I was telling my classes of his experience. He was pleased about that.

202

I last talked with John in late 1963. Parts of that conversation I remember clearly, but other portions are lost to me. I have tried earnestly, and with good reason, to remember our words exactly, but in vain. I remember that John was troubled about his future. I recall vaguely that business school or college was on his mind. But there was one patch of our dialogue that I can summon to mind with clarity very well—too well.

"I'd like to ask you—what do you think of the Marine Corps?" he questioned as he rolled the cart full of groceries to my car.

"I'm a bad one to ask, John. I learned only one trade there, and since I didn't go into law enforcement or organized crime it didn't help me at all in civilian life."

"Have you ever been sorry you joined the Marines?" he asked, looking at me narrowly. Surely he couldn't be thinking of—yet perhaps he was.

"I've always been sorry that I had to take life to stay alive, John. And I didn't like any part of having the dirt chewed up around me or feeling the ground heave with the explosions of mortar shells."

"But would you join the Marines again?" he pressed. I couldn't dodge the question again. I had to be honest.

"I guess so. But, listen, things were different then, John. The country was at war, and I didn't know what I wanted to do with my life. I was pretty much fouled-up—and the service seemed to be a temporary answer. Besides, I was sure to be drafted, eventually."

He looked up from the sacks he had propped up in the back seat. "Do you think that sometimes guys can do better in college after they've been in the service?"

"This much I know. In my own case, I wouldn't have been worth a damn in college right after high school. I suppose that it differs with different people." Now it was my turn to ask a question. "You're not thinking about enlisting, are you, John?"

"I've thought about it some. A friend of mine says that there's something in the Marine Corps that the other services don't have. He says once a Marine, always a Marine. Do you feel anything like that?"

"Your friend doesn't work in a recruiting office, does he? No, I guess I know what he means, but don't ask me to recommend the Corps. For ten weeks they treat you like an animal, complete with tags. But when you come out of boot camp, you're convinced that you could stand anything. Just the memory of your D. I.—your drill instructor—is enough to make you fighting mad. But don't ask me if you should enlist in the Marines. Things are fairly quiet now, but that cold war could warm up awfully fast. I don't know what the Corps 'd have you doing, but when I was in it they were hopping islands and every one of them was a frontal assault."

John glanced over my shoulder to where other cars were pulling into the parking lot. He left hastily, but as I drove out he waved good-bye over a cart full of someone else's groceries. I want to believe that I said the right things to him that evening. I very much want to think that the day he found courage with a monologue and the evening he conversed with a sometime infantryman were not influential in his entering the Corps the following February.

Two years later, on a March day, I was just finishing my sixth attempt to break the literary bank at *Reader's Digest* when I heard the paper boy vibrate the storm door outside my study. As I glanced over the front page of the *Columbus Evening Dispatch*, the print began to blur and run together:

LANCE CPL.

Worthington Marine Killed in Viet Nam

Marine Lance Cpl. ▨ ▨ ▨ Worthington, was to have observed his 23rd birthday Wednesday in Viet Nam.

The Defense Department Tuesday night r e p o r t e d ▨ was one of 44 servicemen killed in recent Viet Nam combat.

HIS PARENTS, ▨ ▨ were notifed Sunday of the death.

A 1962 graduate of Worthington High School, ▨ joined the U.S. Marine Corps in February, 1964. He had been in Viet Nam since last May and was to return to the United States in May.

ALSO surviving are . . .

What price, courage? I whispered as I made out the words. I knew John had made a choice, but I prayed that I had not played a decisive role in shaping his destiny. I tore the article from the paper and carried it with me to Room 106. I couldn't get John out of my mind. Glimpses of the boy kept breaking into my lectures and demonstrations. I knew I had not been the father-image to John, for he had a father with whom he shared a mutual devotion. But the thought persisted—what else could I have represented to the boy that might have taken him to a recruiting office? *Can a teacher ever really know where his example leads or how much of him rubs off on the young with whom he works?*

And now a nightmare called *Viet Nam* had claimed one of mine, had invaded Room 106. *Viet Nam*—another word for *war*. I thought again of that inferno through which I had crept, of the pockmarked harlot Suribachi who lay in her gray vomitus of ash and solidified lava and picked the human flesh from her steel and concrete teeth, and of other sepulchres called the Amphitheater and Meat Grinder Ridge. A sense of impotence swept over me as I pondered the teacher's dilemma, and a poet's half-forgotten words paced dumbly behind my barred lips:

> *Were half the power that fills the world with terror,*
> *Were half the wealth bestowed on camps and courts,*
> *Given to redeem the human mind from error,*
> *There were no need of arsenals or forts.*

Where war and the military are concerned, what is the proper posture of the teacher? Is it for him to dwell upon the flag, the uniform, the regimental colors, the obligation of the citizen to stand for one's country, one's way of life, on far-off soil? To argue for self-sacrifice in an abnegation of reason, a "Charge of the Light Brigade" zeal? Or does the teacher necessarily emphasize the horror of man's killing man, the frightful and incredible waste, the futility that history repeatedly demonstrates? Can the teacher do either or both? Where does the mealy-mouthed failure to take a stand end, and the immorality of indoctrination began? I did not know, I do not know. Still, I remembered a girl who had supposed there was a "hero" in 106 and a boy who had asked me about the Marine Corps, and I wondered whether I had sent a boy to his death.

I kept the clipping on my desk for some time. I was pondering it again when another young man stepped into the room, perhaps a week later. "Hi, Dave. Something I can help with?"

I was always glad to see this student. Lively, self-reliant, high strung, Dave was as well liked as anyone in that senior class. His grade average had not been high enough for Michigan State to accept him, but he was working hard to try to bring up his marks. Dave was always on the go. Hiking, canoeing, climbing were among his favorite activities, and he was one of Worthington's brightest hopes on the swimming team.

Though his great love was the outdoors, Dave liked people, too. And his was the sort of personality that draws attention from every quarter. His laughter and his dark, handsome features kept the girls buzzing, and his sincerity and depth of thought appealed to everyone.

"Hope I'm not bothering you," he half apologized.

"Oh, no, no. I was just thinking about a boy who—do you remember the kid I told the class about when we were getting our monologues ready? You know, the one who was afraid to give one but gave it, anyway?"

"Oh, yeah! The one the football player congratulated."

"That's the one. Well, I can give him a name now. This is what became of him." I slid the clipping across the desk, and Dave leaned over it.

"Yeah, I read this," he said after a moment. "That's a shame. He got over being afraid, and then he died in Viet Nam." He caught the irony right away.

"And now I've got to live with the knowledge that, maybe, if he hadn't come to 106, it wouldn't have happened," I told Dave. I went on to describe my last talk with John.

"Oh, no," protested Dave. "He knew what he wanted to do. If you let yourself think that you sent him to Viet Nam, you don't give him credit for making up his own mind to do what he thought he had to." That was Dave, of course—he had a knack for cheering people up. How many times have students come to 106 for help and then turned out to be of assistance to me, their teacher? It was happening again.

"Dave, you make me feel better. I guess you're right. I wasn't really giving John enough credit." I slipped the news-clipping into a book.

"Besides," Dave continued, "I believe Death finds you wherever you are. I'm not like that Omar Khayyam guy—I mean, I believe in a God that cares—but I think when He wants you, He takes you, whether it's in bed or a swimming meet or Viet Nam or any-where."

"Yes, but think of it, Dave. Not quite twenty-three. I hate to think of anyone dying that young."

"I really don't agree with you, Mr. Rousculp. I mean—look at me—I mean I'm really living, really enjoying myself. When people get older, they lose something. They see their dreams go smash, and the people they love turn on them, and the whole darned world all messed up. At least, that's the way they talk. Me, I haven't had much to worry about. Oh, I've shed some tears, but my life has been pretty carefree. It's only now I have to begin to sweat it. If only people could be like hawks—free and independent and hunting for life. You know, when a hawk can't hunt and be free, he dies. He just sits and waits, dying a little more every day." Yes, the boy made me feel better.

"You may have the right idea, Dave." The bell was about to ring, I saw in a glance at my watch. "Well, so much for Death. Now what can I help you with?"

"It's about my research report."

"Oh, yes—the red-tailed hawk." That was his subject, I recalled.

"I was wondering if my outline—" he began as the bell clanged in the corridor. He said he'd have to run, that he'd see me later about his question. Somehow we missed connections. The spring vacation came and went. Then he was out of school for several days because of illness. And then—then there was no need to answer his question. Dave was killed in an automobile accident and the school was plunged into mourning. Dave and his closest friend, a junior, were hit broadside in a station wagon by a big semi-trailer dump truck not far from a southeastern Ohio town. He and his companion, who died also, had been attending an outing of the Rock Mineral Society of Columbus. The place for his rendezvous with Death would have been of little moment to Dave. *"Death finds you wherever you are,"* he had said.

The funeral home was crowded. I really didn't want to go, but I had to. Not merely for Dave. Another boy had stopped at the desk that day to tell me that Dave's mother was hoping I'd be in. There was a long line of people there to pay their respects. It seemed to me that Death had lost all sense of fair play—Dow Nelson in November, then John, now Dave.

After about five minutes the line had progressed so that I saw the casket and Dave. The accident had been of awful violence—the mortician hadn't been able to conceal all the signs of it. I stood there thinking about Dave and John, of other students of mine whose death had brought shadows into Room 106—the red-headed boy who had died in a plane crash, the tomboyish little girl who died in an L.A. hospital, a teacher's daughter killed in another auto wreck, and all the others—too many. . . .

Then I remembered an image—a red-tailed hawk cutting its swath of freedom and joy and beauty through an eternal sky of youth. "He isn't dead," I said to Dave's mother. "A boy like that doesn't die."

I had to get out of there, away from the mute fact and the mortician's mummery. I mumbled some other things to his mother, then fled. But I couldn't find my way out, and before I located the door I stumbled past the father—a little man, a doctor, standing uncertain and bewildered by his loss. I came out of the funeral home the wrong way, bumping into people who were entering, yet getting past them in time to keep the secret in my eyes. I got to my Chevy before the wet astigmatism clouded my sight.

"Was it awful?" asked my wife.

"Awful," I choked, trying to find the slot on the ignition knob.

As we neared home, she spoke again. "It's terrible, isn't it? So young!" I had had time to think—my eyes had cleared, had washed away the image of Death.

"But he's free, Alice. He didn't want to leave youth and to get on the treadmill we call adulthood. Life doesn't let us follow the stream and wander where we will, and he knew that. There's a wisdom in youth. It would have been Divine cruelty for a spirit like that to be broken and corrupted. And what he was is still alive."

Later, I went to my study, where three sets of papers were lying on my desk. I picked up one set and shuffled through it until I found Dave's last composition. Then I sat down to read it, to grade it, and to enter the mark in my gradebook. Perhaps it sounds foolish that I should have done so, but it was my way of denying Death's absolutism. *Dave is not dead, by God*, I thought. *John is not dead. So cry your eyes out, Housman and Longfellow, over the passing of Youth. Youth lives, nevertheless—if nowhere else, then in my heart, though the pen runs dry and the gradebooks yellow with time. And, Keats, there is a poem, still unwritten, about another urn—this time, an American urn on which a middle-aged man, a teacher of sorts, reaches out to fleeting youth in his desire to teach, to learn, to understand, and to love. This is the Beauty which is my Truth. This is the enduring beauty of the chalk dust.*

I saw him coming toward my room at the close of the open house. There was no avoiding him. Two mothers were telling me that their offspring were enjoying English in 106, and politeness and vanity kept me from excusing myself at a fast trot to the nearest exit. He waited just across the corridor until the women had gone, then sidled up. It was nearly ten o'clock, and my face and chapped lips were smarting from the "PTA smile" I had been wearing for some two hours. Now I had this fringe benefit. Mr. Knipe—my portmanteau incorporates *knife* and *gripe* —was an expert at concealing complaints and pitches with the mien of innocent joviality.

Why he should have picked me out so regularly as a sounding board is still a mystery to me. I seldom conceal annoyance with any degree of skill, and Knipe had a knack for getting under my

Classroom on Wheels

epidermis. In some respects he was a likeable sort, but there were several million light years between his views and mine. He usually wanted to discourse on the "federal monster in Washington." Just the spring before, he had been agitated over Eisenhower's position on federal aid to education.

"You know those Washington bureaucrats—just open the door, and they'll be in here telling you what to teach," he had warned.

"Did they send over people to set up the school curriculum in the '30's?" I had countered.

"Whaddayamean?"

"I mean when this building we're standing in was put up by the WPA?" I usually tried to leave Knipe with a small knot in his oversimplified line of thought, but he always came back for more.

I didn't have to speculate long as to what he had on his mind this time. His insinuations were always as subtle as a mouthful of Worcestershire sauce, but he outdid even himself this time. "I hear Jack Hintern's girl got herself knocked up on the last senior trip," he began with the charm characteristic of his usual phrasing.

"Oh, is that so, Mr. Knipe?" I returned. "Where did it happen— in the National Archives Building or on the floor of the Senate?"

"Now, you know those kids get together in hotel rooms, even if it is against their so-called code." He nudged me with an elbow.

"No, I don't *know* that. With four, five, and six to a room, I would suppose they'd have much less privacy than here in Worthington on the back porch or in the back seat of a car." He had picked a topic which especially vexed me. I liked the girl in question very much. She was in the pregnancy predicament, true, but her principal difficulty was a father whose loud mouth had offended so many people that town gossip about the girl's circumstance became its means of revenge. Now it appeared that Knipe was going to use her as an example in attacking the annual class trip. I began to think how pleasant it would be to caress his bridgework and rearrange his leer, but lost the thought in a huge headline:
★★★WORTHINGTON TEACHER HELD IN PTA ASSAULT★★★

"Those kids really tell some stories about what goes on on that trip," he was adding.

"For instance?" I invited.

"I hear most of them are hitting the bottle in New York."

"Now, we know, Mr. Knipe, what kids are like at seventeen. Didn't you ever stretch things a little to let on what a sophisticated devil you were?" It was my turn rib-nudging. With some satisfaction I felt his favorite panatelas crunch beneath my elbow.

"Then you don't believe any of this goes on during the trips?"

"I didn't say that. I know a few of them get out of line and violate the code of conduct they agreed to follow, but the trip isn't quite the Saturnalian orgy that some make it out to be."

"Well, people in the community are beginning to ask some questions about this trip," he generalized.

"I know how we can make everyone happy—I just thought of it. We'll have you give the girls rabbit tests before and after the trip, and I can make all the kids inflate balloons every night at bed check." That remark ended my interviews with Mr. Knipe.

I defended the senior trip for several reasons. Not the least among these was my friendship and association with the man who had originally organized the project—Frank Lowery. Frank, a veteran of the North African and Italian campaigns of World War II, had been at Worthington since the year preceding my arrival, and we had struck up a close acquaintance right away. He taught the course called "Problems of Democracy," which has since been given the more prosaic label, "American Government." At the time that Knipe and others were busy sabotaging the trip, Frank and I were operating a bookstore as a sideline, and our families frequently spent time together.

It wasn't simply out of loyalty to a friend and business partner that I supported the trip, however. I believed it to be a very worthwhile educational experience for Worthington students, and, feeling so, I participated in it as well. For ten years Lowery and I went East every spring with a "family" ranging in size from ninety to one-hundred-fifty members—the senior classes of 1952-1961. As Frank conceived it, the trip was his "social-studies laboratory," and he did the lion's share of the work in directing the twelfth-grade fund-raising projects which would minimize the costs of the trip for the individual student. Spaghetti dinners, smorgasbords, carnivals—these and other activities regularly found the two of us surrounded by a multitude of laughing, laboring teenagers, many of whom would never otherwise have had the opportunity to take such a trip. Even in the work that preceded the journey, there was a spirit of goodwill, camaraderie, and common interest which, taken by itself, justified the senior trip.

Once in a while minor crises developed at the dinners we served. Once salt somehow got into the sugar bowls and created some consternation among our patrons. Sometimes the home-delivery orders were scrambled or forgotten. The most amusing and alarming incident, though, occurred when one of the boys on the salad-mixing detail lost his class ring somewhere in the culinary delight he was preparing. I spent the rest of the evening expecting someone to wind up with a plateful of molars, but the ring never reappeared.

Frank and I usually took our wives along to help out on the trip. As my wife is a registered nurse, she always took along the school-furnished first-aid kit. It really looked more like a discarded Hopalong Cassidy lunch-bucket which the school nurse had filled with Band-Aids, gauze, tape, an antiseptic solution, etc. A half-dozen or so parents would accompany the seniors, too, and most often they were very cooperative and helpful. Occasionally, though, one of them would add to our worries. Once a woman grew angry and even hysterical because her daughter preferred the company of other students. Another time a husband and wife were at odds with each other from the time we left until our return. In one case, especially, I was glad that a parent did not go. The woman had already announced at home her plan to accompany us when her daughter approached me in 106.

"Mr. Rousculp, I have a slight problem." She was embarrassed and even shaken, I could tell. "My mother wants to go on the trip, and I'm afraid Mr. Lowery will put her name down."

"Well, I know he still needs chaperones. I heard him say so. What's wrong about your mother's going?" I thought perhaps it was just a case of her being upset over some minor matter—young people are often hypersensitive where their parents are concerned.

"There's something that you probably don't know." She was fighting tears now. "My mother is an alcoholic, Mr. Rousculp, and when she's high she tries to make out with any man or boy she's around." She continued with some convincing details, crying intermittently. "I just couldn't bear it if the other kids saw her that way." I tried to reassure her, and as soon as she had left the room I tore down the corridor and up the steps to Frank's classroom. He was sitting there, adding a column of figures.

"Do you have all the parents you need for the trip, Frank?"

"No, we really should have one more."

"Look"—and I mentioned the woman's name—"if she comes in or calls, you'd better say you're all filled up."

He cleared his throat and looked at me questioningly. "What's the matter with her?"

"In the strictest confidence, Frank, she needs two things— prohibition and a chastity belt."

After the first year, the early part of the itinerary for our annual odyssey was fairly well established. Having survived a sleepless all-night train ride, the class would arrive in Washington for a full-day's touring of various government buildings such as the Justice Department, the Bureau of Printing and Engraving, and the National Archives Building. It was the Class of 1953 who first included in their trip the tour of Jamestown and Williamsburg. They were the only class to spend a night in Washington, and the only hotel at which Frank had been able to secure reservations provided for vampires under the mattresses as well as incoming guests of the usual sort.

But it wasn't our complaints alone that alienated the hotel management. While Frank and I took our wives out to find a restaurant, considerable activity was taking place in the hotel. Some of the boys were filling balloons with water and knocking at the doors of other boys' rooms. In this little game whoever opened his door got soaked. Having been particularly gullible and several times the victims of these shenanigans, the occupants of one of the rooms planned a retaliatory stunt. One of them found a fire bucket in the hall and filled it with water. Then, standing on a chair in order to reach the open transom, he waited for another knock on the door and an opportunity to avenge his earlier indignities. Soon there came a light tapping, the bucket was lifted and tilted, the contents poured forth, and from the corridor came sounds of splashing and horrified surprise.

When Frank and I returned to the hotel, there at the desk was the house detective, still dripping wet and foaming at the mouth. From his right hand was dangling the student-body president, whose expression was full of the grief that mice and men experience. I don't know what Frank did to comfort the detective and the manager, but it was the last time our seniors stayed at that hotel.

In subsequent years Frank decided to divide the Washington tours into two phases, between which the Virginia visit would take place. In this way, the second and third nights of the trip would find us on board ship. At the end of the first day in Washington, three to five buses would take all of us over to the pier in Baltimore (or in Washington, before the dock there was closed), and we would embark on the *District of Columbia*, the *City of Richmond*, or another of the Old Bay Line steamers. As a class advisor and chaperone—I'm better suited to the advisory role than to the duenna bit—I found this part of the trip the most enjoyable and at the same time the most hazardous. If we lost one of our charges in Washington or New York, we had a good chance of recovering him. If one of them fell into Chesapeake Bay in the middle of the night and were pulled under the old steamer, the gulls and lobsters would find all sorts of goodies the next morning.

Frank tried always to alert everyone to the dangers involved in hanging out or crawling through their stateroom windows and especially of trying to walk along the side of the ship on the very narrow rail that the ship's crew used for painting and other maintenance purposes. The only instance in which I ever heard my friend use invective in the presence of students happened one year shortly after we had boarded the ship. Hearing laughter outside, Frank slid open the louvered window to take a look. From my bathroom I recognized his shouting: "Garth, you ass! I told you to stay off that damned rail!" Thus another problem in democracy was solved.

Once the staterooms (most of them about 8′ by 12′ divided by three seniors) had been assigned, Frank and I would shave and shower, worrying about someone's luggage that hadn't shown up at the dock or feeling concern about some of the other school groups on board. There were usually a few unsavory characters, too, among the adult passengers—small-time gamblers, deck-walking drabs, and drunks—as well as the usual young married couples, weekend commuters, and adult tourists. One year it looked very much as if I were going to have to spank a young sailor who had apparently spent some time in the cocktail lounge below decks. He had developed an unmistakable passion for one of our girls. She had made the mistake of smiling somewhat too invitingly, and now she was thoroughly frightened by his attentions.

The Old Bay Line served excellent dinners, generally, and afterwards the ship's hostess supervised games, student talent shows, and other entertainment. The classes usually slept soundly that first night on the steamer.

The next morning, the ship would begin serving breakfast at six, and we would crowd outside to see the fleet units at Hampton Roads and watch as the ship pulled into Newport News or Norfolk. Then the seniors, leaving their luggage on board, carrying cameras, and juggling last-minute pieces of jellied toast and souvenirs, would disembark and take buses to the Mariner's Museum. Here, I would annually lose track of myself, my wife, the Lowerys, and the seniors. There is a particular ship model— Nelson's *Victory*, done in ivory and brass—which always calls forth the latent Raffles in my nature. Because of me our bus was always behind schedule when it left for Jamestown.

No one should visit the old church ruin at Jamestown before reading "America's First Great Lady," an account in Donald Culross Peattie's *Journey into America*. Peattie alone prepares the sightseer to sense the ghosts that inhabit that patch of ground. Yearly I had to be dragged bodily from that place and from a display in the Old World Pavilion near the reconstructed fort—the picture of the young Walter Raleigh and his half-brother Hum-

216

phrey Gilbert, who sit in wide-eyed fascination before an old sailor spinning a yarn of adventure.

On the way to Williamsburg, Frank would always enjoy telling the students that they would have pickled pigs' feet for lunch, and every time he would appear dismayed at the audible wave of nausea which swept the bus. Afterwards, when the seniors sat down to baked stuffed pork chops in the Williamsburg Inn, I would see Frank grin at the kids and the kids smile back at him. I could glimpse in those swift exchanges the kind of satisfaction that every teacher wants to experience. The affection he felt for the young was warmly manifest in the way he worked and planned for them, and they knew it. They returned his affection, in spite of all the difficult tests in POD with which he had plagued them through the year.

In Williamsburg the senior classes would watch a movie at the information center; tour the governor's palace, the old capitol, and the powderhouse; take pictures of one another in the stocks outside the reconstructed jail; and crowd around to watch the twentieth-century version of an eighteenth-century blacksmith make horseshoes. Wherever possible, Frank would relate these experiences to classroom materials previously handled in Worthington. Once in a while I could throw in a pitch for literature, too.

When the group returned to the steamer that night, they were always full of life, and I customarily felt a trifle apprehensive during our passage back up the Bay. I believe that through ten years of senior trips I saw every possible prank, every variety of rascality ever invented by the juvenile mind. Of course, there was some conformity along with individual scampishness. Every class seemed to have its own trademark: just as the Class of '53 played with water balloons, '54 used squirt guns, '55 specialized in all-night gambling, '56 covered the lifeboats and the night duty officer with shaving cream, '57 set off firecrackers and nearly gave an elderly lady a severe case of war nerves, '58. . . .

Most of this horseplay was the product of sheer exuberance, but Frank and I took steps, nevertheless, to discourage such goings-on, especially when they worked an imposition upon other passengers. In Washington the next day, Frank and I would put the miscreants through an earthly purgatory by making them open their light-tortured eyes and get off the buses to tour such places as the Capitol, the Supreme Court Building, and the Smithsonian.

By the time they had boarded the train for New York, the all-night-funsters found their seats on the day coaches as accommodating as their little beds back in Worthington. Needless to say, Frank and I were even more exhausted and usually slept, too.

Ordinarily, I would wake to the cry "There's the Statue of Liberty!" or "I can see the skyline!" Like most people, our seniors were excited by the prospect of New York City, and most of them enjoyed their stay in the town thoroughly. Birdland, Greenwich Village, Broadway, Mama Leone's, the Latin Quarter, Times Square—these were magic words to young suburbanites from Ohio. They toured the United Nations, inspected Manhattan by bus, took the Circle Line ride around the island, and saw the current hit shows from *The King and I* to *My Fair Lady*.

Some few did not enjoy New York as much as their comrades. Half an hour before we got to Gotham one year, a young man came to me in a highly agitated frame of mind. "You've got to do something," he said in a quavering voice. "I wasn't going to come on this trip, but my mother talked me into it. I thought I could go through with it, but now I know I can't."

"I don't understand, George. I thought you were enjoying yourself."

"I just can't take high places. I've always been that way. Won't there be any rooms on some of the lower floors of the hotel?" He looked to me as if he were about to go to pieces.

"Well, I'm sure Mr. Lowery can make some arrangement with the hotel manager."

"Will you talk to Mr. Lowery about it?"

"Sure," I agreed. George sighed deeply and lowered his shoulders in obvious relief.

I had never been around a person with an extreme case of acrophobia, but I could imagine the boy's fear. Sometimes, I had been told, such people were seized by paroxysms of dread at the slightest height which could produce a psychosomatic paralysis or even a compulsion to leap. I knew George should be given special accommodations, but somehow in all the confusion of our arrival at the Commodore I forgot to talk to Frank about him.

My wife was unpacking our luggage, and I was lathering my face when the phone rang. Expecting it to be Frank, I stepped from the bathroom to take the call. At first I thought I had a bad connection on the line.

"Hello," I repeated. From the other end, came the vague sounds of someone whispering. Finally, I made out my name. "Yes, this is Mr. Rousculp."

"This-s-s is-s-s G-g-george. P-please—come—get —m-me." With horror I realized what had happened. I had let him down—or let him *up*—as the case probably was.

"Where are you, George?" I didn't have my copy of the room lists handy.

"I-I'm in 2-2-2-2-2-1-2," he choked. It may have seemed to George that he was in orbit, but I guessed that he meant Room 2212.

I wiped the lather from my face and got up to the twenty-second floor as quickly as I could. When I entered the room, the door to which was cocked open with a wastebasket, I found him half-huddled between a bed and a night table with his back to the wall—as far away from the window as he could get. I finally talked him onto the elevator, though it took much persuasion. On the ride to the lobby he gripped my arm until my fingers were numb. Once there, I deposited George in a chair and called Frank. He in turn spoke to the manager. Before the other boys in George's room had got their keys, their room was changed and they never knew why. George had gone up alone without realizing that the first two digits on his key indicated the floor level.

When I got back to him, he was sitting where he could watch the people walking outside the front hotel entrance.

"I'm sure sorry, George, but you're all set now," I told him. "Your new room is 419, and I'll see that your bag is brought down." He gasped and stared at me.

"Clear up on the fourth floor?" he breathed. Despite our later efforts, George did not enjoy himself in New York City.

In only a single instance did a large number of the seniors not fully enjoy their New York stay. A tragic event occurred while we were there in 1953. Frank and I learned that the mother of one of our students had committed suicide back in Worthington. The family asked that the boy not be informed, but that he be allowed to enjoy himself on the remaining day in New York. An uncle would meet him at the station when our train pulled into Columbus. We tried to keep the information from spreading, but through several telegrams from home a number of students heard the unhappy news. The boy was very well liked by his classmates and teachers, and, for those of us who knew about the death, the thought of the homecoming in store for him was very nearly unbearable.

A second tragedy of less impact upon us, but with related irony, happened as our New York Central train sped toward Columbus. We were just inside Ohio and passing a train going the opposite direction. When both trains slowed and stopped for no ostensible reason, some of the group were curious. Our coaches were close to the observation car, and I went with several of the students to see whether we could determine the cause of the unslated stop. We discovered that, moments before, an elderly woman had been struck by the other train as she walked along the tracks and that her badly mangled body was being removed. There was some question as to whether she might have been a suicide. I was standing beside the boy who would soon learn that his mother was dead. Try as I might, I couldn't forbear looking at his face. He was peering sympathetically toward the tracks where the accident victim was being covered, and I heard him exclaim to a friend, "Poor woman! Probably someone's mother." I had to turn my face and get back to my seat in the day coach.

Without a doubt, the main factor that ended the trips was the occasional violation of the senior Code of Conduct. Before the first trip, school officials urged Frank to have the class formulate a set of rules to govern their behavior. From the beginning, however, it was apparent that the Board of Education would never sanction a trip unless the class could agree that no drinking would be permitted, that smoking would be regulated, and that sexual promiscuity would be guarded against by room restrictions and curfews. In other words, the great majority of seniors found it necessary to agree to a code of behavior which would govern dissenters as well. It is not surprising, then, that there were usually a few young people who could not resist breaking the "law," just as adult society numbers its own civil and criminal offenders.

For the most part, the seniors appreciated the privilege of the trip and Frank's exertions in their behalf, and the great majority tried to follow the rules. Smoking was definitely prevented wherever, as on the tours, our students could be identified as part of a school group. The only known offenders of the curfew rule were required to sit in the hotel lobby for a specified portion of their free time. Only twice did Frank and I have unquestionable evidence of drinking. The first time, a student trial, presided over by the class officers, was held in the East Meeting Room of the Commodore, and the chaperones (among whom Frank and I were outvoted) meted out a perhaps too-light punishment to a young man who would soon face far more serious charges before a court in Ohio. In the second instance, two nights before the return to Worthington, the violator was so sick that Frank and I determined not to send him home on a train by himself.

Precautions were always taken to prevent young couples from being alone in hotel rooms, and the trip chaperones never had indisputable evidence of sexual activity apart from some advanced necking. Such evidence is not easily come by. This is a matter, after all, in which society at any level has difficulty in exercising control. I have never once doubted that, where there's a will—well, some young people combine precocity and planning, however artless the result. At the conclusion of every trip, Frank was always hopeful that these youngsters whose insecurity and desire for attention made them brag about what "we got away with" would not bring a halt to the trips. My own power of negative thinking saved me from such optimism.

The senior trip held still other minutes of frustration and anxiety for Frank and me—the girl who dropped her purse over the side of the Circle Line yacht, the young Negro who was deeply hurt by a segregated restaurant in 1952, the teenager who contracted scarlet fever, the boy who took apart a pay radio to get it to play without quarters but who couldn't reassemble it, and other problems kept us well supplied with emergencies. Yet the trip was, without question, one of the finest educational ventures that Worthington High ever undertook for its youngsters. It was, in truth, more than a social-studies laboratory—it was really a laboratory for life. It removed hundreds of young men and women briefly from the fawning, protective arms of their parents and brought them a little closer to the realities of this world. It widened their understanding of our country, its government and its society. They saw its beginnings at Jamestown and Williamsburg, its modern governmental concepts and functions at Washington, and its hub of contemporary culture and commerce in New York.

As in everything else he does, Frank Lowery put all of the sincerity and devotion inherent in his nature into that trip. When transportation problems, class sizes, and community critics like Knipe began to create insuperable difficulties, it was only with the greatest reluctance that he surrendered his "classroom on wheels." I shared in his loss. The trip, like the commencement plays, had forged an *esprit de corps*, a class spirit which contributed significantly to the school spirit at Worthington.

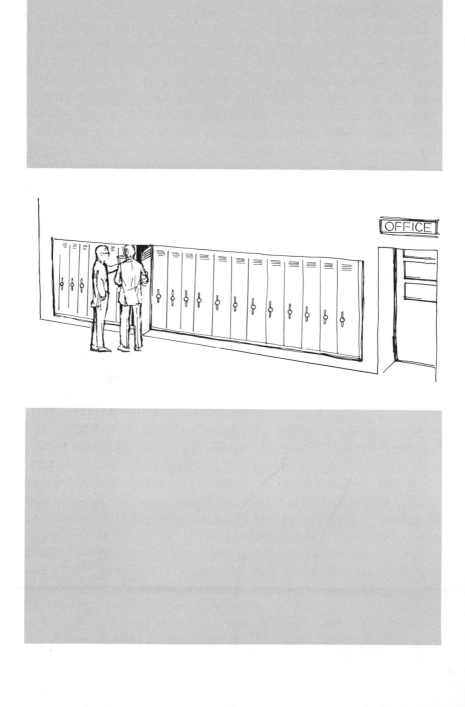

Martin McGrath had entered the high-school principal's office that Monday morning before I arrived, and Bill Lane was greeting him as I walked in. Lane motioned the two of us away from the counter and into his private office a dozen steps away.

"Sit down," he invited, and McGrath and I took chairs. "Greg should be with us in a few minutes." Greg was McGrath's son and the chief subject of this conference. I sat with curiously mixed feelings. I had an ugly, disagreeable task to perform—yet it was one that I had braced myself to do mercilessly. Lane didn't enjoy the prospect of this confrontation, either. He and I both knew that the next half hour would find his office charged with emotion. Neither of us had had an enjoyable weekend, knowing that we had this business to face when we came back. But it had to be done.

The Purloined Papers

Lane began to pace, then stepped to the door to see whether there was any sign of Greg, and excused himself to check briefly on what could be delaying the boy. I hoped Bill wouldn't be too long, for there was really nothing that I could say to McGrath. I had met the man only once before. He had come by 106 to see me when I had had his boy in a freshman-English section. The father's main reason for seeing me had been his son's grades—B's and C's. The man had wanted to know why Greg was not doing A work, though he hadn't come right out with the question. I had been expecting him and had given him a full summary of the boy's work with me. I had felt that the son's performance could and would improve and had told McGrath so. The father had left with a reasonably clear notion of our English program and of my regard for Greg's progress.

Here in Lane's office, the man looked much older. I was surprised to find that his sandy hair had much more gray in it, that there were new creases around the eyes. Sometimes an English teacher, preoccupied with the strains of many eighteen-hour days, forgets about the wear and tear that some executives in the world outside the school experience. McGrath was an extraordinary success in the industrial world. His annual salary amounted to at least five or six times my own, but the company he served was notorious for the nervous breakdowns among its employees at all levels. McGrath was a fine-looking, immaculately dressed figure of a man, but some of the pressure of his work showed through his posture of self-assuredness.

His son—recognized for his leadership in state student organizations and known nationally for his athletic prowess—was the joy of McGrath's personal life. In a few short minutes Lane and I would have to reduce the two of them to the stratum of commonplace father and son. No, there wasn't much I could talk about as McGrath and I sat waiting. I'm no good at small talk with a man I'm about to hurt. Meanwhile, time was a cripple.

As the seconds hobbled decrepitly across the face of my watch, I considered the succession of events that had led inexorably to this early-morning ordeal. The papers had disappeared on Tuesday, April 20. I had been fighting a cold that week and had been out of school two days. My replacement had followed my instructions carefully. When I returned on Thursday, I found her note to me:

Tues.

Dear Mr. Rousculp,

    The classes were all well behaved and co-operative. <u>However</u>, the papers that were handed in in the second period disappeared while I was at lunch and on hall duty. They were on the desk when I left. The only four that are here are the four that came in late—after lunch. I don't know what to do or where to look and I feel very badly about the papers. Maybe they will turn up. I surely hope so.

    I hope that you are feeling better.

Jean Phillips.

Wed.

We had some very interesting discussion on Hardy's works today.   The
papers did not turn up.

                    J. P.

After reading this report, I was not "feeling better." I was more in the mood to go home and crawl back into bed or possibly under the bed. The situation put me into quite a squeeze. First of all, I must tell the second-period class that, except for a handful of themes, a set of papers had somehow got away from the room. Naturally, I put off informing them until I had virtually torn the room apart to be certain the substitute hadn't accidentally mislaid them. She had a reputation for dependability, but I supposed that, like me, she might have forgetful moments.

My search was fruitless. The papers were gone. After explaining to the class, I had to determine what to do about six-weeks grades, soon to be turned into the office. As I already had a number of marks in my gradebook, I told the group that if they wished to do their papers a second time, I would treat them as additional work in averaging grades, but that I would not require them to do the work over.

I was far from satisfied, though. Some of the students had looked disappointed over the missing papers and even somewhat unhappy with me. Moreover, I am the sort of person who cannot tolerate losing things. When I misplace something myself, I usually rationalize my error, preferring most often to blame it on my wife, my daughter, my next-door neighbor, or flying saucers from outer space. I looked over the roster of my second-period section. The people in that class were hard-working youngsters, but some of them were so competitive and so much under pressure as to be desperate on occasion. Could it possibly be that one of them had failed to do the assignment and had tried to cover by making off with the whole batch of compositions? I didn't want to think so because I had had this same group for two years and trusted them as much as my "negative thinking" would permit. Still, I felt responsible for those papers, and I couldn't rest until I had found them.

Then I remembered something. Once before, a paper had turned up missing in that section—Greg's. Had I ever really received it? I had no way of proving that I hadn't misplaced it, and the boy had firmly declared that he had turned it in. In that instance I had assumed the blame and had averaged Greg's grades without that one mark. I trusted the boy entirely. Besides, I had worked closely with him in a play production. Surely he would not have taken a set of papers, but would have come to me. Of course, out of fairness to the others, I would very likely have had to lower the grade on a late paper. Why, though, should he be late in turning in a paper? Perhaps the time he was spending in athletics and in the Thespian spring production had forced him into a corner.

But when could he have done it? The answer was obvious—he was a hall monitor during the lunch period when the substitute was out of the room, and she had had no key with which to lock the door. His post was only about seventy feet away. He could have—

I went back over the roster. Maybe someone else—perhaps it was—no use, there was only one clear suspect with a possible motive and a perfect opportunity. But I still could not believe his guilt. I began to watch him surreptitiously in the classroom and the hall. I studied his eyes when we spoke. Everything in his manner was by this time suggesting culpability.

Intellectually keen, notably sensitive and creative, physically robust and handsome—this boy was a gifted young man in many respects. His father and his sister were proud of him, but Greg believed that his mother was hypercritical and determined that her son should be an outstanding athlete and scholar and should not waste his time on such fripperies as dramatics.

On the other hand, Greg lacked a certain warmth, a capacity to sympathize with others. Some of this deficiency may have grown out of the accelerated English class in which he had competed for six years. Part of his failure to concern himself for others may have issued from his feeling that he had to defend himself from his mother's dissatisfaction with him. One thing was certain—he was capable at times of behaving like an egotistical ass.

I could overlook this last feature in Greg because it so frequently accompanies the final stages of adolescence. Chances are, it was a defense mechanism or face-saving device. If it were not, I knew that life would soon modify his egocentric tendencies—unless he was sick, that is. Sometimes there is a point at which ego surpasses exaggerated vanity and narcissism and begins to feel that its natural superiority places it above the rules that govern others. Mine had been that sort of ego at Greg's age, and I had been guilty of enormities less forgivable and more destructive than the theft of a set of papers. There are too many Raskolnikovs in the world.

I had seen no symptom of the extreme ego in Greg, however—not until May 12, that is. Then something happened that settled the issue for me. In the absence of Ralph Nusken, Greg's American-government teacher, the boy appeared in class wearing a suit and pretending to be a student teacher—a "Mr. Nutter"—who was at present working with Nusken. The substitute teacher sent from the office was completely taken in by the masquerade, for Greg's physical maturity, poise, and knowledge of the assignment were quite convincing. Instead of checking with the office, the substitute merely turned the class over to the boy. Not only did Greg do a creditable job of teaching—of course, the class was delighted to cooperate with the joke—but he also turned out some effective mimicry of Nusken's mannerisms.

For some of the high-school faculty, Greg's act, when it became known, smacked of cleverness and ingenuity entirely. One of the younger teachers, I discovered subsequently, had even loaned (innocently, I hope) the jacket which Greg had worn for his act. Some saw it as no more than an amusing interlude. Even Nusken, wishing not to appear a spoilsport, was inclined to be forgiving. For me, however, the incident did not constitute mere wit and deviltry—it reflected the sort of supreme self-confidence that I had never before witnessed in Greg. As a matter of fact, I was disturbed by the thought that perhaps for several weeks now I had been playing "patsy" for Greg. I had liked the boy and had worked hard to prepare him for college. The more I thought of his impersonation, the more I wondered whether teachers in general had become a joke to him. Not only do I believe in my profession and revere it, but I do not like the role of carpet. There is a certain vindictiveness in me that comes straight from the spleen, but I tried to shake off my anger. It was not easy to do so. For worst of all, I knew now, even without looking, where I would very likely find the missing papers.

Two days later I wrote the following letter:

Mr. Earl W. Lane, Principal,
Worthington High School,
Worthington, Ohio.

Dear Sir:

    You will remember that I reported to you several weeks ago that a set of compositions had been stolen from my desk. These papers had just

been collected by the substitute teacher who
relieved me during my illness. According to her
statement, the papers disappeared during the
time she was at lunch--the first half of the
fourth period. The room had, during those minutes, been unlocked. I do not at all enjoy
informing you at this time that I have what I
feel is quite sound evidence implicating one of
our seniors. With Mr. Taylor to serve as a
witness, I opened and inspected a locker at
approximately 7:00 this morning and confirmed the
suspicion which had led me to take such action.
The missing set of papers was there, intact,
beneath a magazine and various other articles at
the bottom of the locker. The student assigned
to that locker--234 UHMB--is Greg McGrath, a
member of the class submitting the set of papers.
Among the papers there is none written by him.

After explaining the logic behind my suspicions, I concluded
my letter with these comments:

I do not feel any jubilation in finding this
evidence because there is much about this young
man that I had come to like. I dislike supposing that he has come to subscribe to the philosophy now in vogue that one must win by whatever
means necessary, even by cheating. It is obvious, however, that the school cannot do its
job by allowing students to get away with this
sort of thing. As Greg's teacher, I would not
be doing my job if I were to allow him to convince himself that he has put something over on
me, and done so because he has had my affection
and trust. As a matter of fact, I feel deeply
hurt that a student in whom I have heretofore
maintained faith and in whom I have taken pride--
he was one of my cast in the senior play, for
example--should violate that faith and relationship. I have apparently done a poor job of
teaching in this instance.

    I do not know what action to recommend to
you in Greg's case. I only know that this is
not innocuous, "fun" behavior, but, rather, out-
right theft, ostensibly motivated by self-
interest and perpetrated to the great disadvantage of others. This young man may well be ill;
he may be merely a product of our sick society
--whatever his problem, it is to his best interests that we take action that will be meaningful
as well as just.

228

I will be happy to confer at any time with
you on this subject.

Cordially yours,

Charles G. Rousculp
English Department

I had given this letter to Lane on Friday. Now, sitting in the office with Greg's father, I felt worse than ever. I don't like cutting down innocent people. What compounded my sympathy for the father was that he had just recently been contacted by Lane on the matter of Greg's impersonation and had probably begun to relax somewhat in the wake of that business. Now he had been called to the school over some new difficulty. By this time he must surely have sensed the tension in me.

Had Greg's mother been there, I would have felt compassion for her, too. No doubt what Greg often had taken to be belittling comments on her part had only sprung from what she thought was a sincere effort to help him. It is too easy and too much in style to blame parents for all the misdeeds of their young. There is little question, of course, that adults contribute to their children's problems. Yet a high-school senior is not free of responsibility for his acts, especially when he has been given unusual opportunities. Greg's parents loved him and, if they made mistakes as all other parents do, they had, I'm sure, the best intentions always. Yes, I would say that parenthood is a great equalizer—no matter what our station in life happens to be, our young can bring us tears. I would have been sorry for Greg's mother, though it is in me to be particularly moved by father-son relationships.

There was a look of idolatry in McGrath's eyes when Greg came in with Lane and took a seat. Bill began the meeting by reading my letter. At the end of the first paragraph, I felt the spine and heart go out of the father. He put one hand to his forehead, and I saw the look of shock on his face. He was only about ten years older than I, but I knew that sorry kaleidoscope of years through which he peered. It would have been impossible for Bill and me to hurt him more grievously.

Meanwhile, Greg was sitting stonily under that hail of words. He sat studying the floor all the time the letter was being read. Finally Bill finished, and I heard the older McGrath breathe a long sigh. He looked out the window unseeingly, and there was capitulation with life—an unconditional acceptance—written all over his visage. My indictment of his son could never, of course, lessen Martin's love for Greg, but my letter had brought, perhaps, a searing reminder to the father—that his son was, after all, of the line of Adam and thrall to the human frailties that beset us all, young and old alike. Afterwards I was not at all surprised to learn that McGrath drove to a Columbus high school where Greg was to speak later that day, in order to comfort and to reassure the boy, to tell him that in our guilts there lie the seeds of wisdom if we will have it so.

"Well, Greg," Bill put the question, "what's the story here?" Greg was shaken, it was clear, but he wasn't quite ready to give way. No doubt the full realization of what he had done to his family and himself was just now saturating his consciousness. Perhaps he half-believed his feeble denial. He looked across to me appealingly.

"Mr. Rousculp, I didn't take those papers. Honestly, I don't know how they got in my locker."

Lane looked from the boy to me, then to McGrath, who had, himself, begun to stare at the tile on the floor. Bill's next glance toward me indicated that I had the initiative, and I grabbed at it. I had hoped the boy would break right away and shorten our inquisition. For a minute I was angry, though I wrestled with my voice. "Greg, you used a word—*honestly*—and that's the way I want you to talk."

"But, Mr. Rousculp—"

"Greg," I said, and now my voice was a low, hard tone he had never heard from me before, "I want the truth from you. And if you want to graduate from this high school, you'd better talk straight. A missing set of papers is no joke to me. I've played it straight with you and I've worked hard for you. But I take my work seriously, and I'm not about to play tic-tac-toe with anybody on the subject. I don't apologize to anyone for my profession and I don't intend to start. The day I become a fall guy for my students is the day I get out." I turned to Bill. "Mr. Lane, under the circumstances, unless Greg admits he took those papers, I don't intend to certify a passing grade for him in English."

Lane waited and so did I for the boy to wilt. Greg was staring at me in disbelief. Then, for the first time, the smallest and most painful voice of all broke the silence: "Greg, he means it. You'd better tell the truth now if you've ever told it—while you still have some friends left."

McGrath did not look at his son as he spoke, but Greg must have seen on his father's face and heard in that voice the stoicism and grief registered there. He buried his face in his hands and half screamed, "All right! I did it! I did it!"

The hardness went out of me then. I could have wept for the boy and his father. I glanced at Lane again, and he was shaking his head slowly, on his mouth a smile, not of victory but of irony and sympathy. He was probably wondering, too, how soon another such conference would be rapping on his door.

My work was over. There would, of course, be the necessity of spelling out my position on Greg's punishment—in such cases, it is always desirable that a principal not operate unilaterally. When Bill asked me what I felt would satisfy my course requirements, I indicated what I would want from Greg. Then I rose. The boy's face was still hidden in the palms of his hands. I touched McGrath's shoulder. When he looked up, I wished that he hadn't. "I'm sorry," I said, "but I had to do it—as much for Greg as for anyone." He merely nodded. Someone had turned out the light in his eyes.

On May 20, three days after that conference, I received from the office a copy of the letter Lane sent the McGraths:

```
Mr. Martin McGrath,
5966 Columbia Avenue,
Worthington, Ohio

Dear Mr. McGrath:

I wish to summarize our discussions and agree-
ments at the conference held on May 17 regarding
your son, Greg.  The purpose of the conference
was to discuss Greg's recent misbehavior and to
decide the most meaningful and effective pun-
ishment.

  I. MAJOR PROBLEM

    A. Situation

       Mr. Rousculp submitted, in writing, evi-
       dence and charged Greg with stealing a
       set of themes from his room during his
       absence on April 20.  This theft took
       place during the fourth period, when the
```

room was unlocked and the substitute was at lunch.

Greg admitted that he had not written a theme due on the 20th, and that he took the entire set of themes in order to avoid receiving an "F." The reason given for his action was the lack of time to write the theme, due to the pressures of the Thespian play and the State Student Council meeting.

B. Action Taken

It was agreed that the following action would be taken:

1. Greg's grade for the fifth six-week period (the period in which the theme was due) will be an automatic "F."

2. In order to receive credit for English IV, Greg must write the theme and the autobiography (which he maintained had been turned in but which Mr. Rousculp could not find). It was suggested that Greg do some real soul-searching in the writing of his autobiography. Both writings are to be submitted to Mr. Rousculp by June 1.

II. OTHER PROBLEMS REVIEWED

A. Physics Class

Greg's misbehavior and exclusion from physics with three other students was discussed. Greg disobeyed Mr. Hill's instruction to report to study hall in Room 203 upon exclusion and arranged to go to the biology prep room. Mr. Hill suspended Greg from physics for two additional days for failure to comply with his instructions.

B. Impersonation of Student Teacher on Wednesday, May 12

Greg assumed the role of "Mr. Nutter," a student teacher, and took over Mr. Nusken's class during the sixth period. Greg agreed that his actions were disrespectful to the substitute and indirectly to Mr. Nusken. Greg and the class were instructed that such behavior was not

condoned and would not be tolerated. He
was given a strong reprimand, assigned
some after-school duties, and you were
informed of the incident for follow-up
action at home.

Due to his involvement in the above situations,
the honor of being one of three science students representing Worthington High School at
the "Project: Honoring the Science Scholar"
this weekend has been denied him. Greg was instructed to make amends to all parties offended
by his misbehavior. He was also dismissed as
a hall-monitor.

I deemed the disciplinary actions taken in each
situation meaningful, just, and in Greg's best
interest. I hope that further action will be
unnecessary.

If you have questions regarding this summary,
please call me at your convenience.

Sincerely yours,

Earl W. Lane
Principal

Privately, I told the boy that, if I were he, I would apologize to
the other members of the class. Whether he did so, I do not know.
I also indicated to him that I did not intend to discuss with anyone
the papers and who had taken them. I kept my word, so well that
I never knew whether the members of that class were aware of
the whole story.

The autobiography that he turned over to me was one of the
most beautifully written and honest documents I have had from
a student. He *did* engage in some soul-searching, and I believe
that he learned some humility in the effort. Before he graduated,
Greg and I had two very long talks, once in my home and once in
the doorway of 106. I may be wrong, but I think that he will carry
some of the chalk dust in 106 the rest of his life.

Some may feel that the school and I were "soft" in Greg's case.
I cannot think so. Later I told a girl that I expected never to forget
Greg and to hear very great things about him some day. Afterwards, she let me read a portion of a letter that he had written
to her.

Glad to hear about the success of your senior class play. Did Mr. Rousculp direct it? Were you makeup chairman? ....You said that I must have made some "life-long impression" on Mr. Rousculp. You're quite correct — only the impression was that of sheer disappointment. You see, I purloined (I guess that's a polite way to say "stole") a set of essays from his desk because I had not completed mine and could not afford (so I thought) a failing mark. He found out because, not being a notorious or experienced crook, I just stashed them in my locker and never bothered to get rid of them — I guess I wouldn't make a very good robber! (I hope) Anyway, he found them in my locker. Wow! Was that ever a fun week....I really doubt that he has quite as good an opinion of me as you say he does. I wish it were so, but I doubt it. In fact, one of my ambitions is to try to prove to him that I'm not really that sort of guy — or if I was that his intervention in my life has caused me to change....

Greg left his mark upon Room 106 like all the others. I remember best his good qualities which made this one misdeed a particularly trying experience for me. No, Greg, I do not keep a tarnished image of you. My own life has been such that I must necessarily make forgiveness, compassion, and hope my teaching creed.

234

Though we beat a path to the door of the man with the improved mousetrap, sooner or later we discover that someone still has to dispose of the dead mouse. While educators descend en masse upon the shiny new school technique or curricular gimmick, classroom teachers must inevitably deal with the human being trapped by trial and experiment. In the affairs of men there is something that operates rather like Newton's third law of motion—for every action there is an opposite, if not always equal, reaction. Every step that we call progress seems to be accompanied by certain losses. The positive and the negative are bound together in education as in all things.

It was nearly four o'clock, I noted, when I left the typing room and pointed my class-weary 170 pounds toward the main corridor. The halls were almost deserted at that hour. The last classes had

The Kids from B.R.9.G.H.T.

been dismissed, as usual, at 3:05, and on a Friday afternoon the exodus by students and faculty alike is awesome in its suddenness. Only a few stragglers remained to produce distant shufflings and laughter and the far-off slamming of locker doors.

As I made the turn toward my classroom, I saw that someone was standing near the door. Supposing that I had forgotten an appointment or that someone was waiting for me out of some urgent reason, I quickened my pace. Though the lights were out in the hall of the main building, I soon recognized the loiterer as one of my students. "Joan? Waiting for me?"

She was a fairly tall girl, a very pretty person except for her mouth, which never smiled convincingly. Joan was one of the most intense and talented youngsters ever to sit in Room 106. She lived on the very fringe of the school district with parents who were approaching their sixties. In her neighborhood, there were few teenagers whose interests compared with hers in any significant way. Her parents' only other child had graduated fourteen years before Joan became a high-school senior. The girl was fairly active in music organizations, but she spent the great bulk of her out-of-school time alone except for the company of books. Now she stood immobile, her eyes fixed unseeingly upon the opposite wall, her back pressed to the tile between the door of 106 and a row of louvered, dark green lockers. Her whole posture and expression gave me the eerie feeling that she had backed away from something that threatened to devour or destroy her.

"Joan?" I spoke to her again for she had not responded. "Something the matter?" She turned very slowly toward me as if she were waking from some nightmare that still clung jealously to her consciousness.

"Yes," she said in the fashion that one might use to answer the telephone at two in the morning. Then she looked at me with recognition and flushed with embarrassment. "Oh, Mr. Rousculp. No, nothing's the matter. I—I wasn't waiting for you. I was just—just thinking."

"You certainly picked a good spot for it. No one to bother you here except us old school fixtures," I remarked. My self-satire did not amuse her, and I turned my head slightly to flash a might-as-well-tell-me look at her. "Not very happy thoughts, were they?"

"Mmmmnno," she conceded, "but I was just being foolish."

"Being foolish doesn't come easy to you. Now just how were you managing that?"

She juggled the books she held and moved partly away from the wall. "Just thinking about things I have to do."

"Like the paper on Greek drama I assigned?"

"That's one thing, yes, but I have a project in American government, some music to learn, a meeting that I've got to—" She started talking a mile a minute, and I halfway expected her to start to cry.

"You've never really turned in a late paper to me, have you, Joan?"

"No, I haven't."

"All right, just for once let's break the pattern. Take a couple of extra days, compliments of the teacher." She looked at me in surprise. It's a rare event—a reprieve from me.

"But that wouldn't be fair. I couldn't do that."

238

"Look, Joan, it's plain to me that you've worked yourself into a corner temporarily. There's probably not another student in that class who hasn't begged off at some time or other by being sick, and I don't think you're feeling your best right now. What if I tell you that I won't accept your paper on the due date?" I looked at the hall clock. "What'd you do? Miss your bus?"

"Oh, no. I've got to go to the town library."

"There's a game tonight. Don't tell me you're not going."

"I'm not."

"Well, at least you'll make the dance tomorrow night." I spoke in my best matter-of-fact tone, because I wanted her to think that I made such an assumption about her. In reality, I was sure she would never be at the dance.

"No, I'm afraid I have to stay home and do my—"

"Hey, aren't you afraid the young man in your life will be a little put out with you?" Again I gauged my comment according to what I thought she would like me to believe. I was sorry as soon as she responded, for she had no pretenses left.

"What young man? Mr. Rousculp, I've had one date this year, and that was a complete farce from beginning to end."

"Are you trying to ruin my faith in the young American male?" My jests were going over like lead balloons. She was looking at the floor now, lining up her flat-heeled slipper with a crack in the terrazzo. "Okay, so you're not going to the dance. Why don't you make an exception of this weekend and relax a little?"

"It's no use. I can't," she said, shaking her head. There was real back-to-the-wall desperation in her voice.

"What do you plan to do on Saturday and Sunday?" I asked. She gave me a full job-by-job description of the gloomy prospect. Worst of all, she called it her typical weekend—unbroken by anything that sounded at all like fun. After an unsuccessful effort on my part to suggest alternatives, she left for the library to begin her homework with a two-hour stint of research.

Joan graduated in 1965, and I doubt that, apart from her work in *Dear Ruth* and *Camelot*, she will take very many happy memories of high school with her. And I am one of the "heavies" in the story of her stay at Worthington High. She was one of the students that some of my colleagues and I have helped make miserable in an educational development called "advanced," "accelerated," and "enriched" classes. These are currently among the better academic "mousetraps" on the national scene.

I was reminded of Joan and her classmates as I read a journalist's commentary about such advanced groups. There are only a few editorial writers and columnists whom I read faithfully—Jim Bishop, Walter Lippman, and a half-dozen others. Among these, I especially enjoy one woman's remarks, those of *Life*'s "Feminine Eye," Shana Alexander. She is a keenly perceptive social critic whose views are always stimulating. Although I most often find myself in agreement with her, there have been a few instances in which we have philosophically parted company. In a piece called "Neglected Kids—the Bright Ones," she constructs an argument in support of special education for "gifted" children which deserves much applause but which also demands a closer look at the question than Shana had time and space for.

Briefly, her commentary was prompted by her visit to a private school in which the enrollment is made up exclusively of youthful "geniuses." After complaining eloquently of the difficulty public schools have in obtaining funds for such classrooms of high-IQ youngsters, she laments the truth that "excellence makes people nervous," insists that such grouping is not detrimental to either the gifted or the run-of-the-mill student, and argues that the especially bright children are cheated when they are deprived of the mental stimulation and keen competition of others like them. "As to the bugaboo about 'setting children apart socially,' it seems worth recalling that the primary purpose of school is learning," says Miss Alexander. "Socializing," she declares, "can take place at home, on the block, in the neighborhood." The piece ends with a description of the exciting goings-on in a class of supercharged five-year-olds demonstrating their advanced skills in phonics.

The critic's viewpoint is cogently, elegantly phrased and altogether in step with the current thinking of many "experts," but countless experienced teachers will insist that much remains to be said on the issue of ability grouping in our public schools. I don't have the advantage of Miss Alexander's travel and ubiquitous observation, but I can offer some pertinent comments based upon a daily "classroom eye." I cannot quarrel, of course, with her statement that public funds are lacking for accelerated classrooms —every year my own "gifted" seniors are obliged to buy several dollars worth of paperback texts to satisfy partially their capacity and need for broader reading and advanced study. Most of the other schools where such homogeneous grouping has been instituted penalize gifted children and their parents in the same way.

I remain unconvinced, however, that the lack of proper financing for such instruction is the greatest injustice involved. Even in such a select class, the teacher usually finds a surprising range of skills and differences among the students, and these require a more individualized approach. Some teachers may feel, as I do, that perhaps the best handling of the gifted child lies not in his segregation but in individual contacts and conferences with his teacher. Intellectual segregation may breed other kinds of social division and a host of other problems that educational planning has not yet satisfactorily taken into account.

That "excellence makes people nervous" is painfully apparent. Not only does it cause some trepidation among the mediocre, but some of the excellent are as frightened by it as thoroughly as the girl I have described. Well aware of what superior intelligence alone is capable of producing, Albert Einstein warned a graduating class at the California Institute of Technology in 1938:

> Concern for man himself and his fate must always form the chief interest of all technical endeavors . . . in order that the creations of our mind shall be a blessing and not a curse to mankind.

Perhaps he had already glimpsed the ghastly cloud of nuclear destruction. Certainly he had lived long enough to know that intelligence by itself is not enough to assure happiness among men.

Education should bring pleasure to the learner. The youth of unusual intellectual promise should not be made to feel that his gift is his curse. It can be a terrifying realization for an older edition of one of Shana's five-year-olds to see that he and his most immediate associates or competitors are locked outside the rest of the school world and inside a curriculum where they are expected daily to perform according to an impressive three-digit label in order to give proud parents, trail-breaking teachers, and thoughtless theorists something with which to identify themselves.

I understand that my argument is not a popular view. Yet I believe that it is my gift, and not my curse, to cherish the child above the lesson. I do not mean to ignore the arguments in support of homogeneous grouping. But when Worthington High School first initiated the three-level curriculum planning—accelerated, regular, and modified (to avoid the semantic impact and misleading effect of *remedial*) courses—I felt vague reservations, though I supposed that, at 35, I had begun to grow old fashioned. Those same doubts have grown through experience.

First of all, I do not have sufficient faith in IQ measurements to feel that they are as infallible as some would credit them. Every year in my accelerated section I see students who, I feel, do not belong there, IQ notwithstanding. Moreover, to refer, as Miss Alexander does, to "stratospheric mental ability uncomplicated by any emotional or physical handicaps" suggests more penetrating analyses by school psychologists than are presently possible, I think. My own experience in teaching the high-IQ bracket has also led me to the conviction that, even if these students are free of emotional handicaps before entering a sequence of advanced courses, the same competitive atmosphere which some experts praise will become so charged with jealousies and strains as to make some young people ill, even physically ill. Children at five years of age may be less inclined toward ruthless rivalry than high-school students. For the latter, the mounting pressure of grade averages, college selectivity, and scholarships can create conflicts terrible to behold.

The same school pressures which caused Joan to withdraw from wholesome, desirable school activities and recreation were an important factor leading her classmate, Greg McGrath, to steal a set of papers from his teacher's desk. I could not blame myself entirely for the cut-throat competition that existed in the group of talented seniors that included Greg and Joan. They had first come to Room 106 as freshmen, and even then many of them were imbued with extreme self-concern and anxiety over maintaining their laurels and the Almighty Grade.

Shortly after they had begun their ninth-grade work with me, Joan stopped by the desk one day to comment about Katherine, her greatest competitor and eventually the class valedictorian. "That Katherine makes me so mad—she doesn't study nearly as much as I do for this class, and she turns right around and makes better grades. Why, she spent hardly any time at all with today's assignment."

All year long the students in that class played academic king-of-the-hill with a vengeance and with A's representing the crown jewels. Some of them were much too ready to undermine, to hurt one another for me to think of them as entirely healthy young people.

The high school soon discovered that the gifted groups had problems. Could the trouble be alleviated by reducing the workload and by lowering the standards of evaluation? One teacher tried doing so, but only briefly, for the entire class relaxed proportionately. They knew that they were being given A's because of the special section to which they were assigned. Competition and challenge go hand in hand. The greater the challenge, the more deadly the competition. Yet the automatic A produced no more effort in them than it would in ordinary students. IQ and motivation are not natural brethren—they are not even first cousins.

Then, for averaging grades, why not place a higher numerical value on the mark given an accelerated student? someone asked. Other schools had tried this practice. Did it work? After long consideration and a realistic look at the inadequacy of our techniques for screening students into the different levels, the high-school staff opposed assigning special values to the grades of the gifted sections. It would work inequities upon those young people who had the mental capacity to do the advanced work but who had, through schedule conflicts or lack of school facilities, not been included in the high-powered classes. After all, the class rank of graduating seniors—that frequently misrepresentative product of cumulative grades which so often determines college admissions—would be affected. So the problem of competitive sickness goes on, hardly the unmixed blessing that some educator-innovators prefer to see.

In order to remedy the circumstances of the student whose IQ figure is suspect, whose performance shows a marked falling off, or whose attitude indicates that he has given up in the rigorous contest among the gifted, a screening session is repeated every year to eliminate some students and to move others into the accelerated groups. The screening takes into consideration IQ and other testing, the opinions of the guidance counselor, the recommendation of the English teacher, and the principal's review of scheduling problems. The final assignment of a student to such a special section is done with parent approval and knowledge of the courses involved.

For critics of school heterogeneity to say that classroom socializing is not a part of learning is for them to adopt a very narrow, very arbitrary concept of education. If education is to reflect the realities of life, then it should bring us into contact with the broad spectrum of human talents, insights, values, and experiences. Students whose school day is spent entirely among the academic elite are exposed to a highly circumscribed, very unlifelike range of values and interests. Very often such a student is conditioned away from socializing "on the block" or "in the neighborhood," even if he has time for it. He may never develop, through practice, compassion for his less-perceptive fellow man, his less-talented neighbor.

Worst of all, to put a child into a capsule marked "Extra Special" can sometimes result in his being socially ostracized by many of his acquaintances and can even limit his non-social learning at times. Contrary to the belief in some circles, particularly bright youngsters can and do learn much in less-intellectual company, just as I once taught a full professor in economics how to go about changing a tire on his automobile. There is often a common sense, a practicality, a more accurate view of humanity and daily affairs in the ordinary student which can be quite instructive and can teach humility to the quiz kid. Cardinal Newman saw the practical end of education as that of "training good members of society." If one is unpracticed in dealing with his society, it follows that he may not have learned how to assume a constructive role within that society.

Miss Alexander may be correct in saying that there is nothing undemocratic about such grouping in the school. In the sense that it may permit the gifted to develop in proportion to their ability, perhaps it is in keeping with democratic principles in public education. There is only one little closeted skeleton that troubles me in this consideration—the often-incalculable human element. Some of our prodigies seem, after a few years, to fall back into the common crowd, whereas many of history's greatest geniuses have sprung from unlikely sources, sometimes seriously handicapped and even presumed by some early observers to have been dull or peculiar. In twenty years I have been surprised by many a student whose sudden awakening or renascence has seemed to contradict the most sophisticated prediction. I suspect that this capacity of human beings to surmount premature estimates of their individual destinies will never be exhausted.

The genius that has proved most beneficial to mankind has been the creative genius, not the numerically designated mental colossus of the psychologist's file. Creativity, the mark of the true genius, cannot be measured except in accomplishment, and it is never absolutely predictable. Thus, I find among my regular English students many a young person who might profit through some of the time that I must devote to preparing for the work of a special, advantaged class. There seem always to be some students whose capacities and skills appear to be approximately equal to those found in the advanced groups. That the accelerated class works with material denied to students of like promise is bound to trouble a teacher with a sense of fair play.

As a matter of fact, I have seen among the so-called modified groups some instances that gave me similar qualms. One of the boys in a modified class that I taught several years ago was a farmer's son. Earl's shoes sometimes were splashed from "slopping the pigs" or caked with chicken droppings when he arrived at the high school. Like many farm boys, Earl had numerous chores to perform at both ends of the day. Homework sometimes didn't get done because a boy who has plowed the back forty or worked for hours on repairs in the barn may get sleepy later over his books. It had been that way a long time with Earl.

Nevertheless, he liked school and wanted to learn in spite of the classmates who sometimes smiled when he stuttered, as he always did in recitation. When he found time around the farm, he enjoyed reading as much as puttering around an antique tractor. His friends knew him to be a hard-working boy, and his teachers generally liked Earl. Nevertheless, someone recommended him to a modified class because of his shyness, stuttering, poor homework performance, and an IQ figure (undoubtedly affected by some emotional instability and limited cultural background). Besides, a farm boy in a smart suburban school might have looked out of place to some teacher.

Naturally, he needed individual encouragement and help. He sat in a class of severely handicapped youngsters including a boy who couldn't spell his name and a girl still in shock from an automobile accident that had injured her and killed her mother. Intellectually, as physically, Earl stood out like a tower in that class.

One day I was working with the watered-down, far less academic stuff taught in one of those classes when something remarkable occurred. The class had just finished reading a carefully edited textbook version of Faulkner's "Two Soldiers." This story tells of a small boy who tries to follow his older brother into the army just after Pearl Harbor. Groping for some basis upon which to commence our discussion of this narrative, I asked whether anyone in the class had ever experienced a similar separation from some brother or sister. I never reckoned on the response that I would get. When Earl's hand went up, I called on him right away.

Then he began. He talked about his parents' divorce and the division of his family, some of the children going with the mother out West and several remaining with the father. All the time he spoke—and he gave almost embarrassing detail—the tears ran freely down his face and splashed on his desk and his books. The incredible part was that Earl's voice never once quavered and that there was no trace in his speech of the usual stammering. I didn't need a degree in psychology that day to find the taproot in that boy's problems. It wasn't merely the farm tasks that had stood in his way. Unwittingly but dramatically he had demonstrated for me that his academic flaw was not a matter of IQ. I did not know it that day, but Earl's speech impediment in Room 106, at least, would gradually lessen thereafter.

Earl did make me think of another farm boy, a seventeen-year-old boy in Indiana some years ago. Nobody knew much of his father's family. His mother was born an illegitimate child in the mountain country of Virginia. The boy was still quite young when his mother died. His father, considered by some to be a somewhat shiftless man except for his tendency to shift from place to place, did not remarry for several years. The boy had only a bit of elementary education in Kentucky and a year's formal schooling in Indiana.

Were his father to bring him to Worthington today, he would probably be enrolled in a special class, no doubt in what we call a modified section. For the boy was thought not only poorly co-ordinated and backward but emotionally odd. Though he did some reading on his own, he was given to daydreaming, hill-billy superstitions, and vulgar jokes. In our infinite contemporary wisdom we would probably call him culturally disadvantaged and deny that he had the ability to get much from Shakespeare and the standard curriculum. Of course, we would never consider seating him in a class with our "gifted" children. And, armed with our files through which we categorize young people with such despotic certainty, we would never once dream that we might have mismanaged the academic placement of Abraham Lincoln.

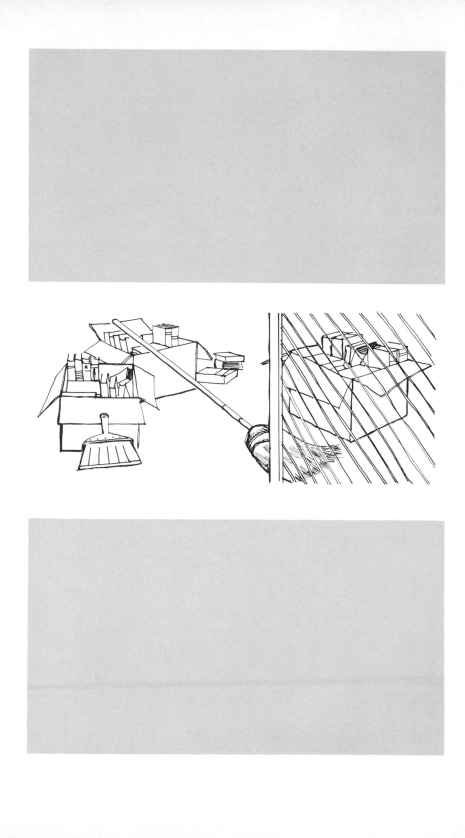

They call it moonlighting. In some places in the country, teachers are reprimanded or even fired for it. In other school systems it is a reality which no one talks about but everyone takes for granted. Practically anywhere, however, teachers find sources of income to supplement their school salaries.

Though the term *moonlighting* suggests after-school or night jobs, the expression here includes most work, even the summer jobs to which teachers turn to help their families live a somewhat better life than their teaching contracts will permit. Sometimes, of course, such extra employment is school related—tutoring, writing, instructing night classes, etc. At other times, moonlighting is fairly unrelated to the schoolteacher's regular duties.

The teacher's need to moonlight is closely tied up with his willingness, or lack of it, to live on a salary which is not commensurate

Chalk Dust by Moonlight

with his training, skill, and service to a community. While teaching salaries in the Worthington School District are, as one might suspect, above the national average, the teacher there nevertheless finds that his salary does not permit him to enjoy the standard of living that a sizable portion of the suburban community enjoys. Thus, there are many teachers who live in houses, drive cars, and take vacations which they cannot afford and who therefore must find extra income.

In surveying my fellow educators, I find a history teacher who has worked as a policeman, a geography instructor who has managed a swimming pool, a faculty member who has been employed by a travel service, a coach who has operated a bulldozer, an administrator who has regularly taken inventories for a hardware store, and a driver-education teacher and shop teacher who frequently clean out industrial grease-pits by night. I could list at least two dozen others whose financial pressures take them into moneymaking pursuits far removed from the high calling for which they spent years in college classrooms.

The nature of my subject-area is such, especially in the large number of compositions I must grade, that I am limited in the kinds of extra-job moonlighting I may undertake. Still, I have in various years been so occupied, and, even if I have disliked the idea of taking time away from my English planning, I have undoubtedly grown in background and valuable experience. My outside-school employment has always been secondary to teaching, and in these purely financial measures I have frequently found potential chalk dustings for my students. In the same way, I have always taken the chalk dust with me to those other jobs.

Of the many nonschool jobs I have worked at during nearly twenty years of professional practice, the most interesting have been my labor as an apprentice carpenter, as an assistant cashier in the Treasury of the State of Ohio, and as the co-proprietor of a retail book store. In these experiences I found myself associated with personality types drawn from every stratum of society.

The carpentry work was the most distantly removed from my usual sphere of activity. In this employment I did much more than the elementary hammer-and-saw bit. I dug ditches for tile, swept floors, was a truck driver in a vehicle with only a hint of brakes, swept floors, was available as a general drudge for just about anyone else on the job—including a hilldweller who spoke in a sort of oral shorthand—and swept floors. Of course, I was totally inexperienced at much of this type of work. I had been a failure even with Lincoln logs as a child; as a carpenter, I made a better butcher. It took real nerve or desperation on the part of my boss to give me any of the more complicated tasks like hanging doors or mitering mouldings. I was ceremoniously stripped of my miter box because of my knack for cutting at the wrong angle. And I could have been drummed out of the carpenters' corps for the terror I created on the rooftops. No doubt people are still getting flat tires because of the nails I half hit and ricocheted into the streets.

The best part of that job was not the $1.50 per hour, but the fringe benefit—an hour or so of euchre played daily during the lunch break or when weather or delay in materials held us up.

I made a lot of friends among those construction workers. They got used to dodging my nails and the two-by-fours I swung around carelessly. At the end of the summer they were still speaking to me, except for the fellow who always got stuck as my euchre partner.

The Treasury job marked my return to the employment that had helped the government and my wife to get me through college. Some of the finest people I have ever known worked in the old Warrant Room, where I spent most of my time punching the keys of an adding machine. Never having learned the keys, I went back to my search-and-stab system, but other operators worked the same way and, having a fast neck, I was as efficient as most.

There's a genuine education in state employ. Among other things, you learn firsthand how the spoils system operates—the "flower fund," the odd jobs the party asks, the special projects around election time, the petitions that must be circulated, the politicians that masquerade with immunity under civil service, and the payoffs in newly created, workless jobs. Because of my experiences in the Treasury and my pre-teaching work as a page in the Ohio Senate, I was in a much better position to teach history, which was still part of my assignment in those early years at Worthington.

Shortly after Christmas of 1955, Frank Lowery and I began talking about the possibility of opening a book store. By early spring, we had got under way. We began without a location—we couldn't afford to pay rent. Actually, we began our business with $150 capital and the commercial potential of both our private libraries. The Senior Class of 1956 added to our capital by providing us a joint gift of more than $100. Whether it was ethical for us to have accepted the gift is doubtful, but in the excitement of establishing a private business we managed to resolve our ethical dilemma by dismissing it from our minds. A trip to the bank and a $300 loan there put us on our way with greater ease.

We began right away to accumulate our stock. Every Saturday morning during the remainder of the school year, Frank and I would visit various Salvation Army and Goodwill Industries outlets. Later, we added the Volunteers of America retailer to our itinerary. In each of these places we would comb over the books available. The prices of these volumes ranged usually from five to fifty cents, and by being selective we managed to gain a fair beginning long before we had a store for our inventory.

Sometimes the stores' employees were very helpful. One sweet little old woman knew us as the two schoolteachers who were collecting books for classroom libraries, and she was always willing to reduce prices for us in the store she managed. In reality, we did in many cases pick up books for classrooms, but not for our own. Frank and I sometimes felt guilty over our subterfuge, but when we would turn around and sell a number of ten-cent books for a dollar or more apiece to textbook stores in the University area, our feelings were always assuaged somewhat.

Not long after Easter, our capital gains permitted us to lease a store location on North High Street in Columbus, about three blocks north of the main entrance to the Ohio State University campus. When we first stepped inside the building, we could only sigh deeply. The long bare room, about 20′ by 60′, had been, in glossier days, a barber shop and afterwards a five-and-dime store. Apart from the gathering of dust, the mingling of oversexed spiders, and the shattering of back windows by bored little boys, nothing had happened in the room for a long time. The toilet in the back corner was unfit for human assumption, the washbasin was an antique, and the floors creaked without the slightest excuse. But this was to be the site of Columbus Bookana, so Frank grabbed something that had once been a broom, and I began to try to wash the windows, though we were never quite able to clean off something that looked like **BARBE** from one of them.

So now we were dirty capitalists—literally, when we hauled in the boxes of books that we had stored in our basements—and for a time Bookana looked as if it should have been named Boxana. Yet our first sales were made from those boxes. After all, we had no shelves. Occasionally a crinkled, curious face would look through the **BARBE** at us to see what was going on in there. Once a student dropped in. "What is this?" he said, looking about at the cardboard chaos. But we didn't care—we were rugged individualists prying open the sacred portals of private enterprise.

Bookana started resembling a book store when my partner and I found an old Jewish gentleman who was closing out his business in the center of a Negro community on Mt. Vernon Avenue. Abe Krakoff was a fine old fellow who had run a clothing store in this location for many years. Now he was retiring, and I could tell he hated leaving that old building. But he sold us his large counters and his sections of shelving for a very small price, and we promptly hauled them across town to our store. Now we could burn the boxes and begin to put our stock into classifications and sections.

It was hard work but fun, getting the big room into halfway decent condition. We painted everything except the walls and ceiling; the lessor had taken care of that job. We got the toilet to work—a relief, to say the least—and here and there it was possible to see the porcelain on the old sink. Once the floor was clear, we could scrub it, and for twenty-five dollars, I think it was, we got a sign painter to print in large letters over the old signboard in front: **COLUMBUS BOOKANA**. Both of us found opportunities to sneak across the street so that we could get a pedestrian's impression of our place of business.

Naturally, our rising status required certain frills. We had business cards printed, got industrial-arts and driver-education teacher Rudy Hitzemann to print stationery for us, bought a used typewriter with a bad *o*, bought a typewriter stand with a bent leg, and purchased a new adding machine on time. In order that we might take advantage of the mail-order trade, we subscribed to the *Antiquarian Bookman*. Our principal extravagance was the bright canary-yellow telephone that we had put in. We needed the phone but not the color.

Frank wanted the store to appeal to the arty element, so we began to bring in picture frames, ceramic jewelry, inexpensive prints from New York outlets, and other merchandise for the look-at-it-over-your-thumb, bloody-Mary-for-lunch bunch. We even invited local artists, Worthington's art teacher Dick Phipps included, to exhibit their paintings at Bookana. We partitioned the store with two-by-four's, and between the studs strung white twine, vertically angled. Then we contacted a dealer in modern arts and crafts and talked her into letting us display and sell some of her foreign and domestic stock on a commission basis. We purchased some fancy plastic lampshades, too, though they proved to be marvelous dustcatchers and turned brown from proximity with the large bulbs we had to use in the store. Our window displays were more interesting because of the various plaster-of-Paris pieces we bought from an old Italian sculptor, Louis Mori. His Easter Island heads especially attracted customers.

Before long we had to expand our book sources. We began to approach junk-dealers and paper-stock people, from whom we could buy books by the pound. Bookana regularly ordered publisher overstocks from several New York jobbers. Calls poured in, too, from people who were cleaning attics or settling estates. Other

253

books were brought in by the boxful by persons who wished to trade or sell. When Frank and I took senior classes to New York, we always spent our free time checking out the old Fourth Avenue booksellers and the Marboro storerooms.

We learned much about books that we had never known before. For example, I had never considered books as something one sold. English teachers are bibliophiles inherently, and I had always cherished books for what was in them. It took me a long time to think of books in dollars-and-cents terms. Even then I felt like a literary madame some days.

There were so many myths to be exploded for both of us. We were shocked to discover that first editions, except for a comparative few, are a drug on the market. Moreover, we learned that the reading tastes of people are unpredictable and unaccountable. The appearance of a customer gave no clue as to his literary interests. Beatniks frequently asked for the most conservative writings, and a clergyman who often came into the store found Jack Woodford and Saber Press novels very palatable despite their emphasis upon sex. We had supposed, also, that the great bulk of our patrons would be college people, but this was not the case at all. Though we endeavored to give Bookana a Greenwich Village air, OSU was too Midwestern for many of the people to find us very appealing. Students would browse, but their stringent budgets and textbook needs most often limited their purchases. After assessing the situation, we expanded our stock of paperbacks, and eventually OSU purchases paid our rent.

Among the greatest pleasures I received in my experiences at Bookana were the many friendships those years brought. One of the first customers to come into the store was a man I knew only as Ramey. Though he had had little formal education, he was probably as well schooled on history as anyone I have ever met. And he knew his books. Ramey was especially keen on materials involving the Civil War and the Old West. The man had been searching for books for more than twenty years, yet his personal library contained only several hundred volumes. The discriminating interest which went into that collection, however, made it worth a great deal of money.

Ramey was of much help to Frank and me, for we had so much to find out about the kinds of stock we needed. In exchange for his advice, we usually gave Ramey the first chance to look over volumes of Americana that we had purchased. I haven't seen

Ramey in years, but if he's still alive I know how to find him. All I have to do is to stake myself out in a bookstore—any one of them—and he'll be along eventually.

If I hadn't realized it before, my days at the book store would certainly have made it clear that the world is filled with people who are lonely, who long for someone to talk to. One day, a very pretty young woman parked her English Ford in front of the store and came in to ask about a book in the window. After she and I had talked for nearly half an hour, I began to realize that the girl was much more in want of companionship than of books. She had a little son, she told me after her third or fourth trip to the store, but she never explained whether she had had an unhappy marriage or none at all. Now, she said, she spent her days typing and avoiding her boss's reach and most of her evenings with her boy. She spent the better part of many evenings, though, in talking, waiting for me to finish with customers, and then talking some more. Frank would look a big "Ha!" at me when she was in there, but I don't really think she was making a pitch for a man. She had too well equipped a trap to have to talk men into it. No, she was interested strictly in an accommodating ear, and I listened to her as if she had been one of the students in my classes at Worthington. She bought many a book she couldn't afford as an excuse for those conversations.

One summer we had a major problem with three little gypsy children who used to haul off whatever they could furtively get their hands on. There was a whole houseful of gypsies just around the corner from the store. Someone told me that they were being hired by a new firm in town—a company which needed employees possessing a highly developed manual dexterity. If this were true, the gypsy children were serving their apprenticeship admirably. I have always thought of the people of Romany as victims of widespread prejudice. Frank's penchant for putting books on a stand outside the door would have provided an irresistible challenge for *any* children on the street, I suppose. Keeping an eye on the little gypsies, however, certainly strengthened my visual skills for my hours in the Big Cage.

The moments of greatest excitement in Columbus Bookana often came with the visits of traveling book dealers. I was always suspicious that we were being "taken" when they bought books, but mine was an apprehension that goes along with having much to learn about the market. Once we sold nearly $300 worth of used books to a dealer. I suppose that material might have been worth $500 or more on the retail market, but the books had cost us no more than $50. In the book market, no one knows everything. About all one can do is to ensure that he makes ample profit himself and accept the idea that more experienced book handlers will get their share, too.

The activity of a small book business, I found, has the rhythm of a convulsive caterpillar. Some days customers came in almost too rapidly to be served, and on other days I had little to do but to sort and dust books and possibly grade student compositions that I had brought from the school. For several months Frank and I could count on a brief boom in browsing about six o'clock every evening. There was a ravishingly attractive blonde who lived in the apartment building three doors north of Bookana. Whenever she came into the store—and she did so often—the place filled with males who had, as if by magic, been smitten by the literary impulse. I told her one day that, if we could afford her, we'd hire her to stand inside the **BARBE**. She knew her power, and I wasn't surprised when she replied, "Well, at the very least you could give me discounts."

University professors came into the store occasionally, and one day I looked up to find old Professor Woodring moving along a row of shelves. He had been a source of personal joy to me at State, and I had to make some gesture. Though his sight had grown worse, he remembered me when I identified myself. He had picked up several volumes of history which had cost the store no more than thirty cents, and I told him his money was no good that day, that I'd like him to accept the books from a grateful student. I'm glad that I had that last chance to say *thank you.*

Frank and I never took more than a small supplementary income out of the store. Most of Bookana's profits went back into the business. By the time we sold the store, we had a stock of nearly 30,000 books. About a third of these were dusty junk— "dogs" in the parlance of book dealers. All dealers have some of these in stock because they sell in spite of their seeming worthlessness. The rest of our stock was mainly composed of respectable fiction and non-fiction, much of it out of print and some of it bound to stay that way. New books comprised roughly 10% of our inventory, and we had purchased these rather selectively with a careful eye to the market. In addition, we had numerous prints and miscellaneous other *objets d'art* on hand.

The principal mistakes we made as co-proprietors grew out of inexperience and faulty assumptions. For one thing, we failed to get up a lighted sign that would extend streetward and over the sidewalk. We assumed that our advertising would be sufficient. Unfortunately, High Street in Columbus is a considerable driving hazard, and motorists are often too busy watching out for little old ladies, college boys, drunks, and indifferent drivers to look from side to side at store fronts.

Our markup on merchandise was probably too high too often. The discount houses today beautifully demonstrate the lesson we were slow in learning—that volume is all important in successful business. We had virtually inexhaustible sources for stock and should have lowered our prices somewhat.

Of course, we had natural, built-in disadvantages, and some of these grew out of limited capital. Where we had to locate, there were no facilities for parking. It was impossible, too, for us to invest heavily in textbooks and thereby attract more OSU business. Some of our problems might have been overcome had we been able to pay more for help. At first, things went well for we had dependable, though modestly paid student help, but we could never afford to have more than one person there on weekdays. Consequently, we did little with the mail-order aspect of the trade, which for many small book stores is extremely important. After we had lost our student employees, we found several older people, and our experiences with them would make up a large volume of anecdotes.

The best of our adult help was J. Y. Smith. He was a tall, slender, bald-domed gentleman of about 65 with an infinite supply of intelligent, enthusiastic conversation. J. Y. was one of the most irrepressible people I have ever met, and his greatest passion was to collect protégés and then introduce them to one another. His wife, a charming lady devoted to her husband and to her own work as a librarian, was just as much an extrovert as her husband. J. Y. did attract people to the store. College students referred to him as "Doctor" Smith out of respect and affection. He was, in many ways, an asset to Bookana. He added much character to the place.

There was just one big problem with J. Y. For reasons I will not attempt to probe, he developed a deep antagonism toward my partner. He would deliberately annoy Frank by changing signs, moving stock, and ignoring my partner's suggestions. Naturally, the animosity became somewhat mutual after a time. At least twice I tried to arbitrate this enigmatic quarrel.

Eventually, J. Y. left, but Bookana's troubles only grew. Our next employee was a woman who hid her wine supply on a dark shelf and who had difficulty negotiating the aisles between counters and shelves. We got rid of her in one day. I found out later that she had set some kind of indoor record—she had fallen over three customers in getting to one book.

Then Bob came to work for us, and he proved to be a very conscientious fellow. His heart condition was such, however, that he couldn't move things. In a book store the size of Bookana, it doesn't take very many boxes in the aisles to obstruct the flow of business.

As partners, Frank and I seldom quarreled. I always knew when I had made him angry—he'd grab a broom and just sweep hell out of the store, the sidewalk in front, and anyone who happened to pass that way. The only real differences that Frank and I ever had grew out of our wives. Both of them looked at the store somewhat as if it were "the other woman." Understandably, they resented the hours that kept us away from our families. Both women tried to be tolerant, but wives sometimes have innate limitations in such matters.

We sold the business—lock, stock, and **BARBE**—for $4,000, a figure which constituted a loss in our opinion. For two weeks we helped the new owner—a man who was looking for a business that his recently widowed sister-in-law could run—by explaining the operation in detail, giving the best advice we knew, and helping them purchase new stock.

During this post-sale phase of my Bookana experience, I had my honesty tested more completely than at any other time in my life. It happened this way. When several boxes of books arrived one day through someone serving as the executor of an estate, I advised the new owner to buy. At a glance, I saw a quantity of good history and Americana in the boxes, and, sorting rapidly through several levels in the cartons, I suggested what seemed a logical bid. For a very little money, the new proprietor got an unbelievably fine collection of books. I figured that he should make, at the very least, a profit of 1000% on his purchase. At his insistence, I went through the acquisition, box by box, and indicated what I felt would be reasonable Bookana prices. Then I found it.

It was wrapped in an old newspaper at the bottom of the box, and I was about to discard the paper when I realized that something was inside it. As I unwrapped it, I saw a paper cover which looked spotted and generally discolored by time. Then the words: *Tamerlaine and Other Poems.* Beneath that title: "By a Bostonian." Finally: "Boston, 1827."

This inscription may be meaningless to others, but the inveterate bookman will probably know what I went through at that moment. For these words comprise the title of what is probably the most highly prized and most valuable volume in American literature. As I knelt there, I was almost certain that I had found a first edition that had auctioned for something like a quarter of a million dollars—a copy of the earliest published work by Edgar Allan Poe. *And now, my God,* I reflected, *it belongs to someone else!*

Then I heard him say, "What's the matter? What's that?" Maybe my hands were shaking. Possibly I had drifted off into some idyll of financial security. His voice reminded me that he didn't know the first thing about books. He had no idea of what I might be holding. Why shouldn't I casually say to him "You know, I kinda like old poetry. How'dja like t'make a fast buck right now offa this old paperback?"

But I couldn't do it. I couldn't even be casual. I supposed I knew then why people like me are not likely to grow wealthy. I handed it to him. "You'd better stick this under the counter, and I'll make some inquiries about it. It may have some value." I knew, of course, that there was always the chance of its not being genuine, *but still*— At that moment, I looked up from larcenous thoughts to my wife and daughter, who had entered the store and would be wanting me to drive them home.

In the car I told my wife. I had the feeling that, by my act, I might have cheated my family. "Oh, well, that's the way with us," she laughed. "I suppose people can die of honesty, but at least it's a clean death."

I was glad, though, the next day, when I learned that what I had found was not the real article. It was merely a facsimile copy which had been sold by Long's Book Store many years before. Maybe I felt better about myself, too. After all, if I had bought the book for a dollar, I would have profited only about fifty cents— not much for the intangible, but valuable something I would have lost in the exchange.

The new ownership failed—it would have even with a first-edition *Tamerlaine*. The new man was looking for something that would make him money without giving him any trouble or taking time away from his other many enterprises. He didn't know about books, didn't care about them. He bought the business at a bargain price, but within a year he wanted to sell out. Eventually, he simply sold equipment, counters, shelves, and stock down to where he gave the rest away.

A few nights ago, I drove past the site of old Bookana. The buildings all along that side of the street have been torn down, have given way to OSU's latest expansion program. I double-parked for a moment and surveyed the open, moonlit ground where the store had been. And I could see it still. It was still alive in my heart and on that muddy patch of moonlight, where the dust from its cluttered volumes mingled with the chalk dust.

"I think that I should tell you I intend to kill myself," she said, looking me squarely in the eyes. If this was Candy's way of saying that she didn't wish to continue her private lessons at Harding Hospital, the widely known and highly regarded psychiatric sanitarium on the east side of Worthington, it was certainly different, anyway. When I stared back at her questioningly, she went on. "Oh, I've already tried—with sleeping pills. Trouble was, I didn't take enough of them. Like a little idiot, I thought a handful would do it. Now I have to find another way." She closed her copy of *Romeo and Juliet* and set the book down on the table beside her. "So it's kinda silly to keep this up, isn't it?"

I didn't answer her right away. Instead, I reached to the record player and lifted the needle just before Mercutio was to be skewered by Tybalt. That we had succored Romeo's friend meant

The Teacher-Errant

nothing to Candy—the villainous nephew of Lady Capulet could have made a shishkabob out of Friar Lawrence, Paris, the Nurse, and the "star-crost lovers," too.

"It's not your fault, Mr. Rousculp. You've been very patient and understanding, but I'm just not getting any better. That's why you have to come here to the cottage now for my lessons. They don't trust me outside by myself or even with you—at least not since the sleeping-pill bit. I've appreciated what you've tried to do for me, but I'm wasting your time, and I—I don't want you to come back anymore."

I hated to see her give up. Maybe I felt even worse about it because I had just that morning received a letter from her mother, thanking me for my work with Candy. "Don't you think you should let me decide when I'm wasting my time? And what makes you feel, Candy, that your life is yours to take? Isn't it possible that your life might have some value to someone else? Can't you see that this perfection-or-nothing kick you're on is really just an 'I love Candy' feeling in disguise?"

"I can't stand myself. I told you that in my autobiography."

"Yes, but it's not true. The person who sits around thinking about suicide is really looking out strictly for himself, isn't he? Regardless of who he hurts or what responsibilities he's going to dodge, he's going to pamper himself—take care of himself with one big permanent nap, unless he believes that the sane suicide is headed for Hell." I threw in that last clause to remind her of something she had been taught in her church school.

"But I'm crazy, or haven't you heard? And I'm going to Hell, anyway. Sometimes I think I'm already there." She looked determined. "No, you can't change my mind, Mr. Rousculp. Nobody can."

I finally left Candy that day with this compromise—that, if she began feeling better and wished me to tutor her again, she should have her counselor call the school. I walked out of the cottage, feeling like a total failure. It takes only one student to make me feel that way. I can have a perfectly good day at the school, and one bad moment can obliterate the other five-hundred minutes. Taking a private-tutoring job at a sanitarium is just begging for such misery, I suppose.

Still, who would have thought that the girl Candy would represent the problem that she did. Both her mother and father were doctors with very lucrative practices in a Southern Ohio town. The girl had just about anything that a girl might want. There were three or four children in the family, and she especially adored her little brother. Candy had received her education in a parochial school, and her grades were practically straight A's. In the month that I had worked with the girl, I was delighted with her mental keenness. Even in her writing, where she had not been given sufficient practice, she was showing steady progress.

Physically, Candy was—or could have been—an extremely attractive girl at 18. She was somewhat taller than average, but nicely proportioned. Her blond hair glinted titian in the sunlight, and her eyes were a startling, beautiful green. Unfortunately, her hair was bobbed much too short for a girl of her height, and she kept her pretty eyes rimmed with red and puffed with tears. Perhaps she was still sensitive about her height (as tall girls often are), for she allowed her shoulders to slump forward. With her hair longer, her posture improved, her tear ducts behaving decently, and her dress properly chosen, Candy would have made any beauty contest a close race.

The girl appeared to love her parents, although she might have resented their irregular hours at home and the demands of their profession. Her attitude toward a brother attending Michigan was paradoxical—it was worshipful yet colored at moments with violent dislike. A word of criticism from him was sufficient to make her withdraw into brooding and self-disdain.

Her autobiography and her occasional comments made it clear that she detested the sisters who had taught her in school. She reveled in Chaucer's satire of the clergy even though I pointed out that he was not attacking the church but merely a few of the people who were not worthy of their positions. But she was generally anti-clerical in her religious attitudes. Especially did she refuse to go to confession. Nevertheless, she believed herself to be the archetype of the sinner. I tried to explain that, though I am not Catholic, I felt that she had absorbed only one side of her church's doctrine and had ignored the other. "Didn't they tell you that we are all sinful, Candy?" I asked her. "Surely they explained the idea of Divine Redemption through Christ. What's so special about your sinfulness?"

At first I thought that possibly she had had some unfortunate experience with a boy—many girls in sanitariums have histories of sexual promiscuity. After spending a few hours with her, however, I dismissed that idea. Though there was a tomboyish quality about her, she spoke of boys with apparent distaste. She felt inadequate and uncomfortable in their presence. Apart from classroom acquaintances and a few parties, she had little contact with them, I gathered.

She never told me just why she saw herself as the chief of sinners. Whenever the issue arose, as it did several times, she would merely turn her eyes to the floor. I don't know whether her doctor ever broke through that barrier. If I were to hazard a layman's guess, I would judge that Candy was a victim of repression, that she had hidden away some experience or experiences in which someone important to her had seemed to reject her and had caused her to feel some enormous, fearful guilt at the same time. Things that she said and wrote led me to believe that the key to her difficulty was her brother at Michigan, or Candy's identification with him. Perhaps I had read too much of Adler, Jung, Freud, and Krafft-Ebing, but I wondered whether the girl's psychiatrist might discover either incestuous or homosexual wishes or experimentation which the child Candy's early religious instruction made her hide away from herself in fright and shame.

Three weeks after Candy and I had called it quits, I received the come-back signal from the hospital's youthful and personable social worker. I returned to the cottage to begin again with Candy, hopeful that she had found light at the end of her dark passage. I saw, though, that there was wishful thinking behind the plan to resume, that things had not really improved with Candy. School work would have been excellent therapy for her, the promise of finishing the high-school requirements for graduation and of getting ready for college might have been conducive to her recovery, but she was not yet ready. The painstaking manicure was gone from her hands, too. Candy was apparently chewing her nails to the quick these days.

At the end of the first week back, I saw her eyes fill with tears as she closed her book abruptly. "It's no use. I can't concentrate," she said, putting her hands to her face. I sat quietly until she spoke again. "Are you getting any work done on your book?"

"Some," I lied.

"Will you write about me?" she asked.

"Would you like me to, Candy?"

"Maybe. What—what would you say?" I could tell she was ready to memorize whatever I might say, and I thought I had better keep my answer in the lightest possible vein.

"Well, I could write about a beautiful damsel in distress and a fouled-up, fortyish Quixote who couldn't do anything more for her than to throw a book at the dragon she was hiding from. How's that?"

She tried to make a convincing smile but couldn't. She looked so pathetic, so alone in her ordeal that I actually wanted to cradle her in my arms. But I have a rule that I follow and I kept the professional wall between us. "If you do write about me, will you use my name?"

"No, I wouldn't. Would you want me to?"

"You can if you want to," she said. "I really wouldn't mind."

I thought that she had given me a great chance to put in an argument for my side. I didn't know that she had just given me a going-away present. "If I use your real name, Candy, and someone decides that he'll publish my *Chalk Dust*, then you'll be alive as long as anyone reads the book. I guess you've stopped that suicide nonsense."

She quoted a pair of lines, then, but not with the declarative inflection: *"So long as men can breathe, or eyes can see, So long lives this, and this gives life to thee?"*

"Sure," I said grandiosely, "just like Shakespeare's sonnet. You get the idea, anyway."

"On paper, I wouldn't mind living, Mr. Rousculp. It wouldn't hurt so much that way." She made herself cold, gathered her books together, and stood up. "Good-bye," she said flatly. The change came so fast that I must have looked dumbfounded. "Good-bye," she repeated in the same tone and turned her head to hide the mist in her eyes. She was holding out her books, and the sweatshirt had slid up her arm so that I saw it for the first time—saw the deep, ugly three-inch scar on her wrist. When I took the books, she reached her other hand to the garment and yanked it down over the tell-tale mark of self-violence. Now I knew that *someone else* had trimmed her nails so closely.

"Candy—" I began.

"Please," she choked. "Please go."

As I walked across the lawn to my car, I couldn't resist looking back at the scene of my latest failure. I saw the drape at her screened window was slightly out of place. She was watching me leave. All she had left was a prayer, and before I drove away from the spring flowers of the hospital grounds I had leaned my head on the steering wheel and breathed my impotence and my petition to the Almighty.

I do not always play the teacher-errant. Every year, I turn down tutoring jobs worth thousands of dollars. Frantic parents, worried students, sometimes even graduate students laboring over theses and dissertations at OSU—they call my home throughout the year, asking for help. Where they've been given my name, I seldom find out—part of it, I'm sure, rests with my long tenure in a school with a somewhat exaggerated reputation.

It is undoubtedly the same with many other teachers. I could use the money, but I seldom have the time, not with the composition load that an English instructor carries home. There is much emotional wear and tear in such work, too. As I have said many times, I cannot teach young people without growing concerned with their personal problems. Sometimes their parents cannot afford me, and I find myself chopping my price, too. Candy's parents could have paid the rate that seventeen years' experience would ordinarily have required, but I wasn't callous enough to ask it of people who were already faced with such a tragedy on their hands. I even worried about Candy's learning that her tutoring cost as much as it did. I was half ashamed of the checks that I received. I felt even worse, knowing that I hadn't done much for the girl.

When I was originally asked to serve as Candy's teacher, I didn't have it in me to say *no.* Two years earlier, I had worked quite successfully with another girl at the hospital. But Patty's situation had been far less serious than Candy's. Patty's breakdown had originated in a mother-daughter rivalry, and the psychiatrist had brought her through very nicely.

The other tutoring I have done has usually been of the ordinary sort—young people who need remedial work in grammar and writing, students who have failed or are in the process of failing English courses at other high schools or at the University. Too often the high-school students are tragically beyond the help of a brief span of special instruction. Frequently, they come to me much too late. At other times, they lack the mental wherewithal to achieve much progress.

The University students are sometimes looking for someone to do their compositions for them, and they are disappointed when I refuse to do more than to look over their papers, mark errors, suggest source references, and explain the patterns of their writing weaknesses and what must be done to remedy these deficiencies. Ethically, a teacher may not serve as a ghost writer for papers assigned a student. Sometimes students need to be shown once how to put a paper together, and I will sit down and outline their ideas with them, discuss paragraph development, or give examples of effective transition. Nevertheless, I insist that the end product be basically their own work. The principal source of frustration in helping college freshmen lies in handling some of the arbitrary and subjective judgments that some inexperienced freshman instructors make in marking compositions. It is a real test to avoid sabotaging the teacher and to find a grammatical alternative that the college instructor might accept.

Some of the calls that I receive for the chalk-dust treatment are fantastic:

Is this the Mr. Rowskoop who teaches English at Worthington? Why, the reason I'm calling is I was selected Miss Ohio last month, and I was wondering if you could help me sometime with a monologue for Atlantic City. You see, I've never done anything else like that, and I hear that you—

I had seen her pictures and I remembered a Marine who would have made an appointment right away, but at the moment I was buried under books at Columbus Bookana and entirely too busy to play Billy Wilder, even if she wanted to pay me in money rather than in the occasional brushing of a 36-24-35 figure.

Uuh, sir, Ah've jus' had a chay-unce t' ge-ut a veruh goo-ud job as a sec'eturry in C'lumbus. An' Ah was wond'rin' ef you c'd he'p me wif mah speech. Y'see, Ah'm fum outa sta-ut, an' Ah—we-ull, you c'n tay-ull thay-ut, cayn'tcha?

I had to tell her that I couldn't help at that time, even though it might have been fun playing Henry Higgins. I didn't feel sorry for her, though, because something in her voice made me feel that she would get the job regardless of her enunciation. Besides, I find the dialects of America very agreeable to the ear. I am one of those who fear that our mass-communication media will some day wipe out our pronunciation differences and leave us linguistically impoverished and colorless.

Mr. Rousculp, this is Mark Marks of Columbus Enterprises. I tried to get hold of you yesterday. My boy is going to be back from Purdue this week and I thought you might have some time to give him some tips on ways to study. I've heard about your course and—

This time I took the job, though I was sorry afterwards. The boy was no more suited to Purdue than I am to the advanced studies in mathematics at Princeton.

There's this theme on Comus *I hafta have in tomorrow, sir, and I just don't know what t' say. I don't even understand the assignment. You ever try readin' that thing? There's this guy, y'see, who's tryin' t' lay this babe, but I can't make out whether he—*

I didn't find time with this one. In the first place, I didn't have the heart to tell him that the girl's brother arrives in the nick to save

269

her niche. It would have ruined the best part of the poem for him.

> *I'm calling from the University, Mr. Rousculp. I understand that you have a program of creative writing in your classes at Worthington. Will you be able to come to my class here one day next week and explain what you're doing? I could give you half an hour.*

I had to beg off. I told him it was my busy schedule. Actually, it would have taken me a week of half-hours.

> *I'm finishing a book on the Indigenous Birds of Peru, and I would like you to look over the manuscript for me. My main problem is grammar—*

I had just collected research reports from my seniors, and I told him that I was sorry that I couldn't help. I felt like saying "Oh, go on!" or, better yet, "Oh, guano!"

Occasionally, these people desiring my aid will overestimate my charitable instinct, and I especially wonder at the well-established, superbly treasuried civic organizations who ask me to speak to their membership but who are reluctant to pay for the time that goes into the preparation and delivery of such speeches. Not that I place high value upon my public utterances. Yet I must pay through the eyes with late hours of grading papers for graciousness unrecognized by gratuities. My wife keeps silent her views on my unremunerated time, but I am assured by her facial expression that an oral rendition of her feelings would make splendid dialogue for Tennessee Williams.

Yet the teacher-errant in me and in so many of my profession finds me doing these amateur recitals many times through the year. My friend, Professor Eberhart, once said to me, "You know, Gene, these people appreciate you more when you put a reasonable price tag on your work." Not long ago, however, I read that he was addressing a group that is notorious for wanting busy people to give freely of their time.

In recent years I have been able to employ more of my out-of-school time with teaching activities that have helped buy groceries. Several years ago George Taylor, who teaches mathematics at Worthington, began part-time work for the Test Development Center of OSU's Bureau of Educational Research and Service. The Center was under contract with the United States Armed Forces Institute, and George was doing math forms, of course. When

Dan Stufflebeam, the Center's talented young director at that time, looked for people to do similar work in English, George suggested my name. Since that time I have worked on several contracts with Stufflebeam and his successors. The test-writing jobs are quite rewarding, beyond the pay involved. Here, just as in the classroom, you know that the results of your efforts can figure significantly in other lives. Moreover, in the reading tests that I helped prepare for one of the country's foremost publishers of educational materials, I have had additional opportunities to practice that other important pursuit of my life—writing.

My employment by the Center was probably what led to my appointment as a communication-skills project consultant for the University. In this role, I was to provide assistance and direction for a group of teachers in a Southern Ohio school district. Every week we would meet in a room at Piketon High School in Piketon, Ohio, and here we would discuss English-classroom activities and materials that could be adapted to the needs of the youngsters in that school community. It was my good fortune that the teachers assigned to me were of that highly concerned and talented variety that make things worthwhile happen in my profession. Since I was the only consultant in the project who was not a University man, I think they were perhaps additionally responsive. We were all high-school teachers together.

I discovered, for the first time, what fun it could be—working with teachers in this kind of situation. A few years after I had begun teaching, Wilt Eberhart had asked me whether I had ever given thought to entering English education, the training of English teachers. I had told him that I felt my best service would be at the high-school level. I hadn't considered that assisting teachers might be nearly as rewarding as I found it to be in Piketon. Nor did I realize that one day I might be working with teachers at Worthington in a somewhat similar capacity.

I had, at one time, run a night course for adults in creative writing. That had been an extremely stimulating experience. There had been a considerable range of talent, experience, and motivation in that group of fifteen grown-ups. The best writer in the class was a forty-year-old man who was regularly doing writing and public-relations work for the governor of Ohio. The least secure member of the class was a woman of approximately fifty who had signed up because she had felt it might be interesting. "Mr. Rousculp," she breathed one night in a low voice, "these other people all write so well. When I signed up, all I wanted to learn or hoped to get out of the course was to write a letter that I didn't have to be ashamed of." That statement of hers moved me very deeply—it was a considerable admission for the wife of a wealthy businessman in Worthington, a suburb that appears as the Mecca of Culture to many people in the surrounding area. Hers was an honest cry for education in an age and area where it is much less surprising to find people pretending background that they do not possess. Needless to say, while the others in the group were experimenting with more sophisticated literary forms, I tried to teach her letter writing.

Every week, members of the class would bring in their short stories, poetry, plays, and articles for study and examination by the group. I would have copies made but without the author's names, and I'd usually throw in something from a professional and once in a while one of my own stories. All of us learned from these sessions of mutual criticism. Even the big-time professionals took it "on the chin," sometimes.

My experiences as a teacher-errant have always been instructive, even if unhappy at times. Just as the minister is seldom, if ever, free of his calling, so the teacher is nearly always associated with his practice in a neighbor's mind. Rudy Hitzemann is regularly called upon to teach driver education to his neighbors' wives. As an English teacher, I often find myself faced with helping others to write letters, interpret printed materials, check their grammar or spelling, or assist them in language issues that have arisen in their classrooms. When I am introduced to people as an English teacher, even well-educated people frequently begin to stammer over their concern that I may be parsing their sentences or judging them by their language, though I make it a point never to do so.

"Once a Marine, always a Marine," the old gunnery sergeant used to say. Maybe, but another aphorism is certainly as valid: *Once a teacher, always a teacher.* Perhaps this is why my moonlit memories picture not only a miter box, an adding machine, and the half-obliterated **BARBE,** but a middle-aged woman who wanted to learn to write letters, a boy who was utterly mystified by *Comus,* and a desperate girl who watched from behind a drape as I walked out of her life.

Somewhere in the clutter which only on the opening day of school looks like a desk is a box of colored chalk. I hide it. I keep it separated from the common white chalk because the colored variety is harder to obtain at Worthington High School. I conceal it for a very good reason—I value it for its contrast and for the emphasis it can give to the chalkboard lessons in Room 106, lessons on Life. Because many of my fellow teachers also prize the colored chalk and as they are somewhat communistic where desks are concerned, I do not put it in an obvious place in my desk drawer. I don't want it to disappear. Hence, I am guilty of segregation, of a type of color prejudice, and of a jealous unwillingness to give up the variety in my chalk-dust existence.

I should hate to think of any monocultured world made up of a monochromatic people living by a monolithic creed. I thrive on

The Many-Splendored Chalk

variety, I treasure diversity, I need opposing views. There is a very sound basis for my position, I believe. I have never been brought into contact with other races, other ways of life, other philosophies without growing substantially in my own thought and perspective.

I must make it clear that I do not defend or wish to perpetuate the disgraceful treatment which man's cupidity and fear have wrought among people whose only "faults" have been racial, religious, and cultural dissimilarities. What some label "civil" rights, I call "human" rights, and I hold that the universal realization of these rights depends upon education, common sense, and good will among men.

Most of the important faces in my past I can reconstruct, can recall in fine detail. But there is one visage for which I reach in vain through the vaporous past. I remember a black face, a broad smile, and a patch of white above the ear—no other detail for the head. Then a great dark hand, reaching across a fence. Then the hand is gone, and I am clutching a candy bar. I peek through the fence at a broad back and a shambling gait. No more than that. For I was not much more than three years old, and that mist-shrouded scene is one of my several earliest memories.

His name was John Brown, and they tell me that I learned to speak his name. He was a handyman employed by the owner of a mansion close by. Daily he brought his gift to me, usually a bar of Hershey chocolate, till the provider's hand, itself, seemed chocolate. Somehow, John Brown merged with St. Nicholas and Jesus Christ in my child's mind. I can remember watching vainly for that old Negro to pass by after my parents had rented a white stucco apartment on the opposite side of town. My loss of John Brown was the first conscious grief of my childhood.

When John Brown had faded with time, and when I had become accustomed to hearing the voices of hate and prejudice around me, I naturally came to use the term *nigger*—until my mother heard me, that is. After she told me never to use the word again, I quickly banished it from my personal lexicon. But still I heard the sound of it in my neighborhood and sometimes with my relatives.

The recollections of my youth nowhere lent themselves to hating the Negro. I remember that the boys in my neighborhood used to play a team comprised mainly of colored children. Their softball pitcher was always a white boy whom they virtually adored. He was their close friend, and later he became a first-rate athlete in the high school I attended. Today he is a teacher and a coach.

How I enjoyed two radio shows which featured a Negro dialect and comedy situations! Like many people, I listened to *Amos and Andy* and something called *The Johnson Family* and felt affection for those characters. It never once occurred to me that such entertainment was anti-Negro, no more than Laurel and Hardy or Wheeler and Woolsey were anti-Caucasian in my thinking. Stepin Fetchit and Mantan Moreland did no damage to the Negro image, except in ignorant minds or twisted thinking, where the damage was already done.

I do not know for a fact but would guess that the Marine Corps was the last of the services to effectively integrate the races. I say this because it seemed to me that the Corps was as dominated by the South as is VMI. I don't mean to suggest that there is greater prejudice in the Southern states, but only that it tends more toward institutional segregation.

When we moved into regular barracks at Stone Bay in North Carolina, some whites from the North as well as those from the South complained that "Eleanor's best" (Negro Marines) had been there before us. Frequently, I heard veterans back from Bougainville speak derogatorily about the combat ineffectiveness of a Negro battalion. On Iwo Jima, I saw what I felt was discrimination of the worst kind. There were three great piles of American dead—separated, possibly, according to the divisions (Third, Fourth, and Fifth)—not to mention a heap of "spare parts" not matched with the bodies from which they had been torn. Two or three times a day, men from a small Negro detachment had to mount those mounds of fetid, decaying flesh and spray them with disinfectant. Faced by that horror, perhaps I missed whites doing the same job, but I cannot recall any at that task.

In the anti-Negro feeling of the Southerners, whose ability as fighting men I came to admire and depend upon, there was a curious anomaly. Many of them were not averse to having sexual intercourse with Negro women. Certainly, they didn't hesitate to talk about such unions. As a matter of fact, I received the distinct impression that, in some sections of the South, interracial coitus was considered to be part of a white boy's growing up. "Yo' ain't growed inter a man," I heard one white Southerner remark, "till yo' gits yo'se'f some Dahk Meat, boy." And the context was not cuisine.

Early one morning I was walking as usual from the home of the girl I was dating in Florida. She lived several miles outside Jacksonville, and I had a considerable trek when I left her house. Along my route there was a particularly noisy if not vicious dog who would leap out at me, always at some unexpected turn, so I kept a match cocked and ready to strike whenever the first low growl came. I was thinking about my canine friend and worrying about whether I could get to Roosevelt Highway and catch my bus for the Naval Air Station in time for reveille when I saw the headlights approaching from behind me. As I reached the Old Post Road, the dilapidated '34 Chevy drew up alongside me.

"Ca-ah fo' a lif' t' town?" came a marshmallow voice. I recognized it as belonging to a bus driver with whom I sometimes rode in the city—a young white fellow of, maybe, thirty. The car was in shadows, but I could barely make out another white man driving the car. I was tired and late and grateful for the chance to avoid Rover down the road, so I hopped into the back seat. There I found myself between two women, who giggled over my entrance.

I knew right away how the group had been entertaining themselves. Everyone was happy and laughing in the car, and, in spite of the odor of stale wine and God-knows-what, I exchanged jokes with them. The car hadn't tailfished very far down the road (or somewhere near the road) before I understood that both women were becoming enthusiastic about my presence. Some whispered quaintness and coyness made it plain that flesh was available and eager on both sides. I tried to sound appropriately appreciative as I turned down the earthily phrased offers. I didn't actually know that the women were Negroes until the car drew up under a lighted section by the old Jax viaduct, where I got out to head for the bus station.

For me the really big surprise came the next day, when I heard that same bus driver order a Negro to move to the back of the bus. Then, without the slightest interval, he said to me: "Goddam niggahs trah theah damnedes' t' set down close t' white people." I must have stared at the back of his neck in astonishment for several minutes. But then I remembered—even in the old car, colored girls rode in the back seat.

Since there were no Negroes in my Marine unit, I had only a few occasions during the war years to observe them and thereby to cancel out the anti-Negro attitudes I often heard expressed. Perhaps that is partly why one event stands out in bold relief as I look back. It happened a night or two before the Iwo landing, and it made an exciting prelude to the holocaust ahead.

As was our custom, Casey, Blough, Burge and I had played pinochle in the galley of the U.S.S. *Napa* (a Liberty transport) till well after midnight. I had left them and had gone to my platoon's below-deck compartment, where I had soon fallen asleep. It must have been two-thirty or so when I was awakened by a horrendous crash and a great lurching of the *Napa.* The whole compartment came to life instantly. Some of the men began to ascend through the ladder well to the main deck even before the instructions were heard to report to our debarkation stations.

To this day, I have no real knowledge of what nearly sank that ship. The story most widely told was that another vessel in the zig-zagging convoy had zag-zigged and had accidentally rammed the *Napa.* There was speculation in my compartment that we had

278

caught a torpedo or struck a mine. Certainly, the ship was taking on water in one of the main hatches and was leaning, if I remember correctly, to the port side.

I tried to get around to check the men for whom I was responsible. Jim Lane, a fine-looking Roman Catholic boy who would die within the month, was still sleeping soundly. I saw that his inflatable life belt was missing. Feeling certain that I would find one lying around, I slipped mine off and shoved it under his arm as I shook him to a sitting position. (It turned out that he was never fully awake and never left the compartment during the incident.) There was another row of bunks to be checked, and when I saw that they had been vacated I made for the deck.

The deck was unbelievable. I couldn't imagine that people could act as they were there. Two lieutenants were fighting over a shoe. A sergeant was stammering badly to his men to get to the boat deck. All around me was consternation. It was almost funny. Then I realized I should try to find a life belt. But was there time to run back to the compartment? I stood swaying in indecision. Then someone tapped me on the shoulder. I spun about to see a Negro face—dark against the cloudy sky-canopy.

I recognized him as one of the stewards or cooks in the galley. He thrust something at me—a life belt. "You're gonna need this, fella," he said and giggled. Grateful, I grabbed at it, but as he swung away and before I could say *thanks* I saw—even in the dark of the deck—that he wore none, that he had given me his own. For a moment, it seemed that I stood by a fence and held a bar of chocolate, instead of the gift of Life.

There were other noteworthy sights on the *Napa* that morning. The captain, walking about in shorts and chewing an unlit cigar as he issued orders; the fastening of a collision mat over the great jagged hole in the side of the ship; the sweeping searchlight of a destroyer-escort moving about the vessel—these are still etched in my memory. Yet, though the dawn was still hours away, any dark doubt that I might have possessed about Negro people was obliterated by the blinding truth of a black man's charity.

Worthington does not have a large Negro population, so I do not find many Negro faces in Room 106. Those that have come to me, however, have made great contributions to the pleasure I take from my work. I would feel cheated if I had to teach in a one-color classroom. Of course, like their lighter-skinned classmates, young Negroes have also brought me some moments of anxiety. One day, some years ago, a young Negro widow called me to arrange an appointment. From the telephone conversation, I knew only that she was very much distressed about something that had happened in my classroom. When she arrived in 106, I could tell that she was hesitant about complaining, even uncertain about talking to a teacher. I tried to make her as comfortable as possible.

"Mr. Rousculp," she began, "when I brought my children to Worthington, I understood that this was the kind of school and town where their color wouldn't make any difference. And people of my color who live here speak highly of you."

"One of the reasons I teach here, Mrs. Jackson, is that there's always seemed to me to be a democratic attitude among the students and teachers in this school. I—"

"Well, Mr. Rousculp, how *could* you have permitted that boy, that Woltzer boy, to give that book report in your class?"

As soon as she mentioned the boy's name, I knew the problem. Dan Woltzer had given an oral book report on Booth Tarkington's *Seventeen*. In the course of the report, he had reproduced some of the author's dialogue in which the young protagonist Willy Baxter is speaking of the Negro odd-jobs man, Genesis. Unfortunately, in that portion of the report Dan had used the expression *nigger* in several places. Mrs. Jackson's son Ben was in Dan's class and had taken personal offense, apparently.

I always ask students to avoid expressions that might wound or offend their classmates, but since I had schooled myself to ignore the word I am not certain that I had noted Dan's repeated use of the term. I explained my position to Mrs. Jackson—that the boy had not used the word with malice, I was sure, and that *Seventeen* does not represent the Negro race unfairly or viciously. "If Genesis is funny," I told her, "he's not nearly so ridiculous as Willy."

My comments did not content the woman. I saw that she wished something else of me. "Mr. Rousculp, Ben says that Woltzer boy did that on purpose because he doesn't like my son."

I told her that I couldn't believe that Dan would do that sort of thing. "I'm honestly sorry, Mrs. Jackson, that the word was used and that Ben was bothered by it. What can I do to make you feel better?" My phrasing was poor. It annoyed her, and little wonder.

"It's not me I'm thinking about—it's Ben. He won't feel comfortable in your class, I'm afraid, till he knows that that boy won't be using that word any more."

"Well, Mrs. Jackson, I can ask Dan if he'll speak to Ben, but I can't promise that he will."

"Do you think he will?" Her hands were tension in teakwood.

"I can only ask him. Meanwhile, I'll talk to Ben, myself."

"I would appreciate that." She was feeling better as she rose to leave. I had to say some other things to her, though. Maybe I wanted the practice—maybe I wanted to try out some comments on her before I talked to her son. "You know, Mrs. Jackson, my first wonderful friendship was with a Negro man, so I have a very natural feeling for you and your family. And do you know what I think are the worst crimes that the white man has perpetrated on the Negro besides slavery? He and some Negro helpers are gradually taking away the colored man's ability to laugh at himself and these same villains have made your people cringe beneath a word. There's an old saying about 'sticks and stones,' Mrs. Jackson, and Ben is going to have to learn the truth of it. Richard Wright and Langston Hughes have found out about words, and they've begun to use some of their own—good language. That's what I'll want Ben to learn in 106—that a person is bigger than a word and bigger still when he's found out how to use words himself. Ben has to learn this just as Carver and Booker T. Washington did." I went on to explain that later in the year *that word* would appear in the literature we studied and that her son should stop hiding from it.

We talked another several minutes before she left, but I don't think she grasped entirely what it was I was trying to say. Dan actually apologized to Ben the following day, and I talked to the young Negro. He was not cheered by our words. For, tragically, there was another factor behind his hypersensitivity—he was badly smitten, moved to the point of adoration, by a young lady in that class, and the girl was white, a young Quaker. He might have seen her smile over the amusing behavior of Tarkington's Genesis. That book report had reminded him of his race, had perhaps seemed to him to widen what he saw as a chasm between him and the girl he obviously fancied.

Though many of my professional colleagues take as much pride as I do in the accomplishments of Negro students and athletes, some teachers are good examples of racial tolerance only, not of an active sympathy for and interest in the Negro. Some teachers, unhappily, are like the old Southern aristocrat, who spoke proudly of "my niggers."

My one great struggle against prejudice had practically nothing to do with my countrymen and did not take into account an entire race. It could be boiled down to a single word—Japanese. "What is the spirit of the bayonet?" the D. I. at Parris Island would shout.

"TO KILL!" thundered the answer. "And *what* do you kill?" intoned our lord and master, selecting his pronoun purposefully. "JAPS!" the drill field reverberated. Parry—lunge. Parry—lunge. Always the leering, big-incisored, bespectacled stereotype. The Japanese were rapists, the Japs were butchers, the Nips were treacherous, the "dirty sons o' bitches" cut off the testicles of wounded Americans. Oh, but there was revenge—the screening fire, then the bazooka shells, then the pack charge to enlarge the hole, and finally the beautiful blossom of the flamethrower and the odor of scorching flesh.

Without taking anything away from the Commando or the Green Beret, I must testify that the United States Marine Corps achieved a mastery in the fine art of conditioning a killer extraordinary. Still, I will not condemn my alma mater. Though I oppose war and though there are souls that I must answer for and to, I have absolutely no sympathy for the conscientious objector who basks in the security of his ideals while someone else makes it possible for him to determine the niceties and proprieties he can support. I recognize the political and spiritual rights of the C. O., but I do not comprehend his rationale, and I certainly would not want him beside me in a foxhole.

On the other hand, one does not learn to hate well one day and to love the next. The Marine Corps taught me to revile and detest the Japanese, and it has taken many years for me to molt away that feeling. Even after my mind had consciously rejected hatred, my body reacted negatively to the presence of Japanese.

The clearest pictures of Japanese troops that I can summon out of the past are those in which the faces are turned away from me. The dead Japanese over whom I stood are without facial features. I remember taking from a Japanese pocket the pictures of the dead man's family. I recall the pose the woman and child had struck for the photographer, but the figures are without eyes, noses, mouths. I think I know the reason for that facelessness. It has nothing to do with time. I had refused to see them as human beings, had determined that it was still the cardboard stereotypes I destroyed. I could put off Truth till that time when I could learn to live with it.

And the Japanese atrocities? They were supposed to be everywhere, to be legion, though I saw only an instance or two. I remember with a shudder a shriveled something (they said it was an ear) that a Marine carried in a jar, the little bag of gold teeth a young man had hammered out of dead mouths, and the murder of a defenseless prisoner. Atrocities happen on both sides in any war, I can better avouch today. Why not? In mass madness one must find individual madness.

Our officers knew that we were animals, essentially. Before they let us come back from the Pacific, they assigned special instructors—psychologists, some of them—to talk to us about things like women and sex and property. I can recall as though it were yesterday the fat little man who discussed the care with which a woman's breasts should be handled. They tried to make us civilized again in two weeks. They were far less successful in getting many Marines to put away the conditioned hate and distrust of Japanese.

I was first put to the test at Ohio State University. On the opening day of my second quarter there, I arrived somewhat early for my morning history class. As the room was empty, I took a seat about midway down on the side next to the window. With nothing to do but wait, I began looking through several books I had picked up at the Derby Hall book store that morning. When several other students entered the room and when one sat down behind me and another to my right, I didn't feel enough curiosity to look around me. Then I heard others entering, and as the bell rang I glanced at those nearby. To my right sat a young Oriental—a Japanese—his eyes intent upon the teacher who had just entered the room.

I may have heard a few words the professor uttered that period, but not many. The remainder of that hour, I sat in a cold sweat, watching my brown-skinned classmate from the corner of my eye. Surely, he must be Japanese-American, like the woman who had done my laundry in Wailuku, like some others I had known. But this one was an unknown quantity, though clearly Japanese. That hour was interminable. There was no relief. My skin crawled, my fingers trembled, my head swam until the merciful bell had sounded.

The seats in that class were not permanently assigned. Thereafter, I was sure never to arrive early. If the Japanese student was not yet there, I contrived to sit where there would be no empty seats around me. Even so, I would find myself looking for him, wanting to know where he sat in that big room.

After many years of teaching, I supposed that common sense and time had rid my being of such unreasoning antipathy. When the Lowerys invited my wife and me to their new home one evening, I discovered that, among their guests, was a Japanese, only a few years younger than I. I made every effort to be polite, yet he may have sensed my extreme discomfort. There was a strain on my part to keep the conversation going. All through the talk, however, I was wondering: *Where were you during the war? What were your father and brothers doing? Are they alive today? Is it possible that they—that I might have—*

That evening was still another trial, but I came a step closer to being fully civilized. I could recall the man's face, his individual physical features, and certain of his mannerisms. Perhaps Frank knew that such contact would be good for me.

The final proof that I was emancipated from my prejudice toward the Japanese came with an American Field Service foreign-exchange student. She was from Hiroshima, and her name was Chie. It was ironic but to my favor that she was the first AFS student to be assigned to Room 106. All the others had taken American literature (normally a junior course).

With Chie, I grew in my awareness of the crime of war—the enormity of man's legalized homicide. She was a warm, vibrant little person for whom all of Worthington High School felt affection. Watching her, I wondered how many such young people had heard the sound of the *Enola Gay* and had reeled with the shock and the fire that followed.

Chie's presence did so very much for me, more than she would ever comprehend. Like all AFS exchange students, Chie left her flag to the school. We keep these flags in a display case at Worthington. I was looking at Chie's just the other day. It is a flag quite similar to the Japanese battle flags of World War II—with one main difference. On the field of white surrounding the sun, there are none of the black markings found on the old battle flags. In the same way, perhaps Chie's smile in my classroom brought clearer sight for her teacher and an absolution for the death-blackened, faceless spectres of his past.

At the end of the year, she said to me, "Thank you so much for most interesting class." I wanted to tell her that her being there had cleansed me, had buried Kato Kiyosama and his bushido with Commodore Perry and his big guns. But she had been born in 1945 and wouldn't quite understand. "Thank *you*, Chie," I replied. "Sayonara."

I keep my colored chalk out of need, a teacher's need. I cherish the memory of colored faces out of affection and another need—a man's need. Each of the races has played an important part in creating the spirit of the chalk dust—the many-splendored chalk.

"They are trying to railroad us into a union," asserted one woman. "This is the attempt of a small group to take over our association!" shouted another. "The whole proposition is in direct conflict with parliamentary procedure," insisted a classroom teacher. "This committee had no authorization to do what they have done," he added. And so it went. When the president put the question to a vote, the result was an overwhelming 82-18 decision to scrap a proposed revision of the bylaws for the Worthington Education Association.

Such outcomes are commonplace among teachers' organizations as they presently exist—the proposed changes would have created a strong professional association that might have been able, through a program of research and public relations, to command the respect of the community at large. The bylaw modifica-

W-E-A Spells AWE

tions would have allowed those who are solely interested in the social aspects of such an organization to maintain *associate*, nonvoting memberships. The revitalized WEA would have built its program to satisfy the aims of an *active* membership, a professional corps in the school district that wanted an organization of professional character and militant concern for improved education. After the vote had been taken, a number of career teachers became convinced that the WEA was destined to remain the ice-cream social that it had been for nearly ten years, or since the Somers affair, in spite of several leaders' efforts.

Much of the early impetus of the Association had come from the superintendent. That an administrator should encourage the development of a professional organization is not at all unusual. If he is to act as a leader of the profession in his school system, he prefers to have a local organization of professionals affiliated with state and national offices to support his recommendations to his board of education for expanded facilities, salary increases, hiring of additional personnel, etc. Not that all boards of education must feel pressure from such professional groups in order to take desirable action, but a board is, of course, directly responsible to a public which may not always share their enlightenment on school matters. If teacher organizations are impotent or nonexistent, the well-meaning administrator is often cast in the role of a monologist asking for appropriations or proposing operating levies which the professional staff seemingly sees no need for. The strength of an administrator, like that of the teacher, is in direct ratio to the strength of the professional organization in any school system.

I had served on the local TEPS (Teacher Education and Professional Standards) Committee that had fashioned the recommended changes in the bylaws, just as I had served years before on the committee which had formed the original parliamentary instrument for the WEA. The TEPS group was headed by a young veteran-turned-teacher, John Hammill, who had already done much to build the Driver Education and Safety program in the state. The dozen or so members of TEPS felt toward John as I did. We had very great respect for his integrity and his capacity for organizational work.

If John has any weakness, it is in the matter of tact and diplomacy. If he has ever run short in this respect—and possibly he has—it was principally because he has learned, as so many other career teachers do, that the greatest reason for education's low estate on the contemporary scene is the unwillingness of teachers to speak their minds. School needs are usually most discernible at the classroom level, and if teachers are gagged by their own apathy or fear the public may not be informed of the classroom state of affairs.

As strongly as Hammill feels about the need for an energetic association, he patiently led the TEPS committee through weeks of research and discussion into a final document which the group felt could implement a strong, dynamic, autonomous organization. The TEPS people were not commissioned to draw up a new constitution, and we saw the parliamentary hazards. We were also aware, however, that the Constitutional Convention of 1787 had no authority from the Congress of the Articles of Confederation to formulate the Constitution of the United States. There were other precedents, too, under which we could justify our work to develop a framework upon which the WEA would become a worthy affiliate of state and national organizations already beginning to see the light.

The committee had not been long at its endeavors when the anti-TEPS faction set up its mill and began to grind out rumors. Curiously, the greatest opposition in the high school came not from classroom teachers, nor from administrators, but from a few people whose positions put them into a limbo somewhere between teacher and official. Most of these people were and remain friends of mine, and though I could not follow their reasoning I could only assume that they opposed TEPS on what they felt were justifiable, valid grounds. In the elementary schools there were some classroom teachers whose opposition to a stronger organization was based either upon misinformation or upon that brand of ultraconservative thinking in education which, among Ohio teachers, is incomprehensible.

Throughout the school system—primary, intermediate, and secondary—the vast majority of the staff were comparatively unconcerned. As I have indicated, many Worthington teachers (some of them of considerable promise) are in the school system on a short-term basis. Naturally, some of these people do not feel the concern for the future of local education and the teaching profession that career teachers do. In addition, some teachers who had formerly been active in the WEA had long since become discouraged over the anemic character it had developed. As they saw it, the organization was a dead horse. To kick it was not merely futile—it created the unpleasant odor of professional decomposition.

Also, there were, as there always are, some who supposed that any effort to resuscitate the WEA must be engineered by rabble-rousers, unionists, or chronic boat-rockers. Some teachers on the staff lived in the community and were afraid of what conservative neighbors might say if they were associated with an outspoken teacher organization. And others felt that they had a good thing, an easy income to supplement a husband's. Teaching can be much *easier* for those who approach their job with a who-gives-a-damn attitude—but, then, persons of this sort do not really teach except by poor example.

The non-professional or apathetic teacher is nearly always aligned with the status quo. He has made peace with himself and has become complacently sedentary. He is the one who always smiles at the true professional and says "Oh, you're not going to change anything. Relax, friend. You're stirring up the dust." His dust, that is. The reason for his smile is that he has found, over the years, that most often he is safely with the majority—including the care-nothings and do-nothings that litter the educational landscape. Mr. Non-professional is honest enough to have very little respect for the label *teacher* which he must bear or for the work he does—he'll even tell you so—and if he could find a way out he'd probably leave. But now he's trapped, as he sees it, and he has stoically set up housekeeping in his miserable quarters. He is, at once, the most tragic and the most disgusting figure in all schooldom—the parasite that feeds on the profession. I once told a student that I do not apologize for my profession, and I don't. Like my fellow professionals, I can only apologize for some of the people hired into the profession.

One of the features of the proposed changes in the WEA that was especially frightening to the non-professional lay in the clause which allowed for a review of the individual's professional qualifications. The legal and medical organizations have established such intra-professional safeguards. Educators will eventually do so, and only then will teachers grow in professional and public stature.

There was a great irony for me in the ballot which nullified the TEPS committee's work. Several months before, I had been asked to speak to the organization on a definition of *professional* as applied to teaching. At that time, I saw no sign of dissent—the heads nodded in approbation and accord. What they were really saying to me was "It's all right to talk about it, but for God's sake don't do anything about it." When that same definition was embodied in the spirit of the recommended bylaws, it was condemned. "How can this organization tell us what is professional and what isn't?" someone cried. The fact was that the TEPS membership was not really telling them, nor would the WEA tell them. Their quarrel was with the statement of teaching ethics and professional behavior that had been adopted by the National Education Association.

I have said before that I am a poor loser. I sat stunned, very nearly speechless, during that fateful meeting. The several comments I did make were brief and feeble, and some of my close friends were disappointed in my poor showing. They didn't know that the heart was out of me for the moment. They didn't realize that I was learning something for the first time, and belatedly. For years I had permitted myself to believe that teachers were hamstrung by external forces—state legislatures, communities, boards of education. Now I saw plainly the real antagonist of the teacher's epic—the teacher, himself.

Through the remainder of the meeting, even the balloting, I stared at that incredible revelation. It was the teacher who kept himself and his calling in bondage. It was he who stood on the sidelines when he should be huddling and driving on the field. It was he who preferred to whisper his complaints in a teacher's lounge when he should be voicing his position and his needs over a rostrum. It was he who, instead of donning the proud mantle of professional responsibility, crept about in threadbare ludicrousness—an Ichabod Crane who did not recognize the headless specter as the projected image of his own tragic timorousness and indolence.

I left that meeting not merely sick at heart. I wanted to vomit. My head was still ringing with the voices—the anger, the hysteria, the derision. These people who had voted had been my friends. At least, I had thought so. People I had worked with for years had accused me—for I could not separate myself from the others on the committee—of trying to railroad them, of doing them wrong, of making trouble, of being a rabid unionist.

That last charge, at least, was substantially correct, I had to admit. Because I have seen what the AMA can do for its members and for medicine, because I have understood the functions of the bar associations, I am indeed a "unionist." Sometimes, one could see selfishness in the other professions, but it did not exist because of the professions, only because of individuals within them. Their associations did much good, and they were "unions." My critics had something else in mind. As teachers associated with a suburban community, they were all snarled in semantics. *Union* was a bad word. Because at present a union-called strike that results in higher wages and escalates prices will leave the teacher in an economic bind, some teachers, seeing this complex effect as the cause of their financial difficulties, are very much anti-union. Many of them have not understood that, if you can not beat a thing, you have in effect joined it, however unwillingly. Once a part of any political and economic system, a group must find its own means of promotion and development. For teachers, the logical *union* is in national, state, and local organizations of teachers. Of course, such organizations must function, not simply exist, and they should recognize the distinction between professional workers and employees of other vocational areas.

My concern and that of the TEPS committee was not centered in teacher salaries and working conditions. We were, to put it succinctly, interested in improving *all* conditions which affect the teacher's practice and the youngster's learning. Like industrial management, the professional teacher is especially interested in his product. The chief difference is that the teacher's product is a human being. Children in a school district are directly affected much more by their teachers than by the physical facilities which house the school. If a school system suffers from an annual exodus of a quarter of its teaching staff, from a need for light industry to reduce the tax burden of residential property owners, *and* from the lack of instructional area in gymnasiums and auditoriums, a functioning professional organization is necessary to keep the welfare of the community's youngsters something more than an ancillary consideration.

No one has stated the teacher's obligation to his profession more pointedly than Ohio's state superintendent of public instruction, Martin W. Essex:

> One of the cardinal responsibilities that we assume when we enter a profession is to give of our time and talent to improve that profession so that it may serve its functions at maximum effectiveness.

I have listened on several occasions to the arguments of the American Federation of Teachers representatives, and I must say that they present a rather eloquent case. I have never seriously meditated membership in this AFL-CIO affiliate, however, because I have always believed that there is a very significant difference between working with things and working with humanity and because I believe that the AFT is bound to reflect its ties with trade and industrial unionism. Still, I must give credit to the AFT. That organization has done much to build a fire under the NEA and its state and local affiliates. The AFT has led the way in taking corrective, united action where teacher-school needs have been at issue. As a result, the NEA and state education associations have begun to employ sanctions in those areas where the profession's voice has been unheard or ignored.

When I speak of an effective professional organization, I am not referring to one which operates in a unilateral, bulldozing manner—a group that calls "Strike!" on the least provocation or which takes action on purely selfish grounds. I am, instead, interested in a teacher organization which focuses, first of all, upon developing the best possible educational program for the young people in the community it serves. Such an organization will recognize, too, that the students' needs are inextricably joined with the teachers' needs. What is good for the genuinely professional teacher is always desirable for the student who sits in that teacher's classroom. An education association will, among other things, undertake to:

(1) establish liaison with community groups concerned with education locally,

(2) keep state and national affiliates informed as to its wishes and its displeasure (when necessary),

(3) keep the public fully informed of teacher views through news releases and advertising,

(4) write letters of recommendation to prospective employers for professional members who have fulfilled their contract obligations and who for various reasons find it necessary to teach elsewhere,

(5) engage in professional negotiations with a board of education in decisions affecting teacher morale and welfare and the effectiveness of the schools,

(6) review qualifications of candidates and support the best candidates in board-of-education elections,

(7) develop a program of financial research in order to be fully informed and then publish these findings to the community,

(8) establish such respect for itself as an organization that its membership will feel a sense of pride and a spirit of professional camaraderie,

(9) evaluate honestly and objectively the total school program and work to improve it wherever and however possible,

(10) censure publicly forces or factors which impede educational progress and which work to the detriment of the profession, and

(11) exert every constructive political influence that can be brought to bear upon legislators—state and national—for the improvement of education and the teaching profession everywhere.

The individuals who had voted against restructuring the WEA had done so for a variety of reasons, some of which I have mentioned. Some few of them held that the revisions would, in the long run, weaken the organization. How they reasoned that the WEA could become less effective than it already was I couldn't grasp. But these opponents were not the ones that had made me ill. Nor did the votes of the apathetic and the few nest-featherers do more than make me angry. What had turned my stomach was the spectacle of the fearful—those who sat in awe over the idea that teachers might even consider becoming a collective force to reckon with in the power structure of the community.

I left the organization. The next year I did not join, for I couldn't, in all conscience.

Then I saw that the decisive meeting had not really ended, that a reaction had gradually set in among the membership. John Hammill was appointed to the vacancy in the wake of the president's resignation. Full of hope for my profession, longing to feel less alone in my work, wanting to renew friendships among my erstwhile accusers, I rejoined the WEA. I want to believe that a new day has begun for those who labor with chalk and pen. I want to know that my profession all over the country has found renewed courage and dedication and pride in its position as the Mother of All Professions. I want to see that W-E-A no longer spells AWE.

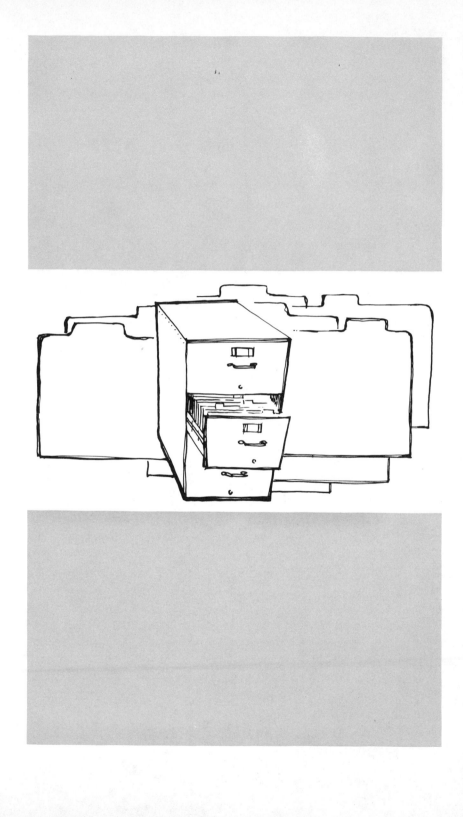

One fall morning, as I was trying to get the papers on my desk into some semblance of order and hoping to find Ivor Brown's *Shakespeare* somewhere under that debris, I heard a light knocking at the door. There was a small girl standing just outside, and I recognized her pixie face and enormous eyes right away. "Come in, Linda. How are you?"

"I wanted to show you something," she beamed as she thrust out one hand toward me. I took the rectangular card she had brought—her report card. Her grades in her eighth-grade subjects were A's in all but one course, and in that one she had received a B. "I never had a report card with grades like these, and I wanted to thank you."

"Now, that's very nice of you, Linda," I replied, "but just remember—you're the one that did it."

The How-to-Study Man

"But you showed me how," she declared. She was referring to her work with me in a summer course labeled "How to Study" which I've been teaching for some years. Linda was convinced that her new academic success had grown out of that eight-weeks sacrifice of summer vacation time, so precious to a twelve-year-old girl. Naturally, I was delighted that her efforts had been rewarded so quickly and so remarkably, but as always I knew that some of the others who had taken the course would show only slight gains or no gains at all.

When she had gone, I opened the file cabinet in which I keep the study-course records and marked a plus sign beside her name to indicate the improvement she had reported. During the five-year period in which I did a follow-up evaluation of the course, I marked a large number of such pluses, but there were a few minus signs (showing an actual drop in grades) and many names where no change in progress was registered. My record is not complete because some students have moved from the school system, and others never attended classes in the Worthington district during the regular school years. Some students have been sent to our summer school from other areas because of the publicity that the study course has received.

The only statistical summary of the course effects was worked up by a team of psychologists in 1961. In their study, the course showed impressively favorable results for students in grades 10 through 12, but negligible changes in the school performance of ninth graders. Since that evaluation, the course has been modified or adapted to accommodate seventh and eighth graders, and my records for these younger students are quite fragmentary.

When my principal, Bill Lane, asked me whether I would like to design such a course in 1960, I agreed to do so in spite of my lack of special training. What came out of my planning was a potpourri of what I believed were practical, common-sense approaches to study efficiency. Admittedly, I sought confirmation and support for my own ideas by turning to such college-level texts as Francis P. Robinson's *Effective Study*. I studied the educational psychologists' writings and tried to synthesize their content and to rephrase it for assimilation by our younger students. In 1960 there was not as yet on the market a textbook which I felt entirely suited to a study-methods course for teenagers. Several publishers had produced materials on the subject, but none that I had ferreted out for examination provided exactly what we needed. Therefore, a significant portion of the substance in the course had to depend upon lectures and demonstrations by the teacher—the poorest of all teaching methods, especially when overworked.

In order to develop greater pupil participation, I found it necessary to allow time for them to discuss their past classroom experiences (successes and failures), to criticize study devices that experts suggested, and to engage in various other activities that would give them added respite from the teacher's voice. I provided writing laboratories in which they could have increased experience in organizing and expressing their ideas on paper and without the bludgeoning effect of letter grades. I asked them to draw pictures or diagrams of the areas in which they studied at home so that, together, we might determine how to eliminate distractions and create better study environments. I got their fall schedules ahead of time so that we might talk about budgeting their hours. Besides brief over-the-shoulder sessions in the classroom, twenty minutes of personalized counseling was allotted to every student. I spoke with each of them about his past grades and about how he thought he might apply the course materials in improving his work.

We spent much time in considering the teacher's role in a classroom. Without identifying individual persons, I gave the students biographical sketches of a number of secondary-level faculty members, emphasizing their more interesting experiences—for example, one member's participation in the Olympics and another's work in breaking up an Italian black-market operation during World War II. I wanted these students to see, moreover, that teachers have as much at stake in their students' progress as the students, themselves. We discussed the motives of teachers and many topics centering upon what makes for good student-teacher relationships and desirable student-student relations.

To show my How-to-Study pupils that their work in school became a matter of public knowledge, I brought into class every summer a number of very old cumulative-record cards from past graduating classes—the cards from which the office prints transcripts for colleges and provides information for prospective employers. Whenever I would read some of the rather blunt, however accurate, summaries written by a former high-school principal, the students would sit wide-eyed and serious. Although some teachers would oppose my using such a technique, this was one of the ways in which I tried to goad students—to move them toward feeling greater concern over the records which *they* were furnishing the school office.

For motivation is very often the cardinal factor in student performance, as we all know. We like to pretend that student achievement falls into the so-called "normal-frequency curve," but our measuring instruments can never truly assess this major unknowable, motivation. Who can say what incentive or lack of it does to intelligence-test scores? Teachers too often make assumptions about student work. Those instructors who grade "on the curve" forget that a whole classroom may be "dragging its feet." Still, I think it is a safe assumption that most students *can* perform more satisfactorily if they *will*. And the teacher can usually inject some fuel into student carburetors.

Of course, the type and quantity of octane for student advance is never certain. Teaching is still more art than science, and I hope that it remains so. We bring our machines and equipment into the classroom, and, though the novelty produces a desirable impact upon students for a time, we inevitably must come back to the teacher's role—his relationship with his students, his ability to stir interest, and that very unscientific, unpredictable phenomenon that causes some fairly well-educated teachers to produce miracles with young people and some superb scholars to plop prone on their probosces when they try to teach.

In teaching, as in many other areas, the more we learn, the more we must return to some of the old verities. Just when science was smug in its belief that the world was round or pear-shaped, orbiting satellites now make it clear that the earth is a geoid, that it does have, after all, the "four corners" described in the final book of the New Testament. When, in our dedication to behavioral psychology, we try to make a Skinner box of a classroom, we soon discover that human beings do not always react precisely like rats, even though history reveals some frightening parallels. Repeatedly, schools have to find out all over again that teaching aids will not substitute for a good teacher and never act as an antidote for a poor one. I knew one teacher, a highly creative person, whose principal weakness lay in her excessive dependence upon recordings and films. Many weeks, she would spend three and four days with these devices, and some of her colleagues felt that a marquee should be erected over her classroom door to read: ☛ AMERICAN LITERATURE NOW PLAYING ☚. One wit on the staff speculated on the efficacy of setting up a popcorn concession just outside her room. To develop motivation, students should certainly get "into the act" more frequently. In life there are already too many people who habitually sit and watch.

The How-to-Study course focuses heavily upon student opinion, argument, and evaluation, but mostly upon their realizing that the best system of study will fail if they don't actively put it to work for good reasons of their own. At the end of the eight-weeks work, the academic future for the individual student is readily discernible. Linda, for one, was highly motivated in her wish not only to please her parents and teachers but to learn. Some degree of success was bound to result from her efforts. The prognosis for other students who sat in class with her was poor. Merle's mother had doted upon the boy since the death of his father, and he had not learned to place any value upon school and his performance there. I wasn't able to change the boy's mind. In his case I failed completely. Other youngsters, better oriented at least to what lay ahead of them and to what would be required of them, showed modest improvement after their summer's work.

The course is too ambitious in its organization, possibly. We try to do so much that the treatment of some materials is superficial or haphazard. A review of arithmetic fundamentals, a brief consideration of grammar, some suggestions for reading improvement, much exercise in note-taking, outlines for studying literature and preparing reports, occasional diagnostic tests and ideas for handling spelling and vocabulary weaknesses, tips on studying for tests and examinations—these are some of the other matters taken up in How to Study. The end of the summer finds my students loaded down with their notes and the materials I have distributed.

Working with this course is not nearly so enjoyable for me as my English classes are, but I have certainly grown in my understanding of the challenges faced by my profession. I had never before fully appreciated the problems encountered by teachers in elementary and junior-high schools. Now I know that every high-school teacher should be given opportunities to watch at close range the young people at work in other grade levels. The proper integration and coordination of a school's curriculum demands such intra-system observations, it seems to me.

I have also learned from the study-methods course that young people, even highly motivated students, can sometimes experience great difficulty in putting more efficient study methods to work for them. Often their problems are in the home, itself—irregular mealtimes, TV or telephones or stereo in their study areas, the student's responsibility in caring for sisters or brothers, parents who entertain through the week, etc. Parents occasionally expect our course to effect marvels when, in reality, they, themselves, have barred the door to improvement.

One night a lady with thyroid eyes and a disproportionately large bust surrounded me at a PTA meeting. "I'm Grace Godot, Mr. Rousculp. My daughter is doing very poorly this year, and I'm going to enroll her in your study course next summer. In the meantime, do you have any suggestions? You see, she has a time problem. Mondays she takes piano in the evenings, Tuesday she always has her church group, every Wednesday night her father and I are expected to go out, and I have to leave Melanie in charge of the two younger children. Of course on the nights she dates I have a regular sitter. I have restricted her dating to three nights a week —that's quite enough for a fifteen-year-old girl during the school year, don't you think? Thursday is just about the only night she seems to have free to study, but these sophomore teachers are just a little unreasonable in what they ask these children to do. I thought you might have some ideas. Margaret Sheldon told me that you—"

I took as deep a breath as her proximity would allow. Even then I hoped that this fleshily dressed woman would not find the buttons on my vest too cold. But I had to break in. If she ran out of breath and inhaled, I'd be impaled on the pencil sharpener behind me.

"Sounds as if you have quite a problem there, Mrs. Godot. Somewhere along the line, something's going to have to give," I said, feeling the pencil sharpener creaking against my shoulder blade. "I've a notion that if we both give it some careful thought overnight we can come up with some answers." When she was gone, I straightened the sharpener and faced the East in silence.

Situations like Melanie Godot's are not the rule, thankfully, and in such cases parents don't really want the advice that I could offer, anyway. The thing that appeals to the PTA's and child-study groups who have asked me to speak on the How-to-Study course is its comparative newness on the public-school scene. The "throw out the old one and get a new one *because it's new*" illness of our society has badly infected some educational circles. By now I have undoubtedly convinced some people that I am a traditionalist, but I don't feel that I am. I don't revere the antique for its age any more than I love novelty for novelty's sake. I believe in educational experiment, but I approach it cautiously because, if it fails, young people may suffer. Education not being a game, children should not play the role of pawns. If the government is to aid education, it should begin by raising the certification requirements and the financial rewards for teachers, not by enriching education's middle-man, the manufacturer of teaching machines and the experimentalist's equipment.

I have just mentioned that study-methods courses are comparatively new on the public-school scene. The methods, themselves, are not innovations for the most part. There is nothing revolutionary in the course I teach, nor in any of the similar courses taught elsewhere. The fundamental methods suggested are rooted in self-discipline, a recognition of what a modern high-school curriculum requires of its students, some perception of what constitutes good working relationships among people, and a realistic concept of time. The specific methods of study which the course endorses and encourages are the same ones that experienced teachers have recommended over the years. The ballyhoo over "independent study" in the 1960's was absurd—the principle antedates Socrates himself. The sole novelty of my course and others like it is that it draws many tested ideas together and tries to utilize that conglomerate to build incentive in young people.

It would be very pleasant for me to hoodwink myself into thinking that I have blazed new trails or worked wonders in my How-to-Study course. But I know better.

When is a teacher actually done with his work? When is he through as a teacher? It is my conviction that he has truly become "deadwood" when he loses his interest in young people. If he lacks that interest in the beginning, he never really begins to teach. Of course, I'm talking about teaching people, not automatons—human beings, not quadratic equations, paragraphing, or chemical bonding. Even a grammar lesson might mislead the would-be teacher. In the sentence *Mrs. Wills taught Jeff reading*, the grammatical indirect object should be the educational direct object.

I must admit, though, that I have seen some of those the education colleges call pupil-oriented teachers lose their interest after a number of dedicated, useful years in the classroom. They do not become callous or withdrawn out of spite or natural distemper—instead, they begin to feel that the changing times have built too

The Hairy Question

great a wall between them and their students. They lose interest because they believe that they can no longer communicate with or understand young people. The weight of age becomes intolerable, the September-to-June stint grows longer, and the summer is all too brief. The monthly check is no longer the mockery it once was because they sense, themselves, that something has gone out of their professional practice.

This calamity does not visit the careers of all teachers—the Dow Nelsons or the Jeanette Frys. But I have seen it happen to so many others. I do not say that it proceeds exclusively from some cultural quarantine blocking the teacher from his students. Sometimes, unsatisfactory teacher-administrator relationships complicate the condition, physical ailments may aggravate it, financial indebtedness may magnify the symptoms. Still, at the root of the

305

matter most often is a longing on the teacher's part for the good old days, when youngsters spoke, dressed, behaved, and studied as they were supposed to.

As I view the prospect of teaching another twenty years, nothing troubles me more than the fear of some day feeling a like incapacity to comprehend and enjoy the young. I have wondered whether it strikes a teacher with warning. Does it set in gradually or all at once? And do the afflicted ever get over it? I was especially troubled by these questions when a something-new strolled under the sword into Room 106. Not so long ago.

I couldn't blame it upon the wrestling vaude*villain*, Gorgeous George. Like the Pilgrims, it appeared to have come from England, but just as the sight of those early white-collar workers must have offended the eyes of many a native of that time, so the Beatle coif distressed me. Over a period of years with chalk dust and lectern, I had seen the teenage fads come and go and had never once been profoundly disturbed. I had never considered, not even for a moment, that any aberration in adolescent dress or appearance could possibly affect my work as a teacher. Of course, I was one of the lucky ones, I confess. None of the Beatle mimics had as yet sat in my classroom. Occasionally one of the ultra-hirsute set would pass me in the corridor, but I maintained my faith that, if I closed my eyes and clutched my gradebook, It would go away. And It always did—until that fateful September, that is. But then, before I could say "Defend us from all sorcerers" in Anglo-Saxon, It came into my room and took a seat.

As I have already intimated, I am the possessor of a rapidly expanding browscape. In other words, where the subject of hair is concerned, I dwell in an all-glass house and am therefore not given to lobbing boulders. Nevertheless, like many adult males in our society, I had grown to associate long hair with transvestism and homosexuality. I realize that such narrowness of thinking speaks poorly for one who has taught literature and history. In self-defense I must add that, on no other matter, have I found myself affected by externals in quite this fashion. Buffalo Bill, General Custer, Ben Franklin, and Sampson notwithstanding, my conditioning as a man and as an ex-Marine had set up an emotional block where the Beatles and their impersonators were concerned. At least, that's how matters stood with me the day my English classroom was suddenly invaded by, of all things, an English-wrought jumper-bumper.

I had complimented myself, I suppose, that no one assigned to 106 would ever come in looking like this one. His appearance matched that of a stereotype that some men even cross a street to avoid. He had the physique of a tall, skinny prepubescent girl, but such a frame is not unusual among boys of that age. He was not a bad-looking boy, but very thin. He stood 5′ 6″ on pipe-stem legs, and in tight jeans he looked like a "before" side of the physical-culture ads shouting: "Look, Ma! No torso!" His complexion, like that of many adolescents, revealed that his androgens and estrogens were engaged in chemical warfare. It was the hair that worked the transformation. The horn-rimmed glasses, the delicate and graceful musician's hands, and the reddish-brown Buster Brown bouffant coincided perfectly and horribly with an image locked in my memory—the deviant who had lived for a time in the neighborhood where I had grown up.

Obviously, I could not "cross the street" this time. However I might wince, he was assigned to my class. I must serve him as his teacher. Even as my gorge rose, I was indicting myself for my prejudice against the newcomer. Moreover, I felt trapped by my own logic. I had always joked with my students about their preoccupation with petty surface impressions. Now, I wondered whether I was not being petty, too.

He was, after all, only a boy—there was documentation to this effect in his cumulative file folder. I had to adjust, to overhaul my thinking. Perhaps I was becoming stodgy and static in my views, fogeyish at 42. What if the next September brought several dozen such were-pups to my classroom? Maybe Darwin was wrong—maybe the human forehead was destined to disappear. I must learn to live with this hybridity just as the Cavaliers had to get used to the Roundheads.

I do some of my best, most serious cogitating when I'm going through the mechanics of shaving in the early morning. If I remember correctly, I was so occupied one morning while mulling over the possibility that the slight increase in radioactive fallout might account for the increasing incidence of Beatle-itis. Then I stopped short and considered what it was that I was doing at that very moment. I was trimming my moustache.

There are only two good things that I can say of my moustache —it covers a portion of a vile visage and, like some other things about me, it is not in style. I am the only teacher in the school with a moustache. Old-timers would scoff at the close-cropped growth on my upper lip, but in modern times moustaches have all but disappeared. Even many of the bearded men do not wear them. *Is it possible that some people might think moustaches on men as outlandish as shoulder-length hair on teenage boys?* This thought occurred to me as I chipped stray whiskers and opened a capillary or two—par for the course.

Naturally, I was concerned with the reaction of other students to the boy with long hair. Most of them, I believe, regarded him with amusement, but some treated him with unconcealed disgust and a little cruelty. Curiously enough, many of the same students who might applaud him at a local "battle of the bands" contest saw him as rather out of place when offstage.

For any school, though, there were and are even worse implications in the presence of the long-haired ones. For a few students in my class, his being there constituted a standing joke on the administration and faculty, who seem even more entertaining when they issue rules prescribing the "legal" length of hair on front, side, and back. In both corridors and classroom, students like the male Rapunzel of Room 106 constitute a distraction, a carnival feature over which school discipline appears to be impotent, apart from arranging periodic, often ineffective sessions with parents and barbers.

Nevertheless, I hoped that the tonsorial regulations might remove the offending growth just as the sartorial rules had reduced the number of *Playboy* fold-outs in my classroom. Faced with a growing number of Them, however, the office was finding it increasingly difficult to enforce hair limits, especially when one of Philip Wylie's Mothers-Who-Never-Really-Wanted-to-Cut-Their-Little-Boys'-Hair-in-the-First-Place got on the phone. It was up to me, I saw, to deal with the hairy question myself—to overcome somehow my antipathy and revulsion.

Unhappily, there were, as there usually are, other factors that hindered my efforts to work with and for the boy. I tried to see him as an undernourished, red-headed Prince Valiant, but as the weeks passed he refused to cast off his masquerade as Princess Dalliant. Yet I persevered. I took great pains to disassemble that unseemly cerebrum to find out what made it sick.

What kind of mind lurked beneath the mold-culture that ornamented it from brow to nape? To begin with, he wanted no part of any classroom. School, he felt, was impeding his progress as a rock-'n'-roll star-to-be. After all, he was playing with an instrumental group who were creating a quite audible commotion with teenagers in the area. They were performing almost nightly and experiencing some financial success. As a result, Rapunzel was a part-time student. Whenever he did choose to grace my class-room with his presence, he would sit there condescendingly, his eyes straining to stay open in the harshness of daylight and his beat-beaten brain absorbing next to nothing. The only excitement he ever felt in Room 106 came with my thoughtless mention of the long hair affected by the poet Shelley. The boy completed only enough work to draw a D during the first semester, and it is pos-sible that my self-accusations and worry over not being fair to him may have assisted him in passing.

The irony of his attitude and performance was simply this: the boy was courteous, pleasant, and capable of doing good work. He was, to be honest, very strong in written-composition assignments when he felt an interest in the subject of the theme. But these occasions were rare. He would ordinarily cross his spindly, jean-encased legs, caress his hairdo with loving hands, and drift off into his reverie of Imminent Stardom and Instant Millions.

Meanwhile, I checked and rechecked his school record in the office files. I talked with guidance counselors and others to find out why I was unable to make any headway with the boy. There was little comfort in being informed that none of his teachers had really got through to the boy. None of my colleagues could advise me further than to add to the disagreeable picture I already knew too well. One of the teachers provided me with a rundown on the problem-student's home life. One parent, it seemed, quaked at the boy's temper tantrums, and both father and mother had presum-ably given up all efforts to guide or govern the boy. Apparently, the only favorable recognition the boy had ever achieved was the applause he found outside the school, with his music. I learned also, from people who are supposed to know about such matters, that the youngster possessed considerable talent with his musical instrument.

I wish that I could close my account with a happy resolution and a foolproof formula for dealing with young people like Rapunzel. Though I continued trying to communicate with the boy through long notes on his papers and several pointed conversations, he was eventually expelled from Worthington High School by an out-of-patience administration. Before that occurred, however, his attendance had become even poorer than before and his attitude had incorporated a peculiar mixture of apathy and persecution complex.

One of the papers he turned in held, perhaps, the key to his point of view. In it he spoke of the school's tyranny in trying to suppress his individuality. When school officials insisted that he have his hair trimmed, they were violating his rights and cramping his individualism, he declared. That he truly believed this, I have no doubt.

His hair was his fetish. It had not served as the cause of his difficulties, though—it was only a symptom, one which reflected not merely his own special illness, but the neurosis of a whole society. How, in the face of all the Beatle emulators, he could reason that his long locks made him an individual is not clear. At the same time, his notion that they did so demonstrated a very widespread delusion in our time—that the proof of individuality rests upon shallow, superficial factors. About the time that the Follicle Follies arrived from Britain, this boy was misreading Thoreau's "Civil Disobedience" and Emerson's "Self-Reliance," as so many have done. Thus we have the Rebel with a Cause, although history will have to remember it as the first cause ever combed, ratted, and sprayed.

The disenchanting truth to which teenagers are oblivious is that, in pursuing fads and purchasing teen symbols, they are often exploited in herds by the Teenager Industry. Teenagerdom has been owned and operated by grown-ups since before they were born. Taking into its domain such matters as dress, music, drive-ins, radios, automobiles, etc., Youth Incorporated has flowered into an enterprise which is worth billions of dollars annually and which has spawned the ridiculous idea that teenagers are something unto themselves and unrelated to the society around them. As things stand, even mathematics has to give way to the teen cult. A child becomes a teenager at age ten or eleven and is expected to act this part until he is sixteen, at which time he is either ostracized as being too old or is taken as a leader through his teenage associates.

Adults help the teen businesses along by assuring a constant turnover in teen styles. The cry today is "I'd rather be young than be President." As soon as adults have "moved in" in their pathetic desire to be teenagers, too, the teenager industries discard the Twist, the Total Look, the "Yeah-Yeah-Yeah," or whatever it is, and produce a new teenage something or other. And so the cycle proceeds.

So before we crucify Rapunzel upon a barber's chair, we should examine closely the adult society which breeds this phenomenon. To what extent does the society of grown-ups depend upon show? Vance Packard, Erich Fromm, and many others answer the question with painful eloquence. In quest of the fast buck, the appearance of status or importance, and the effortless success-that-comes-overnight, how many of us pay lip service to God, democracy, and the hearth as we mill about in the shrine of Phoniness? Sometimes the Phonies teach too quickly and too well, and afterwards the well-meaning parent, clergyman, or teacher is unable to salvage and to rehabilitate. Regardless of my efforts, then, there will, for a time at least, be a young man who nightly wraps his individuality in a hair net.

It is always conceivable, of course, that Rapunzel and his hopeful rock-'n'-roll friends may work their way into that temporary, uncertain emulsion of fame and notoriety known as Stardom. I would be the last to deny them their music and their dream, but I would prefer that they emphasize skill, not scalp. Possibly I have been teaching so long that I have lost my awareness of the value of money, but I know that purchasing power has no more connection with personal worth than individuality has with tangled tresses. True talent sometimes needs a trademark, a special gimmick, in order that it be noticed. Still, the entertainment market is clogged with hair. In fact, it is hard to find some of the bright, gifted newcomers because of all that hair.

On the other hand, talent of every sort should be accompanied by self-understanding and a sound, enduring sense of values. I would like to see this boy succeed, even in the contemporary dollar-sign sense of the word, but I would also like him to recognize that, when the lights of the marquee no longer shrill his name, there is a more satisfying, more permanent something-else in life.

When Rapunzel came to the door of 106 to turn in his English books the day he left Worthington High to avoid a haircut, I felt sorry for him. He would attend night school in Columbus in order to get a high-school diploma, he said. Then he thanked me, God knows why. He had taught me, though not intentionally, much more than I had taught him. He had struck a match and faintly lit an unenlightened grotto in my mind, a brutish place of superficiality and intolerance which I am still laboring to illuminate. As I watched him walk down the corridor, I could see that he was proud of his firm resolve and convinced that the moral victory was his.

What would his future be? I knew that, more than likely, he would survive unscathed the slurs and threats of beatings on the street. I hoped he might avoid the homosexual propositions he would encounter in the entertainment world, where narcissism, self-indulgence, and jaded tastes combine to produce inverts faster than anywhere else, outside of prisons. I saw the awful moment of tragedy ahead of him—when he would have to leave the teen-age world, when the junior-high crowds no longer listened in adulation but sought new Superteens, new bandstand idols.

As he turned the corner and stepped from my sight, I saw him pass his hand gently over his hair. *That hair! How many more like him would come to 106? Would I ever get used to it?*

I still haven't got over the long-haired ones, but I know that I haven't yet reached the place where I no longer understand young people. Though Rapunzel's hair offended my sight, I learned to feel compassion for him and to understand his misunderstanding of me. Had his tresses been his only problem, I would have gradually grown to ignore them. Perhaps I might even have been able to convince him that the great individualists of history grew inwardly, not outwardly. Regrettably, he came to me from a home that merely housed him, from a church that merely provided camps and picnics, from a society that only duped and deluded his pallid, pimpled spirit into trading truth for a one-night stand. But, worst of all, he came to a teacher who failed him.

"Will there be anything else, sir?" the bellhop asked me.

"No, I guess not," I answered and walked to the window overlooking the new plaza that Hartford, Connecticut takes so much pride in. From my room in the Hotel America, I could also see the Connecticut River in the moonlight. As the bellhop closed the door, I turned to examine the room again. It was beautifully furnished. I flicked on the television set on my way to the closet to deposit my bag. By the time I had closed the drapes and undressed, one of the sons of Hercules on the late movie had saved the virtue of an overmammaried Grecian maid who was now repaying his heroism by jeopardizing his own purity.

I lit a cigarette and tried to concentrate on the screen. No, Goldilocks didn't stand a chance. The young man's Muscle Beach narcissism was impregnable, I decided. I knew I couldn't have

Every Man Has His Price

seen the picture before because I couldn't have sat through it. It wasn't long before I was on the villain's side. A twist of the dial gave me the late news—a reminder that it was after midnight and that tomorrow I would need my wits.

A great meteorite had been seen all along the East Coast, the announcer said. Had I followed a star to Connecticut? No, not a star. It had been only an end-of-March thunderbolt in an envelope from Dick, the editorial director who had been responsible for publishing some of my writing. His firm was currently interviewing people for editorial positions, and his letter asked whether I might be interested in applying for an opening on a social-studies publication.

At first, I did not choose to think of Dick's letter as possibly leading to a job offer. I had begun to accumulate rejection slips on short stories once more, but here was confirmation that someone believed in my writing, enough to think I might make an editor. Later, I began to think more about the application form enclosed. It posed a question—one that I could not ignore.

I had received Dick's letter at the school, so my wife did not see its contents till that evening. Even then, I was tempted to put it away and forget about it. But I couldn't. For nearly seventeen years, she had made it possible for me to teach—by working as a nurse, by accepting my long and irregular hours, by being too nice to complain about the demands of my work. When she had read the letter, she was as excited as a child. "Oh, you've always wanted to write," she said, "and maybe another kind of life would be good for us. You've worked so hard teaching—so hard that I've worried about you. I know you can't keep up these hours much longer without killing yourself, and—" She turned her head away and broke off without saying it, that *she* was tired, worn out by her work.

It was for her sake, mainly, that I sent the application to Connecticut, and I spent much time on it so that I could justify the salary I would ask if they should make an offer. I sent a letter with the application form. In it I tried to explain that leaving my classroom would not be easy for me, but that the idea of teaching through my writing was attractive, too. Perhaps that was my way of rationalizing that taking a job in Connecticut would not really mean abandoning Room 106.

The reply from the East came too soon, before I had been able to think, to weigh what such a change in my life would mean. Selfishly, I saw the answer to my application as not simply a promise, but as a threat. Dick's organization suggested that they fly me there for further discussion.

I showed this reply to my closest friends on the Worthington teaching staff. The reaction of Dave Miller, Worthington's outstanding instrumental-music teacher, with whom I planned to collaborate in writing a musical play, was typical. If it represented a big opportunity for me, he thought I should take it, yet he indicated reluctance to see me leave, simply because he was my friend.

All over again, I was climbing a hill—on the other side of which I might find a Sea of Promise or a lonely, topless, thick-trunked banyan tree behind which lurked a nameless, faceless threat to my life. Before I took that final step, I had to look back at the faces of my comrades. But they could only watch and wait.

How many hills were in a man's life? And were they all so ominous? I had once been scared of a hill on an island hell, *but I had climbed it.* And I would climb this one. Faulkner was right when he spoke through his Sam Fathers: "Be scared. You can't help that. But don't be afraid." There *was* a difference—the distinction between caution and panic. The cautious can climb, but the panic stricken must freeze or flee.

At home the tension mounted. My wife, I could tell, was ecstatic over the possibility of a change in our fortunes. "I've heard Connecticut is beautiful!" she exclaimed. When would I go? Of course, I couldn't afford to take her along. Anyway, it would be a rapid 24-30 hour jaunt with no time for sight-seeing or fun. She and I had talked about everything else except the big question. Dick would, I was certain, ask "How much?" And how could I put a price tag on the affection of my students and the respect of a community? How could I put Room 106 and seventeen years up for sale?

A prosperous, hard-headed business executive had told me once "Every man has his price." I had refused to believe it because he was saying, in effect, that any man will sell his integrity and his loyalty. I had often told my classes that I could not accept such a cynical philosophy. Nevertheless, I was about to establish a minimum bid for my service. *I had a price*—I must receive an amount sufficient to purchase happiness for my wife and to offset the loss of things without price. All I had ever wanted to do was to teach and to write. I tried to convince myself that only through this job could I do both. Together, my wife and I decided the lowest figure that I could accept.

My teaching fell off during those weeks. I found myself snapping at people. One day I lost poise entirely during a discussion of Koestler's *Darkness at Noon*. We were trying to visualize Rubashov's cell, and several facetious remarks from my students were all I needed to upset me. I think they knew I swayed under some pressure.

"You'll never leave here," said Harold Hill, my very good friend who combines two professions with noteworthy performance in both. Teacher and Presbyterian minister, Harold was trying to goad me toward something that he felt I should do. "Regardless of what they offer, you'll stay." For my own sake, he wanted me to take that job in the East.

I called Dick in Connecticut and agreed on an interview date. Frank Lowery, who has ties with a travel agency, got plane reservations for me. On a Tuesday I left school in the early afternoon to pack. I didn't carry much with me—an extra shirt, a pair of socks, toothbrush, and razor—but I still very nearly missed the plane. It took two Boeing 707's with a stopover in New York to get me to the Hartford airport.

I twisted the TV dial in the America once more. Hercules' kid had found himself a new playmate, and this one had an even more fantastic center-of-balance. Finally I found another channel, featuring one of those late-night, isn't-our-conversation-titillating shows. I was undressed down to my shorts, but my throat still felt tight—the price tag around my neck. After I had turned out the lights in the room, I opened the drapes and looked across at the river once more. The feel of the glass reminded me of the chill outside. It was an unseasonable April.

Dow Nelson would not see this spring. Jeanette Fry would, but not from a schoolroom window. She had retired. How long could an English teacher last at the pace I followed? If I were to remain a teacher, would I live to retire? If so, what then?

Suddenly I was back watching a lonely little figure walk slowly down a school corridor—a retired teacher, a man who looked as if he had retired from life, itself. Someone had told me once that the students had practically driven him out of the school because of his age-cracked idiosyncrasies. Could that happen to me? Does there come a terrible moment into the life of every teacher when he realizes that the balance has shifted—that his students need him much less than he needs them? Is this a fixed chapter in the saga of a teacher?

They say that, as a man grows older, he loses his capacity to adapt—to accept new challenges. Had seventeen years at one task done that to me? Was not each young person who came to my classroom a something new? Is not the supply of challenge inexhaustible in a teacher's life?

Even if I remained a teacher, I must climb a hill to scan an unknowable horizon and to live with whatever I found there. All men must either climb such hills or else stand trembling in the shadows, blind to a part of the sky, to the stars that dwell there. When the chalk dust and I had mingled with the common clay, there would be little left of me unless I had written. Yet in my beggared, ragged words, there was nothing that hinted even slightly of immortality. In which direction lay the greatest peace and satisfaction? There is only one prayer for such occasions, I think. *"Thy will be done,"* I murmured toward the wind-frayed clouds above the Connecticut.

It was after one o'clock now, and I put my electronic companion to sleep, wishing that I could turn off my thoughts so easily. I stretched across the bed in an effort to do so. But the pictures kept coming. One of Hercules' film-born bastards—and a forbidding hill—and a specially constructed brassiere—and a meteorite—and a schoolroom with a sword and a bust of Goethe—and a letter—and a pair of Eurasian eyes—and a boy hiding a set of papers in his locker—and a teacher dead beside a book still unfinished—and the moon-swathed Connecticut—and a woman in the white of a wedding dress and a nurse's uniform—and finally the opaque serenity of dreamless sleep.

Next morning, my stomach was churning too violently for breakfast. I met Jeff Markheim, who drove me to the little town where Dick's and the publisher's offices were located. Coffee, a tour through the building, an introduction to people I might some day work with, then the talk with Dick.

He had come here from the newspaper business. He had been on Iwo with a Marine special-services group during that campaign. Slender and wiry, he looked at least five years younger than I though he was a year or two older. The only suggestion of his age was in the beginning of gray in his dark hair. Now he pulled on his pipe and looked at the schoolteacher in his office. "I've seen your writing and I like it very much. We've had a fine response to that piece of yours we printed. You know your way around in educational testing, and you've had considerable experience in teaching. The position I have in mind would require the writing of the teacher's supplements to our publications, occasional articles elsewhere, and possibly some traveling." Then he asked the how-much question, and I answered it.

Dick didn't appear to be bothered by my price. Of course, my application had shown my additional sources of income. After a moment's silence, he said, "Well, that's probably in line with what you have to offer. You'll want to hear an explanation of the fringe benefits, of course. First, why don't we take a look around the town, discuss housing, and then have lunch later?"

The town was a disappointment despite its charm. Nobody I met sounded like a New Englander. The countryside was beautiful. I knew my wife would love the rural setting through which Dick drove that day. Eventually, after about a thirty-mile tour, we pulled into a drive and entered a very rustic but very nice restaurant. We began with a drink or two and then ate lunch.

The four hours I spent with Dick were thoroughly pleasant, in spite of my conflicting feelings about the possible outcomes. I sensed that my host was quite favorably impressed with me. Regularly, he would interject subtle, casual questions about what ideas I had relative to social studies and publications pointed toward that area of education. The offhand reactions that I provided seemed to please him.

Before I left his office, he told me that he thought I was exactly what he was looking for, the best qualified among those he'd talked to. While I was experienced mainly in the field of English, my having taught history should equip me for the work, he felt.

Afterwards, I talked to the personnel man—a younger fellow from the Rochester office and, before that, the Ivy League. He was comparatively new at his job. I could tell, because he had a difficult time determining what to ask me. He went over the retirement system, then, and the profit sharing and the insurance plans. Soon he got around to asking about my price tag. When I told him, he indicated some surprise. "To be perfectly truthful," he said, "we don't start editors at that level. In your case, they may, though. I really don't know."

So I had climbed the hill, but found only fog-shrouded suspense. I left for Hartford with the understanding that I would be contacted when the decision had been made. I honestly believe that, had the executive vice-president not been out of town, the job might have been mine that day.

The first part of the wait that followed my return to Columbus and Worthington would have been intolerable had I not put the matter out of my mind as much as possible. I buried myself in work. Daily I would answer my wife's unspoken question and my friends' quizzical expressions with "Still no news." The word had passed, apparently, so I found almost everyone on the faculty asking about the issue of my trip. On a Friday, about two weeks after the interview, Bill Lane was contacted by the personnel office for a character reference. The woman who talked to him believed that "a firm offer" would be made to me the following week.

It was another week and a half before the answer came. This time, the letter came to my home, and my wife had hopefully opened it before I got there. The letter did little more than to justify the sense of relief I had begun to feel, my belief that they would not meet my price. No doubt they had found someone at a lower figure and with a broader social-studies background.

My wife had been crying, and I felt guilty because I did not fully share her disappointment. I had gone to Connecticut for her —the woman who had borne my teaching, my daughter, and my financial insecurity. I had done my best, yet I could not, in my selfishness, be as unhappy as she. But before the evening was over, she had, as usual, begun to emphasize the other side of things. She had, I learned, been accusing herself of selfishness, of wrongly trying to take me out of my work.

I drove to the school earlier than usual the next morning. For one thing, I had a manuscript to get ready for mailing. I would still write. Somehow I would have my cake and eat it, too—I would find a knife to divide it. I would not let some say of me, "He *teaches* literature because he cannot *write*." I might not have the Great American Novel in me, but I still had my Odyssey in the Chalk Dust. This time, I could see my shining Pacific from the top of the hill, and I would embark with stronger faith that His will had indeed been done in my life. By God—no, through God—I would write. For I had something to say.

There was another and probably more important reason for my early arrival at Worthington High. I wanted to look at the room— at 106, with its damnable disarray and its blessed beauty. I had not, you see, dared really look at it for weeks. Because if I had looked at it too long, if I had peered into those file cabinets, if I had dawdled over my desk before and after school, I could never have left it and the 15,000 hours I had lived there. Now I could feed my eyes upon that place with a soul and so many phantom sounds. And I did so.

My schoolroom reverie was interrupted by Dave Dayton, the history teacher, still in his policeman's uniform—his contribution to the teacher's world of moonlighting. "Hey," he said, "hasn't anyone fixed the coffee in the lounge yet?" I went with him to the lounge, and eventually we had cups full of black steam. I told him the news from Connecticut. If I was glad, he was glad, he said. "I heard some of the students were upset over your maybe leaving," he added.

"You mean they know about it?"

"You better believe it, buddy," he declared.

I had to believe it when I got back to Room 106. Someone had been there. On the desk were spring flowers in a small decorated can—as unlikely a sight in my room as a copy of *Vogue*. Under the flowers a five-by-nine piece of cardboard read: "To whom it may concern (over)." I glanced toward the door to be sure that no one would see me handling a bouquet. Then I lifted the can and turned the card. On a yellow background flecked with myriad colors was printed in big red letters **STAY!** And beneath it, in tiny black script the words: *"we love you."*

Even the flowers seemed suited to 106 that day.

What are great teachers made of? I have but two degrees and twenty years of apprenticeship to bring to the question. I continue to grope for the formula in my daily efforts, but there are too many incalculables to be accounted for. A man could have a half-dozen degrees behind his name and threescore years in the school-room and still be filled with doubts about such matters. Even with the aid of the Delphic oracle, a crystal ball, Nostradamus, and the Muses themselves, it is unlikely that anyone could provide a definitive, absolute solution.

But I must *attempt* to reach and to weigh that insubstantial something which—added to training, desire, and experience—makes the really good teacher. I have to essay the task because so many of my students have become teachers or plan to do so. Perhaps after their exposure to me some of them are convinced

The Professional Defined

that the field of education badly needs help. A few of them have even been foolish or kind enough to call me a first-rate teacher.

Observation and personal mistakes have given me some notions as to the composition of a good teacher. But the words come too easily—like so many counterfeit shadows of the realities. And when I see what I have written, I hear the spirit laughter from those I would describe—the peals of merriment from Academy, Gymnasium, Kindergarten, Lyceum, and Little Red Schoolhouse —and then that wisdom of the past, chorusing, whispering somewhere over my shoulder: *"We are such stuff As dreams are made on. . . ."*

The dream of becoming a teacher requires pride and presumption in the dreamer. If he continues long in his visionary quest, he must ultimately learn humility and taste the tartness of Truth. Unless certain qualities are innately a part of his personality, the humbling of defeat and the fact of his limitations will guide him toward some alternative aspiration.

Certainly, a teacher must possess a willingness to share. This requirement is built into his work—not simply the sharing of knowledge, time, and space, but of accomplishment. It is ironic that a teacher is paid for doing a job that he can not possibly do by himself. Education is a bilateral or multilateral process, obviously. Learning can take place without or in spite of a teacher. When it occurs partly through the efforts of the teacher, it requires the simultaneous and cooperative labor of the student. Therefore, whatever success the teacher experiences must belong in part to his student. It may be that herein lies one of the lessons in humility that the teacher must assimilate. Some people do not like to share their sense of accomplishment, and such persons should never undertake to teach.

An equally important trait in him who would teach is *joie de vivre*—a love of life and humanity. The teacher can not be exclusively a scholar—he must be so intensely human as to value people above books and the other tools of education. "And gladly would he learn and gladly teach," writes Chaucer of his Clerk of Oxford, but this poverty-stricken student's scholarship and love of literature offer no assurance that he will *successfully* teach. A good teacher must find both knowledge and people attractive, and his students should discover in him a human vitality, vibrance, and warmth that will make them wish to know him and his secret, even if they must absorb a part of his knowledge to get to the essence of their teacher.

Yet there is a paradox in the teacher's role. Though he must radiate an intensely human character, he can not permit himself to be human at all times. For human beings find favorites in their associations, and they are often tempted to play God in their judgments. Moreover, there must always be that wall—note that I do not say *dais*—that extends between the teacher and his pupils. That wall, however thin or transparent, must stand all assaults. The teacher may reach across it at moments, but he dares not climb over it. The temptation to do so may be great, but the teacher must not join the crowd on the other side.

Another strain upon the human nature of the teacher is the infinite patience and understanding that his task requires. Of course, there is a point at which tolerance must be abandoned—an unknown place without buoy or surface warnings on the sea of classroom relationships.

At the time I had Gustav in 106, he was under the care of a psychiatrist, and his teachers had been instructed to handle him with care. We were no more equipped to deal with this boy than with a radioactive isotope. He was given to violent tantrums and had even threatened to stab one of his classmates with a knife on one occasion. He sat in a special (modified) class that I taught, and I put up with his erratic behavior as best I could so long as it did not interfere with the work of other students. Gustav's writing was tragic in its misspellings, unevenness, and total lack of grammatical logic. He would sometimes start a sentence a half-dozen times, and he would scratch out these abortive attempts and end up with the most fragmentary and incoherent sort of paragraph.

Whenever Gustav was unhappy with me or the class, he would lay his head on his desk arm and mumble. If the class was writing or otherwise occupied, he would frequently sit and stare at his paper or his book until I would go back to see whether I could help him or encourage some effort. At such times, he would often turn his head away from me. Several times I felt like snapping it back my way, but I kept my equanimity. He enjoyed, I think, seeing how thinly my kindliness could be stretched.

One day I handed back to the class some test papers that they had turned in earlier that week. Gustav's grade was a D. There were some signs of effort, but I knew that he could do much better work. With the same poor performance, other students in that group would have had F's marked on their papers. I watched the students' faces as covertly as possible when I returned the tests. I always do because their faces can tell you so much about them at such times. Gustav looked highly distressed.

I had just begun to discuss the test papers when Gustav launched himself toward my desk in wild-eyed fury. "Why—why did you give me a D?" he screamed. "*Why?*" Some of the other students were smiling, and I gave them a scorching eye. "*You don't like me—that's why!* You marked a D on my paper because you don't like me," Gustav went on, his face red and his fists clenched.

I didn't intend ever to hurt the boy, even with words, but a very bad day welled up inside me. I exploded then so that they could have heard me three classrooms away. "Don't you dare tell me, boy, that I marked a grade on your paper because I don't like you. I spend hours on papers. I've leaned over backwards to help you learn. I treat you as fairly as I treat anyone. You did next to nothing on that test." I grabbed the paper from his hand so fast that it was crumpled in my hand. "Look at that—and that—you didn't even answer the question because you had your head on the desk when you should have been copying the board and listening. *Don't you ever tell me again that I've been unfair to you!*"

The class sat subdued and shaken by the sudden and unaccustomed blast of my voice, and Gustav's eyes grew even wider and his mouth hung open. Then, without asking permission but simply propelled by emotion, he flung himself from the room. I didn't follow him. I let him go. Of course I was worried about what he might do, but I had fourteen other students there, and they were frightened of me for the first time. I pulled myself into a teacher's posture with a wrench of my shoulders and, in the calmest voice I could muster, said: "Now, where were we? Oh, yes, Question Number Two. Lynn, how should that one have been answered?"

When the bell had ended the period, there was still no sign of Gustav. It was late in the day when I went to the office. Gustav had gone home, I learned. Whether he had done so on the advice of the school nurse or on his own, I didn't know. I told Lou Koloze, the assistant principal, what had occurred, but I also asked him not to let Gustav know that I had talked about the incident in the office. I felt terrible that I had spewed my anger at a boy who might well have been sick.

Gustav returned to the school the next day. I was in my room at noon, shuffling papers as usual. He burst into 106 in tears. For a time he could hardly talk for sobbing, and finally the seventeen-year-old got out his apology. I was profoundly touched by his broken words and trembling hands. "It's all right, Gustav," I told him. "We all have bad days, and I'm sorry I yelled at you the way I did. Let's turn a new leaf and start all over. Okay?" Thereafter, I had a new friend and a cooperative student in my class.

I do not pretend to have deliberately picked the precise moment where patience had to give way to indignation. Quite accidentally, and at Gustav's prodding, I found the proper time to cease my pampering and to adopt a different tone. Unhappily, I fumble the ball in such instances as often as many of my fellow professionals.

But it is difficult to be a human being, yet not give way to very human impulses.

When I use the word *professional* in connection with teaching, I employ the word in a very limited sense. Plainly, I do not have in mind *professional* as distinguished from *amateur*. Every time I begin to work with a new student, I must start anew—thus, every teacher commences a new year as an amateur to some degree. Certainly, I do not use *professional* with reference to the financial compensation I receive. In agreement with the dictionary, I do not include commercial, mechanical, and agricultural pursuits among the professions.

My definition is somewhat narrower than any of the dictionary's alternatives. I see the professions as being made up of those groups of people who are primarily and actively engaged in serving mankind—law, education, medicine, ministry, social work, etc. Because the professions involve intimate contact between or among people, special rules of conduct—codes of professional ethics—must be observed by any professional practitioner. Because all humanity is in need of (and therefore at the mercy of) its professionals, there is no room in a profession for him whose principal motives are self-aggrandizement and personal advantage. Only the clergyman is completely at the mercy of those he serves—his congregation and his God. For this reason, education has been largely socialized, medicine has found moral necessity in accepting certain of the principles underlying Medicare, lawyers some times serve as public defenders, social workers are on the public payroll, etc.

The true professional of any calling can not be a clockwatcher—he can not take his leisure when he will. The needs of humanity do not manifest themselves at regularly scheduled and predictable hours, and the professional's family can never really count on his time. His time is not his own. Therefore, the ringing of a bell ending a school day, the clock in a physician's office, the calendar of the social worker, and a clergyman's Sundays are merely acknowledgments by the true professional that life for the rest of humanity follows a pattern in which he can not partake.

Still another mark of the real professional is that he has embarked upon a life's work—not merely a brief stint or stopgap occupation. He is, in a fashion, married to his profession, for better or for worse. He believes in his work, reveres his calling. His life is excited and saturated by it and ennobled at the same time, regardless of his failures—the deaths in surgery, the school dropouts, the hypocrites in the first pew, or the conviction and imprisonment of an innocent man. If the professional can conduct his practice in accordance with his profession's ethics, he can lose self and find spiritual peace in the bargain and can provide a lasting example for others in his field.

The honest, dedicated professional does not fear a highly principled colleague, nor his fellow professional's success. The professional does not close his mind to learning or to anything that may improve his practice and profession. He cannot in conscience subscribe to Pope's middle-of-the-road philosophy, "Be not the first by whom the new is tried, Nor yet the last to lay the old aside," for the professional stands always on the frontier of human knowledge and development.

Because he renounces self, he will see his profession horizontally and not vertically. He will, out of his growing insight into people and his professional fellowship, come to understand that quality and not promotion is the measure of all men. He will comprehend that those who stand tall in his profession achieve their stature not through man-made hierarchy but through the simple God-inspired heroism of doing their best for their fellow man.

When I accepted an appointment as coordinator of English, grades 7-12, I did so with the understanding that I would still have a classroom and students of my own. Nor can I interpret my position as being *over* other teachers of English, no more than I can view myself as being *over* my students. I am *with* them, I prefer to think—the youth in 106 and youth in my professional company—and I shall want them all to find the sinewed spirit of the chalk dust.

I just met one of my new colleagues—a young English teacher. I can see in his eyes that, though his past has not been riddled with the errors and the violence in my own, he brings his youthful convictions and scrubbed good looks to the same quest—the often lonely and tortuous path of the teacher's dream. Regardless of all the signs and the press of the crowd, he will struggle with me against the witless traffic of our time, the sicknesses of our society. And if he slips, I must lend him the veteran's hand. I must do whatever I can to show him how the classroom works just as I proved long ago to another boy that a firing pin would function. And in my heart I will bless the young teacher for his uncertainty and apprehension because he will help me to forget briefly the doubt and worry in my own professional day—because he will bring me momentary respite before I begin anew my own awkward attempt to be worthy of the profession I serve.

For now I see that I have been among the most ambitious of men—I have sought to be a teacher. I have wanted to be a *true* professional. I have not aspired to become a great teacher, only to grow into a modestly good one. The simple fact is that I am still a rather ordinary man in my work. Some days I leave Room 106, feeling tall as a ten-story building. On other days I need a jack to lift me over the doorsill. Nevertheless, a single moment in which a student looks up from a book with the light of discovery and understanding spreading across his countenance is enough to illumine a hundred days darkened by frustration and failure.

My definition of a professional may stand outside man's grasp, but it is a worthy goal. Even though I reach for it without success, there is untold, untellable happiness in the straining of my empty hand.

"But I thought you said yesterday that this was a rune," complained a student in the second row, pointing to the Anglo-Saxon "thorn" in the textbook illustration of the original *Beowulf* manuscript.

"That's right—that's what it is." Then I leaned on the lectern and looked at the class, expecting to see them mentally masticating this seeming mystery. But intellectual indigestion had set in from our earlier bout with Saxon "charms"—those anomalous mixtures of pagan ritual and Christian prayer. And we were well into the ninth period, that time of day which produces little more than an occasional cerebral belching.

"But, Mr. Rousculp, you said the Anglo-Saxons used runes for fortune-telling like the Vikings did later."

Epilogue: The Chalk-Blessed Shoulder Shared

"That's what I said, all right. Now, what does that suggest to you?" He and his classmates were still looking blankly at the page as the bell rang. Plainly, we would have to discuss the runic alphabet on the following day. "I guess we'll never know," I told them in mock despair. I nodded dismissal, and a vortex of happy, noisy students quickly formed at the door. It was the third day of a new school year, and summer still prowled like a tardy, unwilling boy outside the building. I walked to the window, where September air was spilling into Room 106 from the bus-filled courtyard.

"How are you?" rang a long-remembered voice, and I turned to see a young woman of about 25 framed in the doorway beneath the old sword. She closed the door on the corridor chaos, then walked to me and answered her own question. "Oh, you're just the same. Like—like yesterday," she said, studying my face intently.

"And so are you," I replied, still marveling that she was not simply a very-favorite phantom that dwells in my classroom. "Well, it's about time you came back. You're the hardest one person I ever saw to run into accidentally."

"It just comes natural to me, I guess," she countered quietly. We spoke for some time, then, of the intervening years, of where she'd been and what she'd been doing. She recited the names of people and places in a dispassionate, obligatory fashion that bordered upon a flippancy I could not associate with my memory of her. Then it happened.

She turned her head suddenly to the back of the room—to the chair at the north end of the fifth row. Wholly delighted and fascinated, I watched her stride back to it with that same quick-slippered, jaunty march of hers. For a moment she stood there and tentatively ran one finger across its desk arm, then promptly spiraled about and sat down. Her eyes swept over the room—the walls, the pictures, the filing cabinet where Goethe perched blackly and frowned—and back to me. "It's just the same," she sang. "It had to be—it just *had* to be. It's almost—almost as if I'd never gone away."

"Yes," I answered her simply and walked to the old lectern—the proper teacher's place. Some little fragments of verse, lines of a poem long buried in my file cabinet, broke in upon my thoughts —a poem with misspellings, and without a standard style, written by an "Anonymous"-but-not-very with a sweetness and sincerity that made me flush all over again with recollection:

> *my knight slays ugly dragons*
> *of ignorance and fear*
> *with words and smiles, and he can fill*
> *a dismal day with cheer*
>
> *my knight is just a jester*
> *for some that do not see*
> *behind the moustache and the vests*
> *a quiet bravery*
>
> *my knight has taken off his sword*
> *and hung it on a wall*
> *but he is armed with eyes that are*
> *the strongest steel . . .*

I couldn't recall them exactly as they were, but I was close—too close, perhaps. I looked up from those words, as real as the thumbnail indentations on my lectern top and the history of classroom tensions they recorded. *I must be detached,* I told myself. "And have you decided what it is that you really want in this world?" I said banteringly.

"Yes," she answered softly, thoughtfully, her eyes fixed on the desk arm, where her finger traced some invisible pattern.

> *my knight will never understand*
> *(cause I dare never tell)*
> *the secret that I . . .*

Must be wise, I thought, *and understanding and—*

"Then, if I know you, it'll soon be yours," I reassured her.

"It isn't all that simple," she declared, nodding her head ever so slightly. "What do people do when the things they want belong to other people?" Now she was peering at me closely, and I knew that the answer was important to her.

> *my knight is someone else's knight*
> *it really isn't fair . . .*

"I'd say that the minute a person starts worrying about who-owns-what he's taken the first step toward reconsidering whether he ever wanted the thing in the first place. Besides, there's always something else that's very much like what we're after, and most often we wind up with something much better." After a moment she rose slowly and moved toward the lectern.

"And is compromise the only way? Is that your formula for happiness?"

"Not entirely. But mine *is* a very happy world."

"Yes," she returned, "this room *is* a happy place. I remember that."

"And my world extends beyond this room somewhat." I felt I must explain its boundaries to her. "Some day you'll find a world made just for you."

"Is it possible that for every person there could be more than one very-special—*very-special* world?"

"I'm sure of it," I told her and looked directly at her. "I'm very sure of it." There was a moment of silent tumult in the room, in her eyes. Same Eurasian eyes, same upstart nose, same elfin other-worldliness—unchanged, unchangeable. Perhaps her war with society had lessened, but the essence of her was unquenchable. Then she turned away her head and fumbled at her purse till she was holding some keys.

"I've got to be going, but I'm glad—I'm glad I—caught you before you left." She stepped toward the door, and I followed and swung it open.

"I'm glad, too. Come back—when you can."

She nodded *yes* and moved down the locker-lined hall. I stepped out and was still watching her over the heads of students when I felt the insistent prodding at my elbow, and I turned, still lost in thought, to the boy who sat in the second row of my ninth-period class.

"I think I understand, Mr. Rousculp—" he was saying.

"*You understand?*" I asked bewilderedly.

"Yeah, about that rune. That thing in the original *Beowulf*."

"You do?" I said, coming around.

"Sure. It means that, if the Anglo-Saxons used some of the old runes in their writing, they probably did it because they thought of writing as a kind of magic," he explained. He might have taken the linguistic outerbelt, but he got to the point.

"You know," I declared with a show of astonishment, "I think you've got something there. How did you figure it out?"

"Well, it seems logical. You told us the other day that nothing really important ever changes with human beings—regardless of what century it might be."

"Yes, I did," I reflected.

"Well, people nowadays find a lotta magic in symbols, too, don't they? So why shouldn't those old Anglo-Saxons hang onto some of their favorites when they started writing?"

"Sounds like good thinking, Rog. Be sure to bring up that point in class tomorrow." His face glowed with pleasure as he promised that he would, then disappeared into the crowd of milling seniors just down the corridor.

Yes, I considered, *a man* CAN *find a magic with symbols and weave their significance into the strands of his life.* Today a young woman had returned, had come back to the chair which had been hers. She did not understand that the girl she had been had never really left this place. She had come back, as others had, in search of self, supposing that out of the bright ravelings of Yesterday she might broider the cloth of Tomorrow. "Let her find that silver skein of fulfillment, God," I murmured half aloud.

I strode into the room and glanced at the chair. Indeed, I had not, myself, fully grasped my reasons for keeping it empty. I had known only that a particular student had sat there, that I must somehow recognize the gift of Love she had brought and the self-understanding she had triggered in me, and that to seat another there would be to diminish or obscure that daily reminder of what the company of Youth had brought my life. Her chair had been still another gift, however unwitting—a rune, a thing of magic central to my classroom. For—and now I saw it clearly, at long last—that chair no longer belonged to one student—it belonged to all the youthful ghosts that inhabit my room: to Doug and Spike, to Nancy and Cathy, to Greg and John and Dave, and to all the others who would join them through the years and the chalk dust.

I turned to the chalkboard. I had to get ready for *my* Tomorrow. Tomorrow would soon be sitting in those other chairs, waiting for something to happen here—here where the past intersects the future. I would have to draw with my inept artistry something that looked like an Anglo-Saxon fortress-home of the sixth century. I picked up an eraser and liquidated Woden and Thor with one swipe. Then I went to work on the other Germanic gods. I rubbed the board furiously, my mouth tasting the gritty dust and my eyes still stinging in the glare of new awareness. And, behind me, hands brushed briefly on a bronze urn, the lectern rocked slightly, the sword trembled against the wall, Goethe grinned from ear to ear, and a chair of wood and metal gleamed like burnished gold in the spell of a sorceress.

A NOTE ABOUT THE PRODUCTION
OF THIS BOOK

The text of this first edition of *Chalk Dust on My Shoulder* is set in Primer, a superbly designed typeface outstanding in its versatility. In the short period since its creation, Primer has become known as an effective, no-nonsense text face in book work and business printing. Linotype began Primer by commissioning the noted American engraver, Rudolph Ruzicka, to design a modern schoolbook face. Though a group of reliable faces had long been standard for this use, Ruzicka succeeded in developing a new text face that possesses a nearly ideal balance of fine qualities. A masterpiece of clarity with evenness of tone and beautifully cut, exceptionally legible italic, Primer is perfectly suited to a work requiring a certain niceness with no loss of readability. It is also interesting to note that there is a striking similarity between forms in the Primer font and certain features of Charles G. Rousculp's own handwriting.

The type was set by Service Typographers, Indianapolis, Indiana. The book was printed by Universal Lithographers, Inc., Lutherville-Timonium, Maryland, and bound by L. H. Jenkins, Inc., Richmond, Virginia. The paper is 49 x 74 420M 55 lb. Pensive Vellum offset; the cover cloth is Columbia, Milbank Linen; the colored endpapers are Peninsular, 80 lb. text. The jackets were printed by Universal Lithographers.

Date Due

FE 21 '72			
NOV 26 '72			
MR 7 '73			
JA 29 '74			
FE 13 '74			
AG 2 '76			
FEB 18 '84			
JUL 13 '84			
DEC 1 8 1984			